Joseph Amato

Mounier

and

Maritain:

A French Catholic Understanding of the Modern World

Studies in the Humanities No. 6
Philosophy

The University of Alabama Press

University, Alabama

To my wife, Cathy,

and our children,

Felice, Anthony, Adam and Ethel

Copyright © 1975 by
The University of Alabama Press
ISBN 0–8173–6616–4
Library of Congress Catalog Card Number: 73-22585
All Rights Reserved
Manufactured in the United States of America

CONTENTS

ACKNOWLEDGMENTS

In the course of this long study, my indebtedness has taken many forms. First, it goes to my wife, Catherine, and our four children, Felice, Anthony, Adam, and Ethel, who had to live, love, and abide with me since the time when this study was originally conceived at the University of Rochester in 1966. Second, my indebtedness goes to my parents and my wife's parents who in various ways have shouldered many of the visible and invisible burdens of a long work. Third, I cannot forget Professor A. W. Salomone of the University of Rochester, who has encouraged, guided, and inspired my work since its beginnings.

Special thanks are in order to Madame Mounier, of the *Esprit* Community at Châtenay-Malabry; Professor Joseph Evans of the Jacques Maritain Library at Notre Dame University; Professor Eugen Weber of the University of California; Helen Iswolsky, teacher and member of the Catholic Worker Community, at Tivoli, New York; Father Joseph Moody of the Catholic University of America; and Professors Wylder, Brass, and Radzialowski of Southwest Minnesota State College; our Social Science secretary, Rita Peterson, members of the college's Word Processing Center, the staff of our library, and my friends and students, Scott Perizo, Tim Fruin, and Art Finnell, who won their spurs as proofreaders. Anyone whom I have forgotten here is forgotten by accident; anyone I have included here is exempted from any errors found within this work.

PREFACE

Emmanuel Mounier and the European Crisis
of Values in the Twentieth Century

Twentieth-century intellectual history is a labyrinth with multiple entrances and, apparently, no exit. In a sense, it has been the desire and drive to enter into that labyrinth in reverse, that is, to hypostatize some sort of teleological "way out" that has tended to enmesh even keen-eyed explorers. The world as man-in-history and the secrets of the universe had become objects of the will to manipulation, if not mastery, no longer subjects of idea in search of understanding. The nineteenth century itself had seemed to lead only to a dead-end marked by a bifrontal sign bearing on one side the ideological warning: "No more metaphysics!" and, on the reverse, the injunction to proceed no longer to understand but "to change the world." Thus it was that, despite frequent exuberating hallucinatory experiences, the new itinerary had led deeper and deeper into the dark forest, further and further away from that bright realm where, in Dante's vision, shines the sun and the other stars. More ominous had been the recurring phenomenon that impelled many a half-blinded wanderer to cry out from the very depths that their glimpse of the infernal flames guided their way to the true light. Other seekers became even more hopelessly lost. Again and again exultant cries of "Eureka!" turned out to be sound and fury accompanying headlong plunges into nothingness.

As one contemplates the miasmic condition of modern intellectual and metaphysical history, the shrieks of Nietzsche's "madman" in the dithyrambs of his *Joyful Wisdom* tear away at the fragile texture of contemporary humanity's tormented spiritual consciousness, and leave it in shreds:

"...Whither are we moving now? Away from all suns? Are we not plunging continually? Backward, sidewards, forward, in all directions? Is there any up

or down left? Are we not straying as through an infinite nothing? Do we not
feel the breath of empty space? Has it not become colder? Is not night and
more night coming on all the while? Must not lanterns be lit in the morning?
Do we not hear anything yet of the noise of the gravediggers who are burying
God? . . . God is dead. And we have killed Him. . . ."

All or practically all twentieth-century systems of philosophy, social
theories, interpretations of history, political "science," ideological doctrines, and, withal, new religious conceptions of the world have had to
start and try to build upon the sands of the spiritual wasteland that
Nietzsche prophesied. For in it lay the debris left by the diachronic
destruction, first, of the primordial Augustinian vision of the "City of
God" and then, in the late phases of post-Renaissance history, the
collapse of the Cartesian ideal of a "City of Reason." Now, the better to
understand the truly nihilistic sweep of this dual "downfall" and its
almost inescapable consequences on the Faustian, indeed at the same
time neo-Promethean and Sisyphean, attempts at reconstruction or in-
novation, at least the fundamental features of the collision and then
mutual destruction of the two successively hegemonic world views that
I am here subsuming under the categories "Augustinian" and "Cartesian" must be delineated in the perspective of their ending.

Behind the inheritance of twentieth-century nihilism lay the playing
out of a mortal dialectic of apparently irreconcilable visions of human
history. Total immanence had been pitted against absolute transcendence; anthropocentric humanism had grappled with and prevailed
against the theology of cosmic order; the idea of historical mastery had
displaced the ideal of secular renunciation; the quest for a *scientia* that
encompassed knowledge and understanding, faith and reason, consciousness and conscience, had given way to deeper and deeper immer-
sion in the parts, in fragments that constituted or claimed to be realms
unto themselves, unrelated to any whole. Mind had proclaimed victory
over spirit and reason itself had been banished by its own progeny—
modern science, technology, industrialism, capitalism, collectivism—
proclaiming the new dispensation of a humanity ceaselessly marching
on toward the horizons of infinite "progress."

A new will-to-believe had enthroned Power at the center of Flux. God
was dead, Nietzsche cried, and Western man had killed Him. So it
seemed at the opening of the twentieth-century crisis of all values.
During the nineteenth century, neither the Romantic rebellion against
reason that characterized the first half of it nor the post-Romantic

revolt against Positivism that dominated its closing decades had succeeded in restoring any kind of organic equilibrium. Before, during, and
after the "great divide" represented by the rich manifestations and
tragic undercurrents of nineteenth-century culture there were not lacking exceptionally keen and prophetic European minds—from Erasmus
to Voltaire, from Goethe to Croce, from Burckhardt to Albert Camus—
who had invoked a *pax spiritualis* to be pursued through philosophical
moderation, intellectual humility, and vital balance as against the arro-
gance of sterile intellect, the hegemony of unreason, and the tyranny of
a History that devours its own children.

By the eve of the twentieth century the marriage of Faustian pride
and Caesarean ambition had been consummated in Europe, and from
their embrace there issued monstrous creatures stamped with the features of new spiritual extremisms, moral tyrannies, political despotisms,
all nurtured in the shadow of the apocalypse. An epochal civil war of
ideas and values now broke fully open in both West and East. (Is there
not more than merely symbological irony in the fact that the cycle of
Emmanuel Mounier's life, 1905-1950, corresponded almost exactly
with the explosive arc of the fearful European crisis?) In contrast to
what had occurred during other long periods of intellectual and spiritual strife (for instance, during the protracted agony of classical civilization from Augustus to the age of Constantine), the modern European
crisis sprang from an inner fratricidal as well as patricidal conflict, not
one between alien cultures but rather between two intimately, almost
indissolubly, related visions of the world. Fundamentally, it was from
their contest that the anarchy of values that had weaned the new Goya-
like monsters of the twentieth century had emerged. The great anarchic
rebellion had sprung from within, not outside, the very matrix of Western history.

A perceptive modern European historical thinker, Hans Freyer, re-
assessed the inner nexus binding the two primordial "protagonists" of
the stupendous spiritual conflict raging at the heart of Europe during
the epoch of its world hegemony. Beyond the petty pace of historical
vicissitude, accident, and chance, he espied the motivating force of a
truth that had lain and stirred at the very foundations of Western
history: In its European manifestations, the kingdom of reason had had
its beginning in the midst of the Kingdom of God and, though it was
something distinct from it, it was "a construction within it, a framework of thought incorporated in belief." Hans Freyer's illumination,

like that of a few other contemporaries of his, among them Mounier himself, came tragically too late and, in a sense, proved utterly ineffectual even in the era of potential reconstruction following the most convulsive phase of the European crisis. But he had tried, with unforgettable lucidity, to recall the intimate connection between the two "kingdoms." In a beautiful, if melancholy, swan song to Europe as the leader of world history, he had sought to recapture the original harmony behind the fertility and splendor of "reason" in its metamorphoses as science, artistic creativity, and the promise of liberation from the unnecessary, dehumanizing tyranny of economic want and social suffering.

Late and too weak, such voices could not undo the tragic dissonance first sounded by Nietzsche. Philosophizing with a hammer, he had long ago revealed the deicidal character of Western civilization. For Nietzsche, the universalized absolutism of European historical reason had been fated to rear a race of destroyers, "the murderers of all murderers" of the very God from whose kingdom their innocent brothers claimed birth and sustenance. Thereafter, few had been able to escape the clutches of the Nietzschean revelation. Thus, in a different way, again, we must ask: By the beginning of the twentieth century, what had the inner drama of Western history been about, what had been at stake, what had perished, who had prevailed? Nietzsche's answer had been frightfully clear. At the heart of that drama, as a function of its momentum and meaning, he had seen the "greatest deed in all history hitherto"—not the "passive" death of God but the "active" murder of God. For the sake of this "deed," he cried, whosoever was born after it had been uncovered would "be part of a higher history than all history hitherto"—or, we must add, conversely, of no history at all. For Nietzsche the dawn of the coming transhistorical day posed an inescapable post-Kierkegaardian Either/Or—either the illumination of a path to be trod by the "superhuman" disciples of the new prophet Zarathustra or the start of a new day so dark that lanterns must be lit in the morning only to reveal the striding of the ultimate barbarian upon the wasteland of a sub-human history. There was no other choice, it seemed, for Europe in the post-Nietzschean "age of the assassins."

Now, the major thrust of Joseph Amato's lucid yet, in a sense, disturbing study on Emmanuel Mounier is that for the young French philosopher of Personalism there came to be a "third way" out of the

Nietzschean Hobson's choice between the superman and the barbarian as sole demiurges of the future of the West. What, in my view, renders Mounier's discovery the more astounding and truly original is the fact that he seemed to agree with the frightening noesis behind Nietzsche's "diagnosis." It is true, to be sure, that Mounier's "agreement" stemmed from different sources, was anchored in different points of reference, and looked forth through different perspectives from those of the prophet of Zarathustra. Needless to say, these fundamental differences of historical origins, hermeneutic procedures, and philosophical points of view are subtly but very clearly elaborated throughout four illuminating chapters of Amato's book (II-V). In them he retraces the "education" from early youth through maturity of Mounier's *forma mentis* and the shaping of his vision of the world. These, Amato shows us, were nourished and molded, enriched and challenged by the intellectual labors, ethical teachings, and religious inclinations of five modern French masters of the mind. Of these, three—Léon Bloy, Charles Péguy, and Henri Bergson—exerted their influence upon Mounier in a mediated way. Their own maturity and the direct impact of their principal works had coincided more or less with the time of birth of Mounier's own generation, even though one of them, Bergson, survived through the period of maturity of the "third" cohort of intellectuals that lived through the explosive stage of the great French and European crisis of the twentieth century. The other two major figures of the French intellectual quintet, Jacques Chevalier and Jacques Maritain, helped directly to shape the fundamental structure of Mounier's thought and, each in his fashion, guided through crucial formative periods the very character and the quintessential direction of Mounier's agonizing quest for personal authenticity and spiritual self-identity.

There is no need, I believe, even to attempt to synthesize the distinguishing characteristic varieties of the philosophical work of Mounier's five French masters. Through his own particularized elucidation Amato has recaptured, with genuine critical intelligence and fine sensitivity to the nuances of motive and meaning, the individual character and contribution to Mounier's formation of each of his masters. It may, nevertheless, not be altogether superfluous to emphasize that around each of those five major figures of modern French thought there had been, indeed continued to be, contemporary circles of like-minded confrères and disciples but also, outside those circles, clusters of antipathetic, if not openly antagonistic, schools of French (and European) ideas. Du-

ring the first two decades of the century these "other" schools and,
therefore, other alternatives in France alone were centered in Durkheim's sociological neopositivism, Boutroux's eclectic "scientific spiritualism," Georges Sorel's antirationalistic vitalism, and Jean Jaurès'
humanistic socialism. Later, during the maturing time of crisis, even as
Mounier was finding his own way, came the sway of the French currents of existentialism under the contrasting varieties advocated, among
others, by the Christian Gabriel Marcel and the atheist Jean-Paul Sartre,
the Marxist Maurice Merleau-Ponty and the neohumanist Albert Camus.
Mounier was certainly aware and even "assimilated" what he felt he
needed from the thought of a number of them, both the older and the
younger, but his own truly existential choice was not pursued on the
traces of their doctrines and ideals.

Mounier's own "choice" was made, it seems to me, in response to an
at-first tormentingly obscure and gradually clearer, then ultimately irresistible, inner calling akin to that of the "active" mystics he secretly
admired. Exactly because he possessed an exceptional mind, a strong
intellect, emphasis on the formation and development of his thought is
not only justified but indispensable for an understanding of the nature
of his work in the world. But exclusive attention to the sources and
forms of his thought can also lead, has indeed led, the unwary—Joseph
Amato is not among these—to misinterpretation of the original character of his moral personality and deepest spiritual motivations. It is, I
believe, necessary to stress this if for no other reason than to clarify the
true influence of his five French masters on Mounier. Though he himself does not seem to have realized or been fully conscious of the real
place they had occupied in his intellectual growth or the function that
had differently served toward the self-definition of his autonomy until
quite late—apparently not before his founding of *Esprit* (1932)—he had
sucked hard, so to speak, at the lymphs of his masters' teachings and
drawn from them all the vitalizing common "food" his spirit needed.
Plausibly simple as it now seems, it was no facile task, not even for
Mounier, to reconcile the particularizing, sometimes distinctively contradictory, characteristics of Bloy's neomysticism, Péguy's passionate
national-metahistorical messianism, Bergson's quasi-Heraclitean intu-
itionism, Chevalier's dogmatic (and political) Catholic conservatism,
and Maritain's Neo-Thomistic "liberal" humanism. In essence, however,
what he extracted and abstracted from them all was a new historical
sense of the vitality and, therefore, for him the immutable validity of

Christian thought and a new philosophical sense of the eschatology of the human condition.

One example alone may suffice to illustrate the play of this dualistic influence—historical and philosophical, both of them, therefore, fundamentally "intellectual"—of one, perhaps the most important, of his masters on Mounier. At one point in his discussion of the unique relationship between Maritain and Mounier, Amato characterizes Mounier's Personalism as both an outgrowth and an independent refashioning of Maritain's thought. Thus, Amato suggests, through an intimate dialectic of absorption and transformation, that Mounier eventually found himself engaged in "one of twentieth-century Catholicism's most profound attempts to rethink the present and to create a new future." That this judgment does capture the essence of a truth in the relationship between Maritain and Mounier seems to me incontestable. And yet a strange reservation lingers in my acceptance of that judgment insofar as, perhaps mistakenly, I read below or within it the assumption of too strong a continuity of Maritain's Neo-Thomism in the undeniable originality of Mounier's organic final version of his Personalist philosophy. For, to me at least, it seems that, while there can be no doubt concerning the permanent impress made upon Mounier by the tormented bio-spiritual vicissitudes of Jacques (and Raïssa) Maritain and his unparalleled contribution toward the Neo-Thomistic revival, the later separation and very serious dissent between Mounier and Maritain can be fully understood only in the context of Mounier's own continuous self-development toward more than a renovated theological system—toward a novel philosophy of life.

Now, undoubtedly, Maritain's work on *Three Reformers: Luther, Descartes, and Rousseau* (1925) was indeed a milestone in the formation of Mounier's historical criticism and philosophical education. Mounier was only twenty when Maritain's impressive critique on the "deviations" of modern thought was published. Without Maritain's "antecedent" organic critique of "the erring journey of modern man towards the contemporary world"—an "erring journey" pursued, according to Maritain, under the guidance of three creators of that modern "individualism" which found itself impotent face-to-face with the onslaught of contemporary "collectivism," whatever its form, shape, or colors during the twentieth century—it can be plausibly supposed that Mounier's first theoretical manifesto, entitled "Remake the Renaissance," with which *Esprit* was launched, is either totally inconceivable or imaginable only in a different form or emphasis even if with similar substance. But Mounier's passionate antihistorical exhortation also raises other important questions.

The phrase "remake the Renaissance" was stunningly impressive but certainly ambiguous. Its essential thrust, however, was unmistakable: it was a call to undo more than four centuries of European history in order to redress the "errors" that Maritain had elaborately dissected and subtly ascribed, in his influential philosophical "syllabus," to the thought and impact of his "three reformers"—Luther, Descartes, and Rousseau. But, it could be asked, if the Renaissance had to be "remade" against that incredibly powerful trio, why not also against other equally significant European minds of similar stature—among them, certainly, Pico della Mirandola, Ficino, Copernicus, Montaigne, Bruno, Pascal, Galileo, Newton, Leibniz, Vico, Montesquieu, Hume, Herder, Kant, Hegel, Jefferson, Mill, Mazzini, Kierkegaard, Marx, Nietzsche. And if against these, too, what was to be done with men of that same error-filled "modern age," many of them of all ages, and among them Machiavelli, Shakespeare, Voltaire, Goethe, Stendhal, Leopardi, Baudelaire, and Tolstoy? All this cannot but seem, as it indeed is, a *reductio ad absurdum* of the young Mounier's desperate call to "remake the Renaissance." But when that call was launched it had to be in the guise of an anti-Cartesian *tabula rasa* of Western history—or not at all. The passion of the moralist would otherwise perish under the distinctions of the philosopher. And yet, in a fundamental sense, at that time at least, it was perhaps only the critical-historical philosophy of his French masters, particularly Maritain, who led Mounier to unleash the force of his moral passion and to release the more mysterious energy of his inner mystic vision of a palingenesis.

Though Joseph Amato himself, cautious intellectual historian that he is, has perhaps wisely not wanted to strain the available particulars of his bio-spiritual reconstruction of Mounier's mind and thought, I feel that these speculations are not totally inconsistent with his implicit documentation and disciplined intimations throughout his book. For further explication, if not justification, let us look a little closer at some larger "facts" concerning Emmanuel Mounier. It is, in the first place, illuminating, as I have repeatedly suggested, to keep in mind that all Mounier's "educators" were not only French but, each in his fashion, Catholic. For many understandable historical and religious reasons, negation rather than affirmation of what the "political Europe" *outside* had brought upon their nation through more than a century and the "philosophical Europe" *inside* had wrought with their church had, almost of necessity, to be their pivotal point of reference. Mounier had not missed this basic lesson not only from them but from the very milieu and atmosphere in which he had grown. Again, those masters and a few others helped him engage, perhaps overhastily, in nurturing a vision of "restoration," at the same time a recourse and return, that, at the moment he formulated and issued his programmatic essay on *"Refaire la Renaissance,"* was essentially negative, a sweeping *gran rifiuto* which, however, upon closer look, reveals itself as of a special type of French-"provincial" intellectual style, at least vis-à-vis the wider spheres of European philosophical and cultural history. Could even a magnificently refurbished system of French Catholic thought really encompass and transcend the complex multitudinous expressions of the whole European mind after the Renaissance and, contrariwise, of the inescapable urgencies of European society and politics on the eve of Hitler's ascent to power? And, lastly, Mounier may have been (as Amato makes emphatically clear) a new model of the "revolutionary," the would-be restorer and utopian in one person. But his ultimate goals went much, almost infinitely, beyond these tasks, for his was a proclamation of faith aiming to exorcise the demons of history through a "drive to resacralize the world." By the time he arrived at this formulation of his mission, his "apostolate," Emanuel Mounier had strangely but fascinatingly come full circle as student and disciple, critic and moralist, and now, finally, "active" mystic and chiliast. In this cycle of Mounier's life must be sought the true meaning and message of a French Catholic intellectual who became a unique European personality during the first half of the twentieth century.

For Mounier the catalyst of this metamorphosis seems to have been the advancing avalanche of contemporary calamity not for France alone but for all Europe during the 1930s. Not only Catholicism but all Christian and non-Christian faiths and the peoples of all nations were now mortally threatened by the rise and strut of the new beast of the apocalypse who, under whatever mask or name—Fascism, Nazism, national or international Bolshevism—had, Medusa-like, at first transfixed and then, from 1933 to 1945, proceeded to tear asunder the last fragments and devour whole the mixed legacy of tragedy and splendor of post-Renaissance European civilization. It was not that, perhaps slowly but clearly, Mounier understood that in order to resist the flood of the new barbarians, and to restore and resacralize the world, not even the strongest theoretical call to "remake the Renaissance" would be sufficient. It was thus that he saw the impelling need to turn and remold his abstract reinterpretation of European history since the Renaissance into an effective philosophy of action that might serve the present needs and sketch out the nature of the means and ends for a renovation of Europe after the deluge. Increasingly, therefore, during the later 1930s and early 1940s, as the shadows of the catastrophe advanced, enveloped, and then slowly retreated in France and Europe, Mounier dedicated more and more pages of his journal *Esprit* to his new philosophy of action. Then he first fully elaborated it in his *Personalist Manifesto* of 1936 and in all his larger works after the fall of France in 1940. Despite momentary flaws in his hopes, attitudes, and activities of the first ten-months phase of the Vichy regime's strange attempt to be the vehicle for a French national restoration (its propagandists spoke of it as a "national revolution"!), practically all of Mounier's later larger works bespoke his new dedication to bring about a real political, social, and moral "revolution" based upon and inspired by his insight into the necessity of an organic revaluation of values not merely for France but for all Europe.

Mounier's new ideal of Personalism as a philosophy of action marked indeed a veritable point of arrival and departure—"arrival" of the theories of philosophical and religious "restoration" that had nourished his mind during his youth and formative years, and "departure" for a self-molded philosophy of action aimed toward a new kind of "revolution," a truly great change in the social and political structure and in the cultural, moral, and spiritual foundations of Europe.

In the last chapter of his book, Joseph Amato offers a relatively concise, yet penetrating and illuminating, analysis of Mounier's Personalism as a "new historical ideal." Keen and clear as it is, Amato's exposition would tend to dispense with any attempt at further elucidation. It may, nevertheless, not prove altogether gratuitous if I make a conclusive effort to call attention, as synthetically as possible, to the nexus between the central themes of Mounier's Personalism and the "location" of his new historical ideal within the larger framework of the great European cultural crisis of the twentieth century that I have sought to make my own guiding thread in this introductory essay.

Had Emmanuel Mounier's temper of mind and person been that of the "pure" theorist or even of the "usual" moral philosopher, his works after the impressive programmatic statement of his *"Refaire la Renaissance"* would have insured him a respectably high place in modern French Catholic thought. Read or re-read with the detachment of time, place, and circumstance, we can now claim, all of Mounier's subsequent larger works—his *Personalist Manifesto* (1936), *Introduction to Existentialisms* (1946), *What Is Personalism* (1947), *The Little Fear of the Twentieth Century* (1948), *Personalism* (1949), and, above all, his earlier *Treatise on Character* (1946)—satisfy, in my opinion, even the severest test that would place him among the most productive and fertile thinkers of the twentieth century. Those works certainly reveal that he possessed practically all the requirements of intellectual rigor, evident features of originality, and, above all, single-minded commitment to philosophy's *raison d'être*—the quest for truth.

Yet, it seems to me, not even from Amato's sympathetic study does the impression that Mounier's total theoretical work would unquestionably place him in the company of the great philosophers of the modern age emerge beyond doubt. I believe that this apparently "negative" impression should not be misunderstood. The genuine philosophers of the nineteenth century—one need think only of Kant, Hegel, Schopenhauer, Nietzsche—and those of the twentieth century—among whom have towered Croce, Dilthey, Bergson, James, Dewey, Heidegger, Husserl, Jaspers, Wittgenstein, Unamuno, and Maritain—have all, each in his fashion, dwelt and labored in a different sphere from that which was Mounier's. In pointing up this difference no invidious comparison is even conceivable. Despite common assertions, the sphere of the "pure" philosopher is neither better nor worse, neither higher nor necessarily more exalted, than that of the genuine searcher for truth whatever his systemic framework of gnoseological inquiry. As scientists, those searchers may grapple with the truth of the world of nature, as historians, with the past of the world of men, as reformers, with the present the human condition, as revolutionaries, with their vision of the future of human society. Each in his sphere strives toward attaining understanding and sometimes "mastery" over some aspect of that multitudinous and ever-elusive quintessential "reality" which is truth—that truth which *ab initio* of Western civilization Socrates regarded as one and whole.

Almost from the beginning Emmanuel Mounier chose for himself a journey of the mind of his own toward the "truth" of his time and world during the first half of the twentieth century. Having made that choice, Mounier had to obey, so to speak, the "laws" of its vital logic.

That logic demanded, above all, that for him no system of thought—not even that to which his birth, education, experiences, and conscious personal urges practically "preconditioned" his intellectual outlook, as modern French Catholic philosophy indeed did—would be sufficient in and by itself unto his deeper, perhaps unconscious, psychic and spiritual moving forces. For Mounier, it seems as if not even the most brilliant and attractive, but nevertheless still passive and abstract, theological foundation could of itself really serve to rekindle belief-as-action from the ashes of modern nihilism. More was needed, he felt, and that "more" implied for him the pursuit of at least two imprescriptible corollaries. First, the sources of theological, even philosophical, faith must be explored ever anew in order to be deepened; they must be challenged, even questioned, in order to be strengthened; they must be expanded to the very limits of secular unbelief (as his study of Nietzsche and the "atheist" existentialists shows) in order to be tested, even tempted, but perhaps ultimately enriched, refreshed, renovated. But—and this for Mounier proved to be the second "corollary"—this essentially intellectual exposure and experience, even fulfillment, could not be integral, intimately meaningful, unless it led beyond. Beyond—to where? Mounier's work and writings after 1932, I am convinced, offer the full answer to this question.

The fact is that Mounier reached his true maturity when, some time about his thirtieth year, he fully understood what for him became thereafter a truth beyond question: his belief, even his faith, would be empty, "egotistical" if not sterile, without his action, and his action would be blind, a suicidal leap into the dark seas of nihilistic activism, without his belief. For Mounier, at the core of the twentieth-century historical tragedy lay exactly the sundering of faith and works, belief and action, that four centuries of European spiritual dissension and moral civil war had ineluctably wrought. In their rebinding, in the healing of that open wound festering at the heart of Western humanity's fate, lay the "mission" of his revolutionary ideal. In its final form, Mounier's Personalism was one of the most passion-filled neo-Christian efforts to turn upside down Nietzsche's dithyramb on the death of God and at the same time to reintegrate the separated major terms of Marx's "thesis"—it was necessary both to reinterpret the world *and* to change it!

Was Mounier's dream of a new city of man reared not against but under, if not within, the vaulting arches of the "old" city of God

fulfilled? Put in this form, the question, I believe, answers itself. For
Mounier had engaged in an impossible task, and he knew it. In the final
analysis, Mounier's self-appointed "apostolate" was nothing short of an
attempt to bring about an all-encompassing reconciliation of the values
of life and the spirit. The sweep of his appeal seemed, and was, ecumen-
ical enough to attract the adhesion not only of a French and European
Catholicism truly conscious of the burden it must bear, of the mission
it must fulfill, in a world of men it claimed to serve, but also of all the
faiths, even those of the unbelievers, in the West. Ultimately, this was
indeed Mounier's impossible vision. Certainly impossible, we see now,
in a Europe, such as his was, gripped by an unparalleled time of trou-
bles, filled with days of unspeakably calculated cruelties and the mind-
less wrath of diabolical, "civilized," subhuman barbarians who scientif-
ically lighted the fires of the "Final Solution" and created the burning
ice of the "Gulag Archipelago." Inexorably, the era of civil conflicts
gave way to the endless years of total war. A dark night of the spirit
truly descended upon Europe and the world it had commanded. And
Mounier found himself among those resisters, alas! only too few vis-à-
vis the literally totalitarian debauchment, who continued to raise their
voices in the wilderness to invoke not an impossible "peace of God"
but at least a truce of reason—a truce of *reason,* now at long last neither
Cartesian nor merely Christian, neither historical nor metaphysical, but
of humanity's right to life. For too long in vain. For the catastrophe
had to proceed relentlessly to its "logical" denouement of mutual destruction in Europe and of the atomic fires of Hiroshima in Asia.

Projected against the "backdrop" of such apocalyptic convulsion,
Mounier's ideal of Personalist revolution cannot but seem at best inno-
cently ineffectual and at worst hopelessly utopian. How could the "mir-
acle" of a revaluation of values be brought to pass in the midst of a
human world apparently self-willed to damnation? Who would be the
true heroes of a new time, an epoch beyond supermen and barbarians,
leading the way to a lasting reintegration, for which Mounier had so
passionately fought, of personality and the community, character and
society, intelligence and history, conscience and power, the self and the
absolute? Europe was broken and divided within itself, surviving in the
shadow of two superstates on its land and oceanic flanks, as it set to
work at elemental physical reconstruction during the brief quinquen-
nium that, quite ironically, ended with Mounier's premature death in
1950. When, how long would it be before the fundamental "restora-

tion," an organic social and cultural, moral and spiritual, revolution, would be fulfilled? A quarter century later the answers to these questions are still not forthcoming.

And yet, despite all this and more, Joseph Amato's characterization of Emmanuel Mounier as a "tragic optimist" still seems redeemingly correct. Mounier foresaw and lived through the tragedy of France, the collapse of Europe, the ruins of Western civilization. Unlike many of his contemporaries—the existentialists and the fatalists, the worshippers of new powers and dominations and the defeatists, the professional prophets of endless doom and the exalters of the sterile joys of nostalgia, the blind reactionaries and the impotent revolutionaries, the nihilists and the terrorists—Mounier tempered his tragic sense of life with the realistic optimism of the shipwreck who, though he sees a shore he cannot reach, will not give in to despair. For him, resistance to the evils of his time was a function of his lifelong defiance of the demons who had polluted the springs of the spirit in the West. After the long murderous night of Europe's second Great War, Mounier's "tragic optimism" inspired him to turn his face to the dawn—to the future. Now, he felt, to "remake the Renaissance" was too much and too little and, at any rate, too ingenuously anachronistic insofar as such an endeavor belonged to a phase of his own and his generation's intellectual commitment to critique and negation of both good and evil in Europe's things past. Instead, the time was at hand "to remake Europe."

The creation of a united humanistic socialist Europe was not only necessary but within the realm of fulfillment. While some of his new intellectual antagonists, among them Sartre and Merleau-Ponty, envisioned an "existentialist" communist Europe, and while his old master Maritain dreamed in his exile of a liberal "Wilsonian" Christian humanistic Europe, Mounier held fast to his new vision of European humanistic socialism as the sole saving means for the reconciliation of the kingdom of reason with the kingdom of Providence, of the city of man with the city of God. During the last years of his life Mounier discovered a trans-Cartesian, vitalistic and historical, reason which, for him, became a new instrument not merely for understanding but for changing the world. Now, only *that* reason might succeed in binding the irrepressible aspirations of humanity for freedom and justice at the very foundation of a new humanistic-socialist Europe. For Mounier this was the final revelation. The fusion of historical reason and his unshaken providentialist chiliasm broke the cycle of his tormented but incomparably fruitful spiritual journey which, alas!, on the eve of his death, was ready to begin anew on a truly higher sphere. In his last vision of a new humanity conscious but not imprisoned by the good and evil of the past, active master, not passive victim of history, lay Mounier's answer to the riddle of the great European crisis of values. And in that answer, in turn, men of a new generation could read the sign of at least one escape from the Nietzschean philosophic "no-exit" that had enigmatically confronted and for too long held in thrall the mind and spirit of old Europe.

In a fundamental sense, it has been Joseph Amato's work on Mounier that has aroused in me, indeed inspired, these reflections, whatever their worth, on the crisis of European values in the twentieth century. I am grateful to him for having stirred my historical thought and enriched my understanding of an extraordinary man and exceptional modern mind. Whatever other, different, critical readings of it may elicit, I have no doubt that there will be general agreement on the fact that Amato's work testifies to a truly rare intellectual sensitivity. Together with his evident capacity for sustained scholarly labor, thought, and style, that sensitivity has admirably guided Amato toward original insights into bio-historical matters of great import. He has written intelligently throughout, in many sections brilliantly, concerning an outstanding intellectual and moral leader within a special French and European community striving to respond to a unique time of crisis and to confront a novel type of historic tragedy.

Amato's book seeks to retrace and reconstruct extremely complicated currents and countercurrents of modern French Catholic thought, aspects of secular European philosophy, and a variety of social and political doctrines during a new age of ideological absolutisms and the hegemonic drive of totalitarian ideas of power and culture. With the thought of Jacques Maritain and the philosophy of action of Emmanuel Mounier as the major threads of his study, Amato proceeds with coherence and clarity in his pursuit of their unique essentials as thinkers and moral critics. It is for this reason, I believe, among numerous other formal and substantive characteristics, that Amato's work constitutes a kind of exemplary "ideal model" of serious and genuinely committed intellectual history. This, for Amato, is not a superficial "intellectualistic" exercise, nor is it an arid and schematic retracing of the "evolution" and convolutions of "pure" ideas spinning in historical (and historic) vacuums. In this book intellectual history is strenuous inquiry into the sources of alternative visions of life and the world; it is a quest for meaning behind fact, event, vicissitude, and change; it is a search for the palpable bonds between ideas and values, history and life, personality and society, philosophic points of view and projects for redemptive action in the world of men. This book, in a word, reveals how two minds, two men (Emmanuel Mounier as well as his student Joseph Amato), have differently grappled with the sources, and the nature and course, of the dialectic between historic tragedy and historical hope at two different moments of twentieth-century intellectual and spiritual life.

University of Rochester   A. WILLIAM SALOMONE
August, 1974

INTRODUCTION

AS FOUNDER AND EDITOR of the journal *Esprit* from 1932 until 1950, Emmanuel Mounier (1905-1950) taught two generations of French intellectuals to understand their times. As chief formulator of the doctrine of Personalism, Mounier proposed a philosophy of our times which still has influence throughout Europe. This study of his philosophy is meant as a way to explore one significant effort at twentieth century self-understanding.

In its broadest sense, Personalism is a diverse intellectual movement of the twentieth century. In part, it belongs to no one school; and in part it belongs to everyone who believes man is a personal and communal being who is mortally endangered by his own political, social, economic, and ideological creations. Anyone, in fact, who in the name of man's worth seeks simultaneously to save man from isolation and tyranny, from the furies of individualism and collectivism, can consider himself, if he wishes, a Personalist. Personalism, defined in this loose sense, includes a whole array of men and movements who, without official program, are committed to man's transcendence and are the enemies of all individuals, ideas, societies, and states that deny man the needs of his body, the dignity of his spirit, the presence and sustenance of a true human community.

Mounier himself, when forced to define Personalism beyond his and *Esprit*'s goals, could do no better than this. In seeking a general definition of Personalism, Mounier always did two things: he defined it first in opposition to what he believed the two most threatening evils of the modern world, individualism and collectivism, and then he related it to a philosophical tradition which found both idealism and materialism enemies. He identified the following contemporary thinkers as creators of this tradition: Lotze, Scheler, Buber, Jaspers, Landsberg, and Berdy-aev, as well as Bergson, Blondel, Laberthonnière, Péguy, and Maritain. Beyond identifying this tradition, and making a few references to an occasional group outside France which broadly opposed collectivism and individualism and conceived of man as both spiritual and commu-nal, Mounier never gave an encompassing definition of Personalism as an existing reality.

In fact, Personalism was rather for Mounier what he believed he and the members of *Esprit* were in the process of forging into existence. In this sense, an understanding of Personalism is inseparable from Mou-nier's biography and his twenty-year effort to create a philosophy of and for our times. It reflects his desire as a Catholic intellectual to find a philosophy that mediates between the divine and the human, the eter-nal and the historical. Equally it represents his and colleagues' dialogues with Marxists, existentialists, and others over the place and purpose of man in the twentieth century. Simultaneously, it is an expression of Mounier's attempt to find an alternative to what he believed the bank-ruptcy of the political right and left, to establish an understanding of the condition of man in his times, to offer a new spiritual perspective in terms of which man could understand his present and order his future. In a word, Personalism was religious, political, social, and all else which Mounier believed constituted part of a proper critique and a solution to twentieth century man's situation. Thus, while Personalism becomes far more than mute biographical data, and cannot be reduced to an arbi-trary and sterile heuristic concept to describe a changing attitude in a changing world, it remains nevertheless first to be understood in refer-ence to Mounier's vocation to his times.

Personalism, on one hand, was born out of Mounier's critical reflec-tions on the events of Europe and the world in the 1930s and 1940s. It expresses his critical analyses of the breakdown of the national and international economic, social, and political orders, as well as his analy-ses of the emergence of totalitarianism in Russia, Italy, and Germany. Personalism, on the other hand, reveals Mounier's efforts to furnish Western man with a new historical ideal for his social, political, and cultural existence. In accord with larger currents of Western humanism, Personalism thus not only decries abuses against freedom and justice in the contemporary world but seeks to articulate a vision of a new human order.

Like any comprehensive contemporary doctrine of man, Personalism has both critical and positive dimensions. As a critique, Personalism first asserts that contemporary civilization has entered into a total crisis. Personalism calls attention to the oppositions, tensions, conflicts, and dilemmas which make up and are in the process of destroying contemporary civilization. Among these dichotomies are: such philosophical oppositions as exist between idealism and materialism, ethics and science; such political and social tensions as exist between nationalism and internationalism, centralization and decentralization and, in particular, individualism and collectivism; such cultural conflicts as exist between faith and reason, work and contemplation, progress and decadence; and, last, such spiritual dilemmas as grow out of the conflicts between tradition and modernity, Church and state, freedom and equality. Each of these oppositions, tension, conflicts, and dilemmas, however, has become, according to Mounier, increasingly and tragically destructive because of the total absence of a guiding philosophy of man in the contemporary world.

As a philosophy of reconstruction, Personalism is essentially an attempt to transcend and reorder these dichotomies by offering a new vision of man. Based upon a belief in the primacy of the person, as a spiritual, free, and rational being, Personalism is antithetical to all collectivisms (Nationalism, Fascism, Marxism) that subjugate man to an immanent order of human thought, society, politics, and history. Equally based upon a belief that man is an embodied and communal being, Personalism opposes all forms of individualism (religious, political, social, economic, etc.) that deny man his place and rights in this world among other men. Thus, Personalism attempts both to define the crisis of our times, and to offer the premises upon which a new human order can be established.

A full grasp of the dimensions of Mounier's Personalism can come, however, only after a historical understanding of the origin and development of Mounier's world view. This, in turn, presupposes answers to such diverse questions as: What are the sources of Mounier's thought about man, society, and politics? To what degree does Mounier's thought reflect the immediate conditions of France, Europe, and the Church in the first half of this century? In what ways is Mounier's Personalism a result of his education as a young man and in what ways was Personalism transformed and contradicted by the different, massive, and awesome events of the 1930s and 1940s? Each of these questions leads us beyond Mounier's individual life and consciousness. Together they lead us to the central problem of understanding the cultural traditions which constituted Mounier's first vision of the world, and the social forces and political events which shaped Mounier's final vision of Personalism at mid-century.

Four men formed Mounier's first adult intellectual understanding of the world. They were Jacques Chevalier and Jacques Maritain, Henri Bergson and Charles Péguy. The Catholic philosophers Chevalier and Maritain gave Mounier his formal education in Catholic and non-Catholic thought. Bergson and Péguy, who were not Mounier's immediate teachers, nevertheless had an equally important influence on Mounier's philosophical and spiritual formation. Bergson gave Mounier's philosophy its inner pulse and form; Péguy, poet and polemicist, was the model upon whom Mounier established his adult identity as a committed Christian intellectual.

All four of these men were critics of their times. In varying degree, each was hostile to contemporary bourgeois culture; each specifically attacked what he considered the philosophical domination of materialism, idealism, and positivism and sought, in contradistinction to them, a new guiding philosophy upon which contemporary man could reform his thought and life. Taken together, the older Bergson and Péguy, as well as the younger Chevalier and Maritain, can be understood as part of a *fin du siècle* cultural revolt against the values of the bourgeois Third Republic. Considered in yet a broader European historical perspective, they can be considered as part of a second wave of Romanticism which came by 1900 to form in its various aesthetic, philosophical, and religious elements a veritable counter-revolution against the ruling values of nineteenth century bourgeois life.

In great part, it was this cultural revolt that constituted the young Mounier's first critical view of his times. His attacks against positivists, materialists, and idealists, as well as his attacks against the bourgeois world, were as fundamental to the young Mounier's critical view of the world as were his studies in Catholic philosophy and theology crucial to the formation of his positive views of existence. In fact, there was already a unity between Mounier's negative and positive views of the world. On one hand, with other religious and non-religious intellectuals across France and Europe in the 1920s, Mounier held the bourgeois spirit accountable for all the disruptions he found in contemporary society, politics, economics, and culture. On the other hand, with so many Catholic and religious intellectuals, the young Mounier suggested this failure of the bourgeois order to be reflective of yet a deeper disorder: modern man's alienation from God.

It was, however, during the event-filled years of 1929-1932 that young Mounier's first views of the world were transformed into his first full intellectual vision of his times, Personalism. This transformation partly resulted from Mounier's growing appreciation of Charles Péguy as both Christian and activist and partly from his awareness that the Church was again open to the worker and the future. That is, Péguy pointed for Mounier the way to a lay vocation of total commitment and service to the truth amid the men of one's times. More important, however, for understanding the emergence of Mounier's adult intellectual vocation and his Personalism was the Depression and the national and international events which flowed from it. These events convinced Mounier, as so many of his European contemporaries, that capitalism was dying, that liberal democracy was no longer operable, that the whole international order was in chaos—that bourgeois civilization was in its entirety in a state of profound and irreversible crisis. Thus, like so many of his own young French intellectual contemporaries, Mounier found it essential to expand what was until then a fundamentally aesthetic-religious criticism of his times into an encompassing economic, social, and political philosophy which would provide a Christian and humanistic explanation of what he considered a total crisis in civilization.

In the act of founding *Esprit* in 1932, Mounier gave his life over to analyzing the dissolution of bourgeois civilization and the preparation of a Personalist civilization. Mounier developed Personalism, thereafter, in relation to the massive forces and events that shook Europe in the 1930s. Because of this, Personalism had a double character. Particularly in the early and mid-1930s, Personalism had a global character since it voiced the reflections of Mounier and the young intellectuals of *Esprit* on the cultural and political impotence of France before totalitarian Russia and Germany and capitalist America. These reflections obviously challenged them to attempt an answer to some of the most profound questions of modern and twentieth century French and European political and social life: right or left, centralization or decentralization, liberalism or Marxism, Locke or Rousseau, freedom or authority? In almost diametrical opposition to the grandiose search for a new Europe and France implied by these questions, Personalism in the late 1930s became more and more empirical and existential as Mounier and the young men of *Esprit* became more and more preoccupied with the hard realities of nations preparing for war.

By the end of the Second World War, Mounier's Personalism seemed considerably different from what it had been in the mid-1930s. In part, a change in context accounts for the difference. Throughout Europe great numbers of Catholic intellectuals called, as Mounier and *Esprit* had, for a whole new world built upon man's fundamental rights and responsibilities. In France, great numbers of intellectuals and politicians alike now admitted that the world they lived in was involved in unprecedented revolutionary change, and they were willing to acknowledge, at least in theory, that the past bourgeois political practices and social policies of the Third Republic must be radically reformed if France and Europe were to survive. In fact, the newly founded Christian Democratic Party (*Mouvement Républicain Populaire*), which was for many the newest and the most promising phenomenon of post-Second World War French political life, at its outset adopted Personalism almost *in toto*. Thus, even though Mounier specifically denounced the Christian Democratic Party and the Fourth Republic for their reactionary social policies and practices and continued to insist on the absolute necessity for a transformation of the entire human order, his voice, when it called for the spiritual and communal rights of man and the need for an alternative to the abuses of capitalism and statism, sounded as if it were but another voice in a whole chorus of nations, churches, and political parties truly clamoring for a new and just world.

Personalism, however, was substantively changed also. Mounier had been educated by the events of the Second World War. It was no longer possible for Mounier to continue to unify Western political, social, economic, and cultural institutions under the comprehensive and encompassing charge of being bourgeois; nor could Mounier any longer employ the blanket indictment of "bourgeois civilization" and thereby describe equally all the evils of the present order and declare the need for a new civilization. This was so for many reasons. France and Europe had grown smaller, and the United States, Russia, and the Third World larger; the fate of France and Europe could no longer easily be assumed to be the destiny of mankind. Power had grown more real; ideas, more abstract. The coming, the waging, and the concluding of the Second World War had offered Mounier vivid instructions in the diverse forces that go into the making and unmaking of states and societies.

But, above all else, the Third Reich and Vichy taught Mounier the most serious lessons: an individual state led by an individual man had committed atrocities greater in evil than Mounier had even imagined in the early 1930s to be the malevolent essence of bankrupt bourgeois civilization. Vichy had shown Mounier how decisively the language of anti-capitalism, decentralization, and community could be used in the same reactionary way in which Mussolini employed the notion of corporate state. Together Vichy France and Nazi Germany had taught Mounier to appreciate both English and French traditions of liberalism. Mounier came to realize that, within these traditions, were embodied more than transitory bourgeois interests; to be found therein were the highest expressions man had so far made of his freedom and liberty. Mounier, thus, was more ready to admit the precariousness of what was good in the present, and less ready to sacrifice it for the ideals of a new civilization.

For all that, it would be wrong to think of Mounier as a type of new liberal or conservative. In fact, his Personalism increasingly enrolled itself on the left. Using momentarily the characteristics which Raymond Aron assigned in his *Opium of the Intellectuals* (1955) to the left in general and members of *Esprit* specifically, Mounier can be said to belong to the left for the following reasons: Mounier continued to think in terms of a revolutionary restructuring of the present. Mounier allied himself unequivocally to the cause of the worker against capitalism. Further consistent with a part of the post-War French left, Mounier strove to find a French and European alternative to Russia and the United States; he tried, obviously unsuccessfully, to stop the growing ideological division between Eastern and Western Europe; and he pursued consistently, but almost always unsuccessfully, a dialogue with the intellectuals of the Communist Party. Last, and most significant in revealing Mounier's broad ties to the left, he identified his Personalism with the socialist humanism which was revived across Europe and France after the Second World War.

Yet in opposition to what Aron makes the determined "myths" of the left, Mounier did not surrender Personalism to a doctrinaire leftism or a vague leftist spirituality. Mounier did not confuse theology with social ideologies, nor did he fail to speak out against the brutal acts of Russian and Eastern European rule. Mounier's independence from a naive leftism was further shown by his refusal to participate in what can be considered the big historical myths. Mounier never subscribed to the myth of inevitable human progress; nor did he idealize revolution as the inevitable and ultimate answer to all human dilemmas. Rather Mounier persisted in surveying man's past, present, and future in terms of "tragic optimism," which on one hand speaks of man's promise and God's abiding love and, on the other, declares that unless contemporary man embody the highest values and goals of the past in a future order, he will continue his descent into violence and destruction.

To understand the transformation of Mounier's conception of his times from its first religious-aesthetic form in the 1920s until its final form at mid-century amounts to no less than mastering a significant part of a half century of French and French Catholic intellectual lives. Understanding the formation and the development of Mounier's Personalism involves grasping the relations that exist between a young man's education and his world view, as well as the interplay between events and consciousness, and the continuity and revolution that go into the making of an intellectual's view of his times. It also equally involves seeking to understand the relation between the abiding assumptions and the radical changes that took place in French Catholic minds as they sought to understand and adjust to the realities of the twentieth century.[1] Inherent, therefore, within the task of reconstructing Mounier's understanding of our times, there is a second task of examining twentieth century French and French Catholic intellectual lives.

In order to establish some of the important unities between pre- and post-First World War intellectual life, a significant place was given in this study to the older Jacques Maritain (1882-1973). Like the Young Mounier, the young Maritain also underwent an identity crisis as a youth and found his search for himself inextricably tied to his search for the meaning of his times. His search led him before the First World War from Jaurès and Péguy, to Bergson and Bloy, and then Catholicism, Thomism, and the *Action Française*. After the Condemnation of the *Action Française* in 1926, which is second in importance only to Maritain's conversion in determining his view of the modern world, Maritain sought a new philosophy of society and politics. In the 1930s, Maritain articulated his Integral Humanism, which is nearly identical to Mounier's Personalism; and in the 1940s Maritain came to be a broad adherent of Wilsonian Liberalism in the same sense as Mounier could be termed a broad adherent of Jaurèsian Socialism.

However, in addition obviously to furnishing numerous valuable contrasts and parallels with Mounier, there were other reasons for giving Maritain a particularly large place in this study of Mounier. First, Maritain profoundly influenced Mounier's philosophical and historical criticisms of bourgeois civilization, encouraged Mounier's decision to found

Esprit, and guided Mounier in his first decisions as the head of *Esprit*. Second, Maritain, who was in the United States almost steadily from the middle 1930s until the late 1950s, is far better known to an American audience, especially for his important influence on natural law and democratic political theory. But third and most important is the fact that Maritain was French Catholicism's and Rome's foremost lay thinker in the first half of the twentieth century.

"Maritain," wrote Mounier on this point, "is the principal artisan of the Catholic Renaissance in France since 1918."[2] As no other, Maritain in the 1920s and 1930s defined the meaning of Catholic philosophical orthodoxy as Thomism, while at the same time determining the contours of Catholicism's dialogue with non-Catholics, and the nature and forms of Catholic participation in culture and the arts. Because of this, even such prominent French Catholics as Blondel, Marcel, and Bernanos do not rival Maritain's role as shaper of twentieth century French Catholicism. To bring Mounier and Maritain together in a study is to bring together the two thinkers who have done the most since the First World War in teaching French Catholic intellectuals to understand their place in modern times.

Together Mounier and Maritain represented one path French Catholicism followed in seeking a second rapprochement with the Republic and the modern world.[3] It fell to Maritain and Mounier to rethink the relation of Church and society in terms of democracy and in relation to the revolutionizing events of the 1930s and 1940s. In turn, as part of the intellectual elite of the French laity, Maritain and Mounier formed one of the exploratory vanguards by which the Vatican sought to understand and determine a course of action in a world for which neither Pius IX's reaction nor Leo XIII's tentative rapprochement had prepared it. In other terms, Mounier and Maritain reflect the spirit of twentieth century Catholicism as it continues to seek its place in the modern world.

CHAPTER I

THE SELF AND CIVILIZATION:
AN INTRODUCTION TO MOUNIER

MOUNIER'S CHOSEN VOCATION was to resolve what he considered a total crisis in civilization. From 1932, the year in which he founded the journal *Esprit*, until his death in 1950, Mounier attempted to help mankind in its passage from one civilization to another. For the French philosopher, Jean Lacroix, long associated with *Esprit*, Mounier is a polemicist, educator and prophet who is comparable to Nietzsche and Marx, Péguy and Bloy.[1] For the Protestant philosopher, Paul Ricoeur, who joined *Esprit* after the Second World War, Mounier's "great force is said to have tied at the origin [of *Esprit*] his manner of philosophizing to a conscious awareness of a crisis of civilization, and to have dared to envision beyond any school of philosophy a new civilization in its totality."[2] Even though both of these claims for Mounier may appear exaggerated, all biographers of Mounier must first approach him in terms of that unique unity that existed between his life and thought, and his role as critic and reformer of his times.[3] It is this unity that characterized Mounier's intellectual vocation and was the essence of his two major accomplishments, the creations of *Esprit* and Personalism.

Esprit's creation in 1932 was the younger Mounier's response to what he believed to be the meaning of his faith and his times. To *Esprit*'s founding, Mounier brought his entire being; his deep senses of friendship and human mortality; his desire to serve God and his fellow man; his belief that man only becomes himself by becoming more than himself. To *Esprit*'s founding, Mounier also brought his and his generation's hopes to find an alternative to what was conceived of as moribund adult bourgeois society. In essence, Mounier infused into *Esprit* all he had learned and experienced to that point in his life.

No less than in founding *Esprit,* Mounier dedicated all his intelligence, will and energy in keeping it in existence. For *Esprit* to survive, Mounier had to perform not only the common but difficult tasks of raising money, increasing circulation, and inspiring contributions, but the less common and the more difficult tasks of providing leadership on issues which constantly threatened to split the Catholics and non-Catholics, activists and non-activists, the philosophers and the politicians who made up the *Esprit* group. Aside from these enduring tasks, Mounier proved his commitment to keep *Esprit* going, by two more dramatic acts. He chose to publish *Esprit* as long as possible under the Vichy regime, even though this meant inevitably going to prison (as Mounier did for a short while in 1942) and, more dangerously, incurring the suspicion of a government that neither guaranteed due process nor, worse, was its own master. After the Liberation of France, Mounier chose to reissue *Esprit* as quickly as possible, even though this meant rebuilding a new inner circle to staff *Esprit,* as well as once again placing himself at the frontlines of events and issues that not only created rifts in journals but divided nations and worlds.

In fact, almost every aspect of Mounier's life can be understood as part of his service to *Esprit.* He rejected a promising academic career in order to found *Esprit,* and what teaching he did throughout his life was done to support himself at *Esprit.* While happily married from 1935 on, Mounier never allowed his marriage and family to deflect him from his service to *Esprit.* While Mounier was unquestionably orthodox in his faith, he once prepared himself, on the basis of a pending condemnation of *Esprit* in the mid-1930s, to accept excommunication if necessary rather than to cease publication of *Esprit.* Even the facts of Mounier's death testify to the continuous sacrifices which he made for *Esprit:* he died poor, and he died young from a second heart attack caused by overwork. Indeed, *Esprit* was more than a journal for Mounier; it was, instead, an identity and a destiny.

The depth impulse which brought *Esprit* into existence was no less than Mounier's desire to create a new human order. At its outset, Mounier intended to make *Esprit* not only a literary substitute for Gide's ruling *Nouvelle Revue Française* but the prophetic voice of an intellectual and spiritual movement which would provide a new body and soul for European civilization. From its beginnings, *Esprit* expressed Mounier's call for a new civilization. Boldly, Mounier titled his first lead article in *Esprit,* "Refaire la renaissance"; its aim was no less than reversing the course of five centuries of European history.[4] It declared that contemporary civilization in its entirety was not in the service of man, and it proclaimed that only a twofold revolution could bring about a just order of human existence: a moral revolution that would give man an image of himself as a spiritual and communal being, and a material revolution that would restructure man's political, social, economic, and cultural institutions in accord with man's nature. This call for revolution was the first and most abiding voice of *Esprit*.

The history of *Esprit* and the writings which came out of it, no less than *Esprit*'s beginnings, reveal Mounier's search for a new civilization. In 1936, Mounier published the *Personalist Manifesto*, a work that summarized the ideological development of *Esprit* during its first three years.[5] Drawing in the *Manifesto* on such diverse but major nineteenth and twentieth century prophet-critics as Marx and Proudhon, Nietzsche and Kierkegaard, Maritain and Berdyaev, Mounier fused parts of their thought into a comprehensive indictment of bourgeois civilization. Bourgeois civilization, according to the *Manifesto*, distorted on all levels man's feelings and art, thought and culture, work and economics, friendship and society, spirit and religion. And at the heart of what Mounier called "its established disorder," there existed a destructive individualism which fragmented contemporary man and society and thus opened the way for the emergence of the new and more awesome collectivisms of capitalism, Bolshevism, Fascism, and Nazism.

In a series of works written during and after the Second World War, which resulted from his vocation to his times and his experience as head of *Esprit*, Mounier set forth his most mature analyses of contemporary society. In his *La petite peur du XXe siècle* (1948), he declared that what hope man had depended on a constructive attitude towards the future.[6] Mounier especially argued against an almost popular and a near-pervasive despair, which, in his opinion, would serve contemporary man no better than the facile doctrine of progress had served as a guide for the expanding nineteenth century bourgeois civilization. In his *Affrontement chrétien* (1945), Mounier again forcefully urged his fellow Christians to accept the validity of most of Marx's and Nietzsche's criticisms of bourgeois life, and to free themselves intellectually and institutionally from this destructive order that confused Christianity's truths and man's needs with its own myopic view of them.[7] In his *Introduction aux existentialismes* (1946) and his master work *Traité du caractère*, Mounier critically examined and drew upon existential thought and depth psychology in order to strengthen and refine the philosophy of man which was at the heart of his Personalism.[8]

As do Mounier's writings and *Esprit,* Personalism also expresses Mounier's vocation to his times. As is best characterized in his *What is Personalism?* (1947) and *Personalism* (1949), Personalism is a philosophy of man in our times.[9] Committed to the primacy of the person as a free and spiritual being, Personalism denies all attempts to reduce the human person to any immanent order of society, politics, and history. Committed to the person as an embodied and communal being, Personalism equally denies all doctrines that deny man's temporality and historicity in the name of a transcendent order. In its metaphysical impulse, Personalism thus aspires to be a new realism by recognizing equally man's spiritual and material nature. In its spiritual inspiration, Personalism affirms that man's freedom is fundamental, but that it is realized only amidst other men in their social and historical conditions. In its ethical and political aspirations, Personalism seeks to affirm the existing unities between thought and action, person and community, community and historical situation.

As a philosophy of man, society and politics, Personalism denounces without reservation the theory and practice of all individualism and collectivism.[10] It contends that neither preserves the real tension between the temporal and eternal, immanent and transcendent orders of human existence. Together, individualism and collectivism are understood to form the destructive poles that characterize and have historically formed existing contemporary bourgeois civilization. That is, since the Renaissance, individualistic bourgeois civilization defined man in all ways (philosophically, politically, juridically, socially, and economically) as an autonomous being. This has had the double consequence of tearing man from his older and more natural communities with other men and leaving him materially and spiritually vulnerable to the collective forms of society, economics, and state that emerged since the French Revolution to replace the dying individualistic institutions. For Mounier, the final consequence of this destructive dialectic is twentieth century man's alienation from himself, mankind, nature, and God, and his increasing subjugation to various forms of totalitarian thought and practice. Personalism, hence, is not a fixed and static world view. Rather it is made up of the premises and analyses that Mounier believed were essential for the creation of a complete philosophy of man in our times.

Personalism, however, cannot be understood only as a philosophy of man in the modern world. Rather, it must be understood that Personalism progressively became for Mounier a vehicle through which he could express his concerns for man in an age of crisis. Beneath the various alterations Personalism underwent as a critique of modern times, it voiced Mounier's constant will to aid man in finding a life more fitting to his nature and promise. "Personalism in so much as it depends on me," Mounier wrote

> will never be an abstract system, nor a political machine. We use this conven-
> ient term to establish a certain perspective on human problems, and to accent
> certain exigencies which have not been emphasized in solving the crisis of the
> twentieth century. . . One can be a Christian and a Personalist, a Socialist and
> a Personalist. I object in advance to any attempt, out of historical laziness, to
> utilize "Personalism" to defend a civilization which history has condemned. I
> object to the temptation, which is very strong on the part of some, to use
> "Personalism" for their own incapacity to sustain a long discipline of action.
> The best fate which could befall Personalism is: having awakened enough men
> to the total sense of man, it would disappear without trace as it became part
> of the daily behaviour of everyday life.[11]

As revealed by Mounier's two major accomplishments, Personalism and *Esprit*, there was a remarkable unity between his conception of himself and his times, between what he believed his personal mission to be, and what he believed were the needs of contemporary man. This unity made Mounier's vocation what it was.

One way to penetrate Mounier's vocation is to examine the principles and beliefs by which Mounier understood and gave value to his own experience. Nothing, in turn, so illuminates this inner anatomy of Mounier's thought as his psychology, which obviously reveals the assumptions and concepts which Mounier believed essential to describe and value human experience.

Of all Mounier's works, the *Treatise on Character* best states his psychology. The *Treatise* was not only a psychology but it is Mounier's most scholarly work. Yet, as Mounier declared in its preface, the *Treatise*, like all of his other writings, is but one aspect of what he believed to be his battle for man:

> *Treatise on Character*, not a *Treatise on Characterology!* This is a purposeful
> distinction. Certainly, it is hoped that this work will fill for its part a regret-
> table gap in French psychological literature, and be a work of science. If only
> because of the date when it was written [1944-1945], it would poorly disguise

its pressing goal. We are entered into one of those periodic crises of man, wherein man seeks in agony either to maintain the traits of an image of the self which is being defeated or to recognize the image of man in a new face which appears. It is necessary to choose vigorously . . . what it means to be a man, a man of this time, and then to will it forcefully, attaching ourselves to it with all fidelity and imagination. We have chosen. We have chosen not only to treat man in our research but battle for man. . . . Our science, an honest science, is nevertheless, a combative science.[12]

The *Treatise* can be presented in terms of two principles which underpinned all of Mounier's thought. The first principle is the refusal to reduce man's meaning to any singular facet or definition of his experience. Man must avoid theoretical and practical approaches to human existence that claim to be total. The second principle, which follows from this rejection of reductionism, is: man must open himself continuously to the diverse dimensions of human experience. Taken together, these two principles meant for Mounier, that man must suspend his own efforts at absolute self-definition, and he must enter fully into life. In poetic terms, man must leave the castles of his dreams, and encamp himself on those fields where reflection and action contest for the meaning of one's life.

On another level, Mounier's faith transformed these principles: the first principle, the irreducibility of human life to any of its parts, voiced Mounier's belief that it is God alone who establishes, gives, and measures meaning. The second principle, the need of man to open himself to the diverse dimensions of human experience, had its final end in Mounier's vision of a Christ who gave his life to teach men that they too must lose themselves in this world in order to find themselves truly in another world.

To grasp fully these principles, is to agree with historian and close friend of Mounier, Henri Marrou, when he writes: "That Mounier was in the deepest and most authentic sense a Christian thinker is testified to by every page of his work. That his Christian and Catholic faith animated not only his thought, action but entire life . . . is clearly known by all who lived near him."[13]

A broad development of these two principles, especially in conjunction with the *Treatise,* leads to the heart of Mounier's thought. By first developing these principles on the plane of man's nature, then on the plane of man's spiritual nature, it is possible to reconstruct the unities and hierarchies that existed between Mounier's reason and faith, his self-understanding and his understanding of his times, and thus penetrate the essence of Mounier's vocation.

For Mounier, man by his nature is an active and willing being who is meant to enter into the world around him. As Freud, Adler, and most ego psychologists aver, Mounier treats man's expansion into the world, dominance over things, and yet dependency on other men, as natural. The child's egocentrism, which is made up of need, desire, and assertion, is the first given form of the self. The challenge of becoming a person—the theme and drama of the *Treatise*—is, for man, given the realities and complexities of human emotions, relations, knowledge, and action, to transform this first and abiding egocentrism into his service as a life and value affirming person.[14]

With anguish, Mounier dwelt in the *Treatise* on man's failure to attain a full personhood. Again and again, Mounier describes how men, for diverse reasons of personality and circumstance, fail to go beyond their natural egocentric tendency "to take themselves for being the center of the world," and how, because of this failure, they progressively succumb to a self-destroying adult egotism, "which instead of turning them towards men and the world," turns "everything towards themselves."[15] While written in contemporary psychological and existential language, much of the *Treatise* painfully reminds one of Dante's trip through the Inferno. A host of men are seen fragmented, bound, frozen in the emotions, traumas, fixations, repressions, and vices of adult egotism. These men are seen as incapable of separating reality from their view of it, and unable either to give or receive. The most serious live by constantly denying their bodies, families, experiences, and nature; the most tragic end by either totally withdrawing from life or committing suicide.

Mounier's abnormal psychology carried with it a judgment of the modern world. As with Nietzsche and Freud, or Fromm and Marcuse, to choose two of Mounier's own contemporaries, psychology was a means to analyze the pathology of the modern world.[16] Analogous to the aberrant growth of the individual, Mounier also conceived the destructive evolution of bourgeois civilization from the Renaissance to his own times in terms of a destructive passage from egocentrism to egotism. This process of deterioration, briefly described, led the bourgeois spirit from its seventeenth century youthful confidence in its own existence and capacity to know nature to the dangerous nineteenth century illusions that contemporary institutions and values are the true goal of history, the sole measure of the present, and a perfect design for the future. Under the sway of nineteenth century bourgeois rule, the human relations of family, sex, and work were reduced to the impersonal mechanisms of production and profit; politics was subjugated to bourgeois interest and aggrandizement; and religion and ethics were distorted to fit bourgeois rule.

The twentieth century bourgeois was for Mounier the culmination of the bourgeois' destructive historical passage from egocentrism to egotism.[17] Lacking the vitality of his more hearty and willful nineteenth century predecessor, the twentieth century bourgeois revealed the final stages of advanced egotism. In Mounier's opinion, which is so similar to that of Péguy and Bloy, and in fact to so much of twentieth century French Catholic literature, the twentieth century bourgeois was a man who "had lost a sense of being," a man "who moved only amidst things," "a believer without inquietude," "a non-believer without passion"; a man for whom comfort was what "heroism was to the Renaissance and sanctity was to mediaeval Christianity."[18] Depicting him as senile, selfish, fearful, avaricious, and atrophied, Mounier argued that, as an individual person and a class, the bourgeois thought like a spoiled child who was unable to separate reality from his wishes, fantasies and fears. This illusionary state of mind further explained, according to Mounier, why contemporary bourgeois man paranoically interpreted the massive dislocations of modern life as personal attacks upon himself, and why he sought relief from this situation by making brief excursions into mediocre religion and art, unleashing sporadic acts of violence against the poor, and continuously practicing his old and well-learned habits of avarice and indifference. In sum, the twentieth century bourgeois demonstrated to Mounier the spiritual bankruptcy of the present order.

In great measure, Mounier's abnormal psychology developed out of his hate of the twentieth century bourgeois. The bourgeois was for Mounier an anti-ideal. That is, Mounier saw the bourgeois in all that he thought and did as the antithesis of all that man could and should be. In accord with hosts of European intellectuals before and after the First World War, Mounier understood the essence of contemporary Europe's situation in terms of the self-destructiveness of the bourgeois spirit. In turn, in accord with so many young thinkers of his generation, Mounier explained the domestic and international failures of the Third Republic in relation to the impotence and indifference of the bourgeois spirit. In sum, understanding the bourgeois mind was tantamount for Mounier to grasping the pathology of the modern world.

The bourgeois intellectual especially revealed for Mounier the spiritual sickness of the contemporary order.[19] Bourgeois intellectual egotism, according to Mounier, took the form of a consciousness that made itself the center of existence. The bourgeois intellectual's *cogito* (first act of consciousness) was the sovereignty of the self and the primacy of the mind over all else. When the bourgeois intellectual sufficiently disengaged himself from his reflections so that he could act, he did not even then experience any new dimensions of reality but simply found more material for fueling further self-reflection. In fact, Mounier found the cultivation of the self to be the essence of bourgeois thought.

The bourgeois intellectual was for Mounier the alienated man, *par excellence.* He could, in Mounier's description of him, neither grasp nor live with the tensions which exist between body and mind, thought and action, truth and situation. For Mounier, he mirrored better than anyone else the spiritual sickness of his times. That is, the bourgeois intellectual revealed clearly those divisive antinomies between rationalism and irrationalism, materialism and idealism, activism and spiritualism, that were destroying bourgeois culture.

This alienation of man from himself and reality, revealed by bourgeois civilization in general and the bourgeois intellectual in particular, was the sickness Mounier's Personalism and psychology sought to cure. Expressing in his *What is Personalism?* the gravity of the spiritual and material sickness that he saw within the twentieth century and the nature of the cure he sought for it, Mounier wrote: "Marx and Pascal, existensialism and personalism, are unified in the first appraisal that we make of twentieth century man. He is profoundly alienated; it is essential to return him to himself and his destiny."[20]

On the level of the individual person, a successful cure of this alienation did not lie for Mounier in an abstract admission of its evil, but rather demanded an unflinching recognition of the human condition. At the core of this recognition there must be a radical acceptance of the fact that life is both material and spiritual. On one hand, man must accept life on the conditions of having one body, one family, one milieu, and one age; to do otherwise is to cut himself from the sources and roots of his life. On the other hand, man must accept the trusts and values of his inner life; not to, is for man to divide himself against himself. If, according to Mounier, a man treats his inner world as a simple coordinate of the exterior world, or he does the reverse by making the exterior world a simple expression of the interior world, his course is nihilistic. To elevate either body or soul to the point of denying one or the other is to deny both the nature and conditions of man. On this basis, it can be said that the *Treatise* gains its form as a psychological analysis and an ethical inquiry by tracing the genesis, nature, and results of these exterior and interior nihilisms, and by suggesting that, only at the price of his being, can man lose himself to the world or lose the world to himself. [21]

For Mounier, man's freedom—a subject central to his psychology—is always with conditions. Freedom is not a thing or an object. A man's vocation takes its form and gains its destiny in a given body, family, milieu, class, country, and epoch. Man's freedom is the freedom of a person situated; it is also the freedom of a person with values. With reference to a given being in a given world, a man must seek to live and decipher his and his world's meaning. A man must continue to feel, think, imagine, judge and will; no elevation of a man's thought or acts at one point in time releases him from thinking or acting at another point in time. No potential of human freedom or application of will heals the wounds caused by the anguish of solitude and the fear of death.

Self-knowledge, which must arise in part from an awareness of these limits to man's freedom, was one of the crucial subjects around which Mounier's psychology took its form. Because of the importance Mounier attributed to self-knowledge, his psychology should first be understood in terms of Christian moral philosophy and the classical French moralist tradition which extends from Montaigne and Pascal to Sartre and Camus. In contrast to contemporary empirical psychologies of behavior and measurement and contemporary existential philosophies and psychologies of the self, Mounier consistently asserted that the self cannot be known as simply another object in nature, understood as the sum total of its exterior manifestations, or derived from a constant and inward directed self-reflection. While each of these modes of analysis is of use, the self can only be known progressively through the unfolding unities of its living activity. The self, to formulate Mounier's approach in other words, is seen as a developing reality which is known only in depth by a living exploration and experiencing of it. "The self," Mounier specifically wrote, "is lived before it is seen, and is only adequately known in its lived activity. The principal merit of Freudianism and the first German personalist psychologies is . . . to have shown that a bundle of verifications by the third person . . . will never grasp the existence of the first person."[22]

The self for Mounier, to remain yet momentarily on this theoretical plane of discussion, could be understood in three different manners. First, concurring with Freud and other German ego psychologists, Mounier asserted the self must be grasped as an *I*; that is, the self as the elemental and primordial willful expression of the individual's needs, wants and desire. The self, second, is a *me*; that is, the enduring and irreducible presence of a being to all that he experiences. Third, the self can be understood philosophically as that part of our being that constitutes and structures our experience of the world.[23] While revealing aspects of the self, each of these approaches to it is limited, for the self as an existent comprises a profundity which refracts discursive reasoning about it; and the self as an object of knowledge demands simultaneously a radical and unique experience of it, a full affirmation of its existence, and a progressive and guided discipline for its understanding.[24]

While it was not Mounier's intention to foreclose a rational and scientific approach to the self, he consciously sought to convince man how limited his knowledge of himself was.[25] By asserting that the self cannot be totally defined, Mounier affirmed that the self is of greater being and potential than man's knowledge and experience of it. In Mounier's own words: "The person is not being, he is the movement towards being."[26] Or in Gabriel Marcel's words, which Mounier quoted: "I am more than my life."[27] In saying that man never had a complete contact with his own self, Mounier challenged modern man's egotism at its heart; he questioned the assumption that man alone knows, defines, and judges himself.

When man truly experiences a type of Socratic ignorance that radically challenges his first knowledge of himself he is, in Mounier's opinion, able to enter upon the path to true self-knowledge. Only this act of self-doubt permits man to be reborn, for it alone liberates him sufficiently from his past conceptions of himself so that he becomes able to re-experience and re-value his self and the world. In effect, he becomes free to become another man. Life, so understood, can become an adventure in self-discovery. By continuously opening himself to new situations, actions, and goals, man experiences the unfolding and formation of his own being. Freed from the inferior egotistic and one-dimensional realms of self-praise and self-accusation, man's self-knowledge begins to serve his real human and personal growth.

As Mounier cautioned, however, the processes of self-knowledge and self-affirmation are precarious. Man's body can weaken; his emotions, tip out of balance; his creative acts, slip into routines; his successes and failures, destroy his equilibrium; and above all else, the drives for exteriorization and interiorization can gain destructive preponderance over one another. There is the constant temptation for the person's natural egocentrism to be transformed into an egotism that turns what was once wisdom into a rigid self-identity, makes patience and temperance cowardice and indifference, and replaces courage and fortitude with irrationality and self-interest.

The positive affirmation of the self in its two dimensions of interiorization and exteriorization, according to Mounier, can only be completed by a third dimension, the self as intending *(le moi en intention)*. Man, Mounier proposed, must accept life as tension filled, and in earnest marry himself to the Nietzschean formula that man is created to go beyond himself. As an airplane, to use an analogy chosen by Mounier, only gains its nature in motion, so man only takes on his nature by his forward movement. As the *mystique* can rigidify into a *politique,* and the open society become the closed society—to paraphrase central ideas of two of Mounier's masters, Péguy and Bergson—so a man who is not advancing in life is retreating from it. In the principle of transcendence *(principe de dépassement)* Mounier saw the beginning of man's real self-affirmation:

> We have seen that exteriority and interiority can end in fixed behaviour, and both of them dissolve into depersonalization. They . . . contribute to his equilibrium only when they exist as a movement of going beyond or a continual transcendence of the given. . . . Man remains standing only by overflowing the banks of the given, the ordinary, the acquired.[28]

With the dimension of transcendence opened, the person as a value affirming being comes into existence. Through action and communication, the person consciously and openly leaves the realms of egotism and brings his egocentrism into the service of his will and intelligence. Willing to sacrifice his self and his images of himself, he is able to risk, trust and sacrifice himself for others, and he thus enters, in Mounier's eyes, the ultimate realm of the person: "The person is . . . definitively *movement towards a transpersonal* that announces the experience of communion and that of valorization."[29]

In accepting his place among men, man cuts the egotistic knot of self-reflection. With his gaze detached from himself, he can share in the experiences of other men. He is able to give and receive, and even to love. Within the act of loving, Mounier believed, man finds his greatest certitude, the existential and irrefutable *cogito*: "I love, therefore being is, and life is worth the pain of having been lived."[30]

In these progressive steps, which lead from egocentrism and egotism to self-transcendence, and then to communication, community and love, Mounier found the key premise of his and all personalisms.

> If there is an affirmation common to all personalist philosophies . . . it is, that the essential advance of the world of persons is not the isolated perception of the self *(cogito)* . . . but the communication of consciousnesses. The person is not in opposition to the *we* which establishes and nourishes him, but to the impersonal and tyrannical *they*. . . The adult, like the child, conquers himself in rapport with others and with things, in work and brotherhood, in friendship, love, action and experience, but not as a given in himself.
>
> This fundamental fact . . . sovereignly commands the perspectives of personalism. It sets it in opposition to contemporary individualism, and forbids it from being an imitation of any form of liberalism. The personalist is not an isolated man, rather he is a man who is encircled, caught up, called. It is the great sin of the West to be so dangerously far from this first truth.[31]

With this vision of person as a member of the community of persons, Mounier believed that action could be restored to its full and proper place in contemporary man's life.[32] Action, which is fully brought into the service of the person, cannot be simply movement amidst an absurd world, an expression of self-aggrandizement, or a cultural manifestation of an irrational activism; instead, in its contemplative, ethical, political, and economical dimensions, action affirms both the material and spiritual existence of man. As an intellectual activity, action operates freely in and upon a multidimensional world. Its goals are structured with reference to distinct persons and specific human communities rather than separated individuals and impersonal collectivities. Action, so understood, is no longer antithetical to thought and values, but the means for men to experience and realize their potential being.

Revealing his ideal of the intellectual vocation, Mounier believed that prophetic action is the highest of all forms of action.[33] It is, in Mounier's opinion, prophetic action that joins the contemplative and the practical domains of action. The agony of prophetic action, an agony

Mounier knew well, is the loneliness that goes with pursuing and professing the truth. The glory of prophetic action is that it calls men to the highest truths of their existence and, at the same time, the most pressing and fundamental needs of the temporal human community.

However, regardless of the great step that man makes in self-affirmation through action and especially prophetic action, Mounier formulated his ultimate view of man in terms of the concept "tragic optimism."[34] Mounier's optimism for man in both his natural and historical dimensions was limited. Aside from his own psychic equilibrium, his optimism had three sources: his belief that man as a being is naturally led out of himself into contact with other men and life; his awareness that certain men go far beyond themselves in courage and love; and his hope that man would experience the worth of surpassing himself, and thus evermore enter into the combat for a full life. Contrariwise, it would seem that Mounier's sense of tragedy about man's temporal existence was almost overwhelming. For Mounier, sicknesses of mind are as common as diseases of the body; human thought and works are at all times precarious; no certain progress guards either the child's growth, the adult's health, or mankind's destiny. That man is future bound was for Mounier optimistic; but, that man in going forward, cannot redeem the human losses of the past or avert the inevitable failures of the future was tragic. Refusing both a naive optimism and a despairing pessimism, Mounier defined his "tragic optimism" as an attitude to meet our times:

If we trace with a kind of triumphant amplitude the vast destinies which open to the work of personalization, let us not forget that its future is not automatic. It is at each moment, in the face of new difficulties, called into question by the personal choice of each one of us, and each of our surrenders compromises it. Matter is rebellious, not simply passive; offensive and not simply inert. . . . Everywhere where freedom is taking its flight, it is held back by a hundred ties. Everywhere intimacy is proposed it is being exteriorized, divided, generalized. . . . Nothing which exists between the relation of persons and the world evokes a Leibnizian harmony. Insecurity and trouble are our fate. Nothing permits us to foresee a near end to this battle; nothing encourages us to doubt that it constitutes our condition. Consequently, the perfection of an incarnate personal universe is not the perfection of an order. . . . It is the perfection of a militant freedom and a toughened combatant. . . . Between the impatient optimism of the liberal and revolutionary and the impatient pessimism of fascists, the proper path for man is a tragic optimism wherein he finds his just measure in a spirit of grandeur and struggle.[35]

Why did Mounier call this tragic optimism, rather than—to use the concept of Mounier's friend and Protestant contemporary, Denis de Rougemont—"courageous pessimism"? How, to ask yet other questions, did Mounier give himself over to doing all that he could to help man, given his limited optimism? What thought, beliefs, and psychological reserves permitted Mounier to continue to hope at all, given his life which led him simultaneously on voyages across the nightmarish events of the 1930s and 1940s, and ever deeper into man's heart? These questions lead to the most basic beliefs by which Mounier lived and gave meaning to himself and his times.

To offer the simplest and yet most accurate answer to these questions is to say that Mounier was a Christian and a Catholic. The axis of his life was his faith; his faith preceded and formed the heart of his awareness of his age. Like all Mounier's thought, his psychology was Christian in inspiration. The questions of how man comes to believe in God, and why contemporary man has forgotten God, were always present to Mounier. As Bergson, Freud, Marx, and Nietzsche furnished Mounier with concepts to explore man's nature, and as Chevalier, Maritain, Péguy, and Pascal directed Mounier's inquiries into the relations of the natural and the supernatural, it was the Gospels, the Church Fathers, and the sixteenth and seventeenth century mystics, like John of the Cross and Francis de Sales, who gave Mounier's thought its depth and spiritual direction.

The two principles which were used to describe Mounier's psychology of natural man receive their full meaning in conjunction with his spiritual vision of man. The first principle, the irreducibility of human experience to any of its parts or singular definition of it, expresses Mounier's deeper profession of the lordship of God, and the consequent blasphemy he saw in any attempt, like that of bourgeois civilization, to separate man from his Creator. For Mounier, man's final meaning comes from God.

The second principle of Mounier's psychology, the need for man to open himself to all dimensions of life, expresses Mounier's Orthodox Catholic belief that God and His creation are good. Life is to be accepted, for in its deepest meaning, it is part of a loving God's creation, providence and redemption. On this point, Mounier belongs to a family of Catholic philosophy which includes Aquinas and Maritain, Dante and Chardin.[36]

Self-knowledge and self-affirmation, which Mounier found so perplexing and precarious for natural man, find a positive basis in this religious and metaphysical optimism. In depth, Mounier established his understanding of himself and man on Augustine's belief that God is more intimate to a person than a person is to himself. Man's end is not to know and be himself, but it is to see and be with God. Only by responding to God can man become more than himself. Only by asking that God's will be done, not his own will, can man transcend his own egotism. Trust and fidelity, so essential to man's growth, are translated by faith and charity from their tentativeness in the temporal order to the enduring realm of the eternal. If all of Mounier's psychology and thought were to be rendered in terms of his understanding of one Christian truth, that truth should be: "He who finds his life will lose it and he who loses his life for my sake will find it."[37]

Mounier's final model for understanding was Jesus Christ. In His incarnation, Mounier found his own and man's highest disposition towards life. This central belief gave Mounier that type of Catholic consciousness that finds the path to God in all that is human. It is a belief in Christ's incarnation that registers at every level of Mounier's thought:

> The duty of incarnation obliges us at every moment of time to hold simultaneously the most contradictory positions; to die to the world at the same time as engaging ourselves in it; to deny the daily world and to save it; to grieve the world of sin and to rejoice in the new man; to count of value only the inner world but to expand ourselves into nature in order to conquer the universal life for the inner world, to recognize in ourselves our nothingness and our princely freedom; and beyond all else and beyond everything else, never to hold any of these divided situations as substantially contradictory and as definitively resolvable in the life of man.[38]

For Mounier, the imitation of Christ carried a man to the limits of his humanity. To know oneself is to know God; to affirm oneself is to affirm God; to be with men is to be with God; to lose oneself is to find oneself with God. In effect, all the themes with which Mounier had treated natural man took on their final significance for him in the person of persons, Christ.

It was this faith that furnished the ultimate bases for Mounier's understanding of himself and his times. Neither human misery nor error preclude salvation; neither the immense evils nor the impending collapse of contemporary civilization deny man's place in God's creation. The tragedies of the contemporary world did not silence the hope of Christ's promise; and it was because of this hope that Mounier was able to give his life over to calling man to a higher self and a better world.

As if he were describing his own vocation, Mounier wrote in the *Treatise*:

> Whoever chooses *le parti de l'intelligence*, does not choose an easy life. The duty to bear witness to a transcendental truth means he will struggle against the limits and passions of his friends; the duty to be engaged means that at each step he will violate those fidelities most intimate to him. He will never be able to deny the one nor the other; nor will he ever be able to find a faultless harmony between them. Perpetually, he will be forced to run from the one to the other. Here accused of betraying the rules of effective action, there of doing injustice to the truth, he will be torn within his own conscience before every choice. But without weakening he must hold to both extremes.[39]

As one who had chosen *"le parti de l'intelligence,"* Mounier found it his vocation to bear witness to the crises of his times and to seek a Christian resolution of them. In this vocation, Mounier's understanding of himself, his age, and God were inseparably bound together. In fulfilling this vocation, Mounier lost his life in order to find his life. Within this vocation resided that fusion of the temporal and the eternal, the human and the divine, which made Mounier's life what it was.

However, it would be wrong to conclude by anointing Mounier as prophet of our times, and thereby elevate his thought beyond the world of men, ideas, values and events that gave his intellectual vocation whatever unique substance and worth it had. For even beyond this, it would be wrong because it would ignore the obvious fact that every dimension of Mounier's thought expresses his place in the twentieth century world. Mounier's psychology for instance reveals the growing influence of Freud and depth psychology on the European mind as well as the profound effects of twentieth century man's deepening recognition of the reality and importance of the irrational. Mounier's philosophy also reveals yet other facets of the contemporary mind. It shows not only the direct and immediate influence of such forerunners of existentialism and phenomenology as Bergson and Nietzsche, Blondel and Scheler, Berdyaev, Jaspers and Marcel, but the overall influence of life philosophy *(Lebensphilosophie)*, which, with its claim to be authentic to man's condition and experience, has dominated much of twentieth century European thought. Mounier's religious concerns also reveal the twentieth century spirit; his accent on the interior dimensions of faith, his hope for a faith that will be true to the situations of living men, his deemphasis of theology and dogma, his preference for cooperation with believers and non-believers in temporal matters—each of these aspects of his Christianity speaks of the modernity of his faith. Taken together, Mounier's religion as well as his psychology and philosophy bear the spiritual imprint of twentieth century thought by their profound recognition that man is a being who lives amidst circumstances.

What Mounier suffered was perhaps even more revelatory of his place in the twentieth century than what he produced in the form of systematic thought. Nearly all levels of Mounier's thought reveal his encounter with a world which he senses is in chaos. For him, man is caught up in a radical change and he must go forward into a threatening future; contemporary institutions are no longer operable in the present or viable as a model for future institutions; the Church, to survive, must radically disassociate itself with the present system and help prepare a new order in which man and faith, the temporal and the eternal, can find a new accord. Each of these ideas, which are so essential to the very structure and spirit of Mounier's message, voice a belief which was at the core of Mounier's understanding of his times: the belief that the present world order was in absolute crisis.

In essence, Mounier experienced what so many twentieth century intellectuals have, the sense that contemporary man is without any order; he is broken free from the past, and before him is the possibility of total annihilation. Myth or truth—it was this view that sparked Mounier's consciousness and spurred on his intellectual vocation. It was this sense that joined him broadly to all those diverse twentieth century intellectuals who in ever greater numbers from the turn of the century onward openly denied man's progress and hence questioned the worth and future of his science, society, and politics. Inescapably, Mounier was one of those many young European middle class intellectuals who, brought up in the aftermath of the First World War, was destined to experience the cultural disillusion of the 1920s, the social and political disintegration of the 1930s, the fighting of a Second World War, and what seemed the preparation for a third world war in the 1940s.

Mounier, therefore, was part of a world that lived within the throes of permanent war and revolution, a world that is yet to see its way beyond them, a world wherein France, the Roman Catholic Church, and Europe—once the very makers of this world—have had to learn to accept their diminished stature and to question their very significance. In seeking a new line of thought and force for his times, Mounier's search was in great part France's, Europe's, and the Church's search for a meaning and place in the twentieth century world.

CHAPTER II

THE EDUCATION OF JACQUES MARITAIN

BY THE TURN of the century European intellectual life seemed to reach its limits. All the major disciplines of human thought had been defined, and all had been in part challenged. No one perspective—religious, scientific, philosophical, or historical—commanded man's view of himself or his times. No one orthodoxy—religious, economic, social, or political—ruled. By the turn of the century, it seemed as if everything was being tried and nothing was being believed. Surely, consciousness was turning upon itself.

The intellectual, if he can be spoken of as one, looked to himself and his world, to thought and action, to past and future, to science and poetry, to politics and art, for certainty, or relief from his uncertainty. The intellectual seemed burdened to ask—perhaps, in fact, he was defined by his very asking: who am I and what are my times? Around these questions, of the self and time, all else pivoted. Optimism or despair, progress or decline, science or faith, cynicism or dogma—such were the abstractions in the name of which intellectuals sought an education and an identity in a world caught up in radical change.

Maritain was one of the intellectuals who began his search for himself and his times at the turn of the century. The first stage of Maritain's search was ended by his conversion to Roman Catholicism in 1906. His conversion completed his passage from youth to manhood, gave him his first adult identity, and formed his conception of himself and his times. The conversion gave birth to Maritain as a Roman Catholic intellectual, and it marked the point at which Maritain passed from being an ally of the forces of revolution and progress to being a proponent of religion and anti-modernity.

The Maritain, thus, who helped Mounier found *Esprit* and was the voice of liberalism to many Catholics in post-Second World War Ameri-

ca and South America, was born out of reaction. To examine his formation as a Catholic intellectual is to grasp the historical and cultural
dimensions which went into the making of the Catholic mind in France
at the turn of the century, and to prepare the way for a similar reconstruction of the formation of Mounier as a French Catholic intellectual
in the 1920s. By tracing Maritain's passage from socialism and symbolism, Péguy and Bergson, to Bloy and Catholicism, Thomism and the
Action Française, it is possible not only to begin to trace the course of
a half century of a French Catholic understanding of the modern world,
but it is possible to introduce the man, ideas, and dilemmas which
shaped Mounier's first understanding of his times.

A Young Man's Poetry: Socialism and Symbolism

Jacques Maritain was born in Paris in 1882 into a cultured upper-
middle class Republican family.[1] His father, the less dominant of the
two parents, was a lawyer. A Lamartine scholar and one-time secretary
to his father-in-law Jules Favre, he preferred the quiet life of Burgundy
to that of Paris. His strong-willed mother, who had Jacques baptized
Protestant for the sake of Republican tradition, was an ardent lifelong
supporter of the causes of mankind's progress.

At the early age of sixteen, Maritain began to look beyond the immediate world of family to socialism for his identity. The young Maritain
declared: "I will be a socialist and I will live for the revolution." Yet, in
the same breath, he asked:

> [Do] I have the right to be a socialist and to enjoy, consequently, the joyous
> socialist hope—I who enjoy at the same time bourgeois privileges—since social-
> ist joy, the happiness of the revolutionary hope, should be reserved to the real
> oppressed workers alone, to those who work, to those who suffer, to those
> who constitute the only real mankind? [2]

And in way of resolution of these doubts, Maritain went on to affirm:
"Everything I will think and know, I will consecrate to the proletariat
and to humanity. I will use everything to prepare the revolution, to aid
the happiness of humanity."[3]

The young Maritain's ambivalence regarding his bourgeois background
and his dedication to the worker were symptomatic of a young intellectual in search of an identity. By assuming the role of socialist, he was

able to give himself a new identity and to join himself, at least imagina-
tively, to the cause of mankind's destiny. In effect, socialism was nothing other than his first venture in conscious self-definition.

Maritain was not alone in finding in socialism a poetry of the self and
an adolescent life style. Perhaps like no other doctrine in the latter part
of the nineteenth century, socialism provided young men throughout
Europe with a means to envision themselves as the proponents of mankind's progress. The young men of the Third Republic turned to socialism not because of a proletarian background, but because socialism was
seen as the sequel to the heroic and great revolutionary tradition of
France, and to quote Jaurès himself, "the climax of all the civilizations
humanity had engendered since the beginning of time."[4] "What many
amateurs appreciated in socialism," wrote the historian Eugen Weber,
"was the spur it applied to their imagination. The great socialist trib-
unes this time were humanists and rhetoricians like Vivani, like Jaurès,
for whom socialism had partly abolished the frontier between dream
and reality ... A means of salvation, a poetry of action, a kind of
surrealism, eventually a deliberate myth: such is the image of *fin du
siècle* socialism."[5]

Socialism, however, was not the only doctrine which provided the
young intellectuals of Maritain's generation with an identity and a critique of what they believed to be the uninspiring and decadent bourgeois values and politics of the Third Republic. For example, the three
major critics of the Republic—Maurice Barrès (1862-1923), Charles
Maurras (1868-1952), and Georges Sorel (1947-1922)—express the climate of ideas amidst which Maritain matured, and demonstrate how
interrelated the research for one's identity and one's philosophy of
one's times had become for many *fin du siècle* French intellectuals.[6] In
Barrès' intellectual evolution from the cult of General Boulanger, who
was expected in the 1880s to rescue the French Nation from the evils
and scandals of the Republic, to his later nationalism based on the cult
of the dead, the earth, and the *province,* there is no clear division
between his writing, his activity in politics, and his personal search to
find meaning in a world which he often found to be absurd and purposeless. In Maurras' conception and leadership of the *Action Française*—an extra-political movement created during the Dreyfus Affair,
which purported to save France from the Republic, socialism, and Jew-
ry, and proposed the restoration of monarchy and the formation of a
hierarchical society—it is not easy to distinguish between his political

and social commentary on France and his own personal desire to have France conform to his vision of Athens and Classicism. Likewise, in George Sorel's continuous quests after the rejuvenation of civilization, which led him from Marxism to syndicalism, from the notion of the general strike to positing the need for a moral elite, there is no point at which his analyses of contemporary bourgeois society are altogether free of his personal concerns to defend traditional morality.

The young Maritain entered this world of Jaurès, Barrès, Maurras, and Sorel. In this world, most intellectuals in varying degrees considered themselves not only thinkers and philosophers but prophets of their times. Socialism was the young Maritain's first public identity and his first philosophy of his times. Socialism, however, was only one doctrine through which he gained entrance into the intellectual life of his times. While Tolstoy, Nietzsche, and Spinoza inspired the young Maritain, it was Baudelaire who captured his heart: "I was crazy," he wrote later, "with Baudelaire."[7]

Baudelaire and the whole decadent and revolutionary tradition associated with him under the generic term symbolism, beckoned Jacques. As for the youth of his generation and the generations before, symbolism seemed to call them from the confines of bourgeois life to the music of the inner soul; to death, to fate, to loneliness, to destruction, to the point where the individual self becomes the source of the universe and the universe but part of poetry of the self—to the point where every feeling receives a form and every form evokes a feeling, where life and art become one.[8]

The young Maritain's mind and imagination were given over to the poetic models and sensibility of his times:

> Oh death, old captain. It is sweet assurance to know that you sail the ship and you will guide us to port. . . . Impenetrability of consciousnesses. Windows! But always closed! . . . . Like a fish in an aquarium.[9]

Or in a longer passage from Maritain's *Carnets*, written in 1901-1902, one sees how Baudelaire, Pascal, Tolstoy, and others were grafted into the confused poetry of a suffering youth:

> The void. Night. A host of gathered forces.. I am more valuable than they, since I know them and they do not know me.
> A wrecked universe. Such a weak instrument, the human brain. What good does it serve? Savage beasts, beasts. . . . In improving itself humanity improves its vices and uglinesses, which pertain to it by definition. Suffering, pain,

shame, always in the depths. . . . To make the beautiful out of the ugly is still possible. . . . But to make success out of the wrecked, to transform one order to another—something of the "supernatural." What can be made out of infinity? The peasants call me "the Apostle" in order to make fun of me.

And then, the Eternal nothingness, ignorance. Objective truth fleeing like objective beauty. Doubt. Real doubt, doubt even upon itself. Reason turning on itself. *Moulin à cafe* which turns in nothingness.

I am pulled by my hair. Upwards. Upwards toward a land created by my eyes, toward songs produced by my ears.

I have made a great city on the void, a great light on darkness. My will sustains itself in nothingness.

I have my soul, and there it was, most beautiful. We two are to live amidst the eternal vibration which passes through the night. Alone!

But how to reanimate the void from below? How to conquer in the realm of action the most brutal forces? I can disdain the universe; we laugh at it in this country, where it holds no power over us. NONE!

But it has us by other ties. Struggle. Struggle. It is essential to be stronger than the infinite. Integrate everything into the self.[10]

Uncertain of his self, the world, and his place in it, the young Maritain thus was swept up in those underground currents which flow from romanticism and De Maistre through Baudelaire, Rimbaud, Verlaine, and Mallarmé, and which from the 1880s onward threaten in the name of symbolism to erupt over the banks of Western ethics and thought.[11] Henceforth, susceptible to Ibsen, Dostoevsky, Nietzsche, and Swinburne, and whomever or whatever else an age in search of itself cast forth, the young Maritain's self was thrown into currents of *fin du siècle* culture. Within him there inhabited two conflicting visions, poetries, of the world: a socialism based on a rationalistic and collective optimism about man's future, and a symbolism which proposed that man was alone and without ultimate purpose. If Maritain, thus, were to find himself, it meant not only a resolution of his crisis as a young man but also an interior resolution of the cultural crisis of his times which in good measure had become part of himself.

Péguy and the Ideal City

Neither socialism nor symbolism, however, deflected Maritain from the expected paths of an intelligent son of the upper classes. While continuing, probably not unlike many of his contemporaries, to seek inwardly after truths that education did not formally teach, Maritain, after being a student at *Henri IV,* 1898-1899, one of the most celebrated *lycées* of his times, went on to the Sorbonne to study science and philosophy. At the Sorbonne he met his future wife, Raïssa Oumansoff, a Russian Jewess whose family had fled Russia in the 1890s. Thereafter, their lives and thought, and even their conversions, were in great measure inseparable. In his "Confession of Faith," Maritain wrote: "The best thing I owe to my studies at that time is that they let me meet, in the School of Sciences, the woman who since then has always, happily for me, been at my side in a perfect and blessed communion." [12]

Together, Jacques and Raïssa hurried from concert to concert, lecture to lecture, and in art galleries, from the paintings of Duccio and Giotto to Manet and Rousseau. They read Corneille and Pascal, Nietzsche and Spinoza, and wrote poetry. They were engaged in criticizing the highest expression of contemporary French academic thought in discussing the personalities and lectures of their teachers, such as Rappaport, a Kantian collaborator of Juarès; Le Dantec, a prominent materialist and biologist who held particular sway over the young Maritains; Lévy-Bruhl, a neo-Comtean and definitely one of the universal and popular philosophers of this time; Victor Delbos, the eminent historian of philosophy; and Emile Durkheim, one of the fathers of modern sociology. The world had never been so much theirs, yet they were discontent.

Long after their conversion, they retrospectively saw themselves as two young and honest souls in search of the meaning of their existence, a meaning which they believed their teachers could not and did not furnish:

> Seventeen! Only seventeen, and already the deepest needs of the mind and soul are raising their voices. A whole life has already been lived, the life of childhood, the life of boundless confidence. Now adolescence is here with its own special power of totally needing and asking. Truly adolescence confronts the universe, challenging it to appear in court, to explain and justify itself, for already youth indicts life. Youth confronts its teachers, with clear eyes, with ardent spirit, its hands open wide, empty as yet of all the fruits of knowledge and learning, but clean as the gaze of its eyes.
>
> If only teachers would remember a little of the soul of their own youth, how they would tremble before that ingenuousness which comes to them with the confidence still of the child, but possessed now of the rights of a just judge. But the teachers of those days, good, devoted and able as they were, seemed to have forgotten everything; the teachers themselves had long since lost their way. Generation after generation they had traveled farther and farther away from the great needs of the human spirit. The dazzling development of the natural sciences and the infinite hopes it had awakened had caused them to

belittle the disciplines of wisdom—that wisdom to which we aspire before and after and above all knowledge of particular sciences.[13]

Retrospectively, they viewed their teachers as the representatives of a spiritually depleted secular Western culture. The Sorbonne itself was seen as more than a building, more than an institution, more than the embodiment of a given culture; it was seen as the symbol of the bankruptcy of a civilization which had lost God.

If any one person had been initially responsible for having given form to and generalized Maritain's hostility to the Sorbonne, it was Charles Péguy, Maritain's first mentor. For many of both Maritain's and Mounier's generations, Péguy expressed their disillusion with the Sorbonne, its "failure" to respond to the needs of society, to provide a "real mission" and "sense of purpose" for its students.[14] Throughout almost all his writings, Péguy depicted the Sorbonne and its teachers as the pinnacles of personal vice and intellectual error.[15] The *Sorbonnarde* was increasingly made by Péguy to epitomize the non-heroic and cowardly, as well as the bankruptcy of positivism, materialism, idealism, sociology, history, and the academic life. In sum, the *Sorbonnarde* and the Sorbonne in large part became youth's anti-ideal because of Péguy and his writing.

Few can study pre-World War France without encountering the person of Charles Péguy.[16] Péguy's intellectual development led at the same time from a humanistic socialism to a mystical Christianity and from a passionate internationalism to a fervent nationalism. In the wake of the Dreyfus Affair, Péguy founded the *Cahiers de la Quinzaine* in order to defend the moral integrity of French socialism, and the *Cahiers* became not only a journal, but a *foyer* at various times for such independent thinkers as Romain Rolland, Georges Sorel, Daniel Halévy, and Julien Benda. Péguy's own powerful and evolving criticisms progressively took aim at those whom he felt betrayed the Republic, socialism, Christianity, and France; his polemics, at different times, found their target in historian and sociologist, clergy and parliamentarians. In 1905, in his famous essay "Notre Patrie," Péguy began to exhort his fellow countrymen to prepare themselves for what he believed was an inevitable war with Germany, and he himself lost his life in one of the first battles of the first great World War.[17] These are some of the reasons why Péguy occupies such an important place in the pre-First World War intellectual life.

Jacques and Raïssa met Péguy in 1901. The older Péguy, born in 1873, immediately attracted Maritain. Péguy was the first writer Maritain had come to know well. He was, not unlike Maritain himself, an impassioned defender of social justice. He was a convinced *Dreyfusard,* and a man who heroically and singularly had taken it upon himself to found a journal in order to defend what he considered justice. That Péguy in all ways opened the *Cahiers* to the young Maritains and Maritain's sister, Jeanne, was but another reason why the young Maritain found in Péguy his first guide. Maritain made himself Péguy's disciple, and Péguy came to consider "Jacques as a younger brother who would succeed him and carry on his works at the *Cahiers de la Quinzaine.*"[18] Maritain and Péguy were to remain friends until, as will be seen, a series of misunderstandings and quarrels beginning around 1907 eroded, and then destroyed their friendship.

The Péguy whom Jacques and Raïssa met in 1901 was rethinking his life. Disillusioned by the outcome of the Dreyfus Affair, angered by the compromises that the Jaurèsian branch of socialism had made during the Affair, and unsure if the recently founded *Cahiers* could survive, Péguy was reviewing his past and his future.

What was called into doubt were the ideals upon which Péguy had established his first adult identity. Péguy had clearly expressed these ideals in three works written in 1897 and 1898—*Joan of Arc, Socialist City,* and *Marcel: First Dialogue on the Harmonious City.*[19] In *Joan of Arc,* written during a year's absence from the *Ecole Normale,* Péguy professed his belief in the mystical unity of man, France, and God. In his *Socialist City,* and in his *Harmonious City,* Péguy set forth his belief in an ideal human city.

On one level, both works reveal his profession of faith in Jaurèsian socialism. While critical of capitalism and colonialism, Péguy's socialism rejected the orthodox Marxian doctrines of class warfare and economic determinism, and in accord with the larger traditions of French humanistic and revolutionary thought as proposed by Jaurès and Michelet, Péguy's socialism affirmed the ultimate unities between France and humanity, the Revolution and the future.[20]

On another level, one which surpasses any specific political position or cultural influence, the *Socialist City* and the *Harmonious City* reveal Péguy's desire for a perfect state of existence. In the *Harmonious City* especially, Péguy depicted a state of existence, an ideal city, wherein man would be in total harmony with himself. Within this city there would be no substantial distinctions among men, and thus there would be no authorities, wages, prestige, sales, wills, competition, vanity, ambition, anger, lies, war; and no need for words like equality and justice, and political forms like democracy, parliament, suffrage, and the right of the majority. Within this city, work would not deform the body, nor power deform human relations. The machine would not dominate either man or beast. Each man, thus, would be restored to himself, other men, and being. All of man in all of his activities would be restored to all other men in all of their activities. Humanity, in its broadest sense, would be, according to Péguy, its own end:

> The harmonious city is for citizens, all living beings with souls . . . because it is not fitting that there be souls that are strangers. Also all the men of all the families, all the men of all the lands, all the men of all the races, all the men of all the tongues. . . . all the men of all the cultures . . . all the men of all the beliefs . . . of all the lives . . . of all the fatherlands, are to become citizens of the harmonious city because it is not fitting that men be strangers.[21]

In quest of his own lost youth and in search of an existence free of conflict, Péguy expressed here in the *Harmonious City* a vision which surpassed in hope Plato's *Republic*, More's *Utopia*, and Rousseau's *Social Contract*, and synthesized the highest aspirations of eighteenth and nineteenth century humanism for a perfect city. His youthful desire to unify himself and all men in a city, a state of being, beyond the divisions of feeling, thought, time, power, circumstance, and necessity, pointed clearly towards the limits of man's hope, and surely forewarned of his disillusionment.

This first faith of Péguy was brought to its climax, tested, and denied by the Dreyfus Affair. In January, 1898 Zola's famous article *J'accuse* declared to the world that a Jewish Captain, Alfred Dreyfus, sentenced in 1894 to a life in prison as a traitor, was innocent, and that the war office was guilty of dishonesty. All of France, thereupon, was divided in two. What was at stake was justice and the truth—as well as the credibility of the government, the prestige of the army, and the survival of the Republic itself.

By signing a petition for retrial in early 1898, along with such intellectuals as Léon Blum, Anatole France, Daniel Halévy, and Lucien Herr, and then by wielding his pen as well as swinging a stick, Péguy plunged headlong into this Affair. For Péguy this was the moment when one's truth and one's action must correspond. The innocence of Dreyfus was the question; all of the past and future were in play for Péguy. When

Jaurès entered on the side of the *Dreyfusards,* Péguy felt that history had reached a turning point—that the "Revolution" was at hand.

Disillusionment, thus, was almost certain as Péguy's hopes for an ideal city were juxtaposed against the acts of men caught up in what can be considered the European intellectual's first civil war.[22] Péguy witnessed another aborted trial for Dreyfus; diverse groups of Republicans, Radicals, and Socialists choosing to follow a middle path; and the emergence of a government for Republican defense under Waldeck-Rousseau (June, 1899) which tactically gave Dreyfus a presidential pardon rather than a new trial and the full acquittal Dreyfus merited.

With disillusionment there came to Péguy the sense that the French nation had betrayed itself.[23] Leaving aside the Church, the army, the majority of the conservatives, the *Ligue de la Patrie Française* (comprised of such intellectuals as Charles Maurras, Léon Daudet, and Maurice Barrès) and all of those who unconscionably or unscrupulously were against Dreyfus, Péguy reacted most strongly against those elites of the Sorbonne and socialism who, in his opinion, preferred compromise and unity to justice and truth. Most devastating for Péguy was what he saw in the Socialist Party and at the Socialist Party Congress of 1899.[24] For the sake of party unity, the socialists compromised away the Dreyfus Affair; and for the sake of unanimity and the defense of the "purity" of the doctrine of class warfare, they censored the independent socialist Millerand for compromising them by taking a post in the government of Waldeck-Rousseau. When Lucien Herr, friend and guide of Péguy since his early years at the *Ecole Normale,* restricted Péguy's right to report on the Congress, Péguy withdrew from the socialist publishing house of which he was part owner with Herr.[25] To use Péguy's language, the *mystique* of socialism at this point became for him a *politique.*

As Péguy steadily gravitated further and further away from socialism, he separated himself more and more from the man whom he most admired, Jean Jaurès. It progressively appeared to Péguy that his mentor, the man who in his opinion more than anyone else embodied what was best in the modern world, had succumbed and been corrupted by the habit of political compromise. It was, in Péguy's opinion, expediency of the worst sort that led Jaurès to accept the vindictive of anticlericalism of 1905, and it was the continued practice of expedience that, in Péguy's opinion, left Jaurès on the eve of the First World War an impotent and traitorous propounder of pacifism and internationalism. A friend of Péguy's youth had become an enemy of his maturity.

In the immediate wake of the Affair, Péguy began his meditations on it, meditations which during the rest of his life returned to and dwelt upon the fact that only he and a few others had understood what the Affair had meant and had remained loyal to its meaning.[26] The Affair, which had tested and denied Péguy's youthful hopes, did not, however, disintegrate his person. The Affair had rather made Péguy a solitary and unique man, a man who, in H. S. Hughes' opinion, belonged intellectually to no school.

> Péguy's own ideological position is so special that it fits into none of the conventional categories of French politics. He shared with Maurras and Barrès the role of a nationalist prophet—yet he insisted on his republicanism and his socialist aspirations. He agreed with Alain in championing the rights of the common citizen against the bureaucracy—yet he differed totally with Alain in his judgment of Jaurès, the Radical party, and the anti-clerical legislation of the period 1901-5. Durkheim he hated as one of the supreme pontiffs of the "intellectual party" that from its fortress of the Sorbonne ruled the cultural life of France—yet in the tumults of the Dreyfus case he had shouted "rally" and set off with his heavy stick to defend the sociologist's classes from the attacks of nationalist students. Péguy was perpetually cutting across one or another of the cleavages that divided French life into neat compartments. His changes, like Sorel's, bewildered his friends and admirers. Yet in some sense that he alone fully understood, he remained true to an intensely personal concept of what his life and work meant.[27]

The final consequence of the Affair had been to make Péguy a man without a place in his own times. Because of the Affair, Péguy came to occupy a prophetic post not without similarity to that of Dostoevsky and Nietzsche:

> We are the last. Almost beyond the last. Immediately after us begins another age, a quite different world, the world of those who no longer believe in anything; those for whom this is a source of pride and glory.
>
> Immediately after us begins the world which we have just mentioned, that which we will not cease to call the modern world; the world of the know-alls; the world of the intelligent, the advanced, of those who know, of those who can't be taught a thing, of those who can't be fooled; the world of those to whom there is nothing left to teach. The world of the know-alls. The world of those who are neither dupes nor imbeciles, like us. That is: the world of those who believe in nothing, not even in atheism, who show neither devotion nor sacrifice for anything. Exactly this: the world of those who have no mysticism; and who boast of it. Let us not be misled and consequently, let no one rejoice, on one side or the other. The movement for de-republicanizing France is profoundly the same movement against mysticism. It is of a same profound movement that this people no longer believes in the Republic and that it no

longer believes in God; that it no longer wishes to lead the Republican life and that it no longer wishes to lead the Christian life. It is fed up. One might almost say that it will no longer believe in idols and that it will no longer believe in the real God. The same disbelief, a single disbelief reaches idols and God, at the same time reaches the false gods and the real God, the gods of antiquity, the new God, the old gods and the God of Christians. A same sterility petrifies the city and Christianity. The political city and the Christian city. The city of men and the city of God. It is properly modern sterility. Let no one rejoice, seeing misfortune come to enemy, adversary, neighbor. For the same misfortune, the same sterility are his.[28]

In summary, the Péguy whom the Maritains came to know in 1901 was a person without a clear creed or a certain future. Expressing the spiritual and political dimensions of his self-examination, Péguy had dedicated three issues of the *Cahiers* to the problem of immortality, and the relation of collective and individual immortality.[29] However, in spite of all the incertitudes which came in the wake of the Affair, Péguy was not shattered. He had already found his inner force and movement. His manhood had been initiated by the Affair. While it had broken his first vision of the city of man, it had not broken his person and his energy. Péguy still had hope, strength, and his faith that on some plane of existence man, France, and God were truly one.

Maritain, nine years younger than Péguy, shared his friend's and mentor's attack against the Sorbonne, clericalism, politics, and the spiritless knowledge of the academics. He probably concurred with Péguy and the other dean of the circles gathered at the *Cahiers,* Georges Sorel, that the present order was politically and morally bankrupt, and that there was a need for a revolution that would change the very essence of man's heart, life, and society.[30] But Maritain was still only a young man, a bright student at the Sorbonne, a beginner in arts, literature, philosophy, and science. Neither his ideals nor his politics had been tested by events, and he had not yet found the axis of his life and thought.

Henri Bergson: Youth's Philosopher

"One summer afternoon in 1902 Jacques and I," Raïssa wrote,

were strolling about in the *Jardin des Plantes. . . .* We were not happy. . . . We had been reviewing the results of our two or three years of study at the Sorbonne. No doubt a rather considerable amount of specialized scientific and philosophical knowledge. But this knowledge was undermined by the relativism of the scientists, by the skepticism of the philosophers. . . . Along with the rest of our generation, we were their victims . . . .

Already I had come to believe myself an atheist. I no longer put up any defense against atheism, in the end persuaded, or rather devastated, as I was by so many arguments given out as "scientific." And the absence of God unpeopled the universe. If we must also give up the hope of finding any meaning whatever for the word truth, for the distinction of good from evil, of just from unjust, it is no longer possible to live humanly.

I wanted no part in such a comedy. I would have accepted a sad life, but not one that was absurd. Jacques had for a long time thought that it was still worthwhile to fight for the poor, against the slavery of the "proletariat." And his own natural generosity had given him strength. But now his despair was as great as my own. . . .

Before leaving the *Jardin des Plantes* we reached a solemn decision which brought us some peace: to look sternly in the face, even to the ultimate consequence—insofar as it would be in our power—the facts of that unhappy and cruel universe, wherein the sole light was the philosophy of skepticism and relativism. . . .

Thus, we decided for some time longer to have confidence in the unknown; we would extend credit to existence, look upon it as an experiment to be made, in the hope that to our ardent plea, the meaning of life would reveal itself, that new values would stand forth so clearly that they would enlist our total allegiance, and deliver us from the nightmare of a sinister and useless world.

But if the experiment should not be successful, the solution would be suicide; suicide before the years had accumulated their dust, before our youthful strength was spent. We wanted to die by a free act if it were impossible to live according to the truth.[31]

"It was then that God's mercy caused us to find Henri Bergson," so Raïssa began a new chapter of her *Memoirs*.[32]

In 1903, Péguy for the first time led the young Maritain and Raïssa, along with Georges Sorel and Ernest Psichari, to the most famous lecture hall in all of France.[33] Within this room there sat such young Catholic intellectuals as Etienne Gilson, Charles Du Bos, and Jacques Chevalier, Mounier's mentor; and such young non-Catholic intellectuals as Daniel Halévy and Marcel Proust. At the podium was Henri Bergson.

Bergson had come to this post of lecturer at the Collège de France in 1900 with prestige. He was the author of two influential works, *L'essai sur les données immédiates de la conscience* (1889) and *Matière et mémoire* (1897), he had just finished lecturing at *Henri IV*, 1889-1897, and the *Ecole Normale,* and in 1901 he was elected to the French Academy.[34]

Berson, an assimilated Jew, born in 1859, attended the *Ecole Normale* during the years 1878-1881. He was in the same class as Jaurès and Durkheim. While there, even though he had elected philosophy over mathematics, he sided with the scientists rather than the spiritualists; that is, he adhered to Mill and Spencer and a type of empirical materialism rather than to such French idealists as Lachelier, Boutroux, Ollé-Laprune, and Renouvier, who professed the primacy of man and spirit.

A few years later, while teaching at the *Lycée Blaise Pascal,* Bergson underwent a decisive experience which is purported to have altered his entire philosophy up to that point and set the lines of all of his future philosophical inquiries.[35] While technically its starting point was Bergson's reflections on Zeno's paradoxes, the substance of Bergson's experience was a single philosophical experience.[36] Motion cannot be understood in reference to space. Motion, that is, pertains to the realm of being and quality and is hence indivisible; whereas space, which is used to measure motion, pertains to matter and quantity and is, therefore, infinitely divisible. That is, to state this insight in yet other terms: what changes, and change itself, ultimately cannot be grasped by spatial and quantitative means. As a series of portraits of a person do not grasp his living and dynamic unity, so, to use a single example, sciences, insofar as they are based on a series of exterior observations at diverse points in time, do not penetrate the inward essence of being in time. A true science, for Bergson, must penetrate the interunity of beings in change, time, and existence; a true philosophy must grasp the *durée* of existence.

This insight, on one level, was simply Bergson's formulation in contemporary terms of the perennial truth that all rational knowledge is partial. In equating geometry, mathematics, logic, and reason to the science of his times, he was engaged in attacking what he conceived the rule of mechanistic and positivistic science. In stressing the superiority of a true philosophy of intuition over a science of reason, he was reformulating in his own terms the existing cultural polarizations between rationalism and Romanticism.

On another level, Bergson's intuition into the inadequacy of human knowledge transcended any specific cultural formsl and determinants of his times and confronted questions of a universal nature: if there are intuitions, he had to ask like Plato, Kant, and others, how are they related to other modes and forms of knowledge? Is it essential, as Dilthey and contemporary neo-Kantians thought, to postulate a radical difference between self-knowledge and knowledge of nature? Are, as Aristotle believed, the realities of change, motion, and growth separate and distinct? Do they reflect an enduring structure and source of being? How, in turn, does one, after having dismissed Zeno, escape Heraclitus' world of flux without subscribing either to Plato's doctrine of forms, Aristotle's four causes, or the Judaeo-Christian conception of God? These questions, so similar to the ones which furnished the bases of the mature Maritain's criticism of Bergson, were directly or indirectly important at each stage of Bergson's development.

In his first two major works, *Time and Free Will: Essay on the Immediate Data of Consciousness* (1889) and *Matter and Memory* (1897), Bergson concerned himself with the subjects of freedom, and the unity of the person. In *Time and Free Will,* Bergson demonstrated that deterministic psychologies fail to understand human freedom despite their claims to be absolute sciences resting on an intelligible universal causality.[37] When, Bergson argued, they are confronted with the case of a given person in the process of making a given choice, they must wait for the completion of the act until they can offer an "explanation" of how and why it was committed. In *Matter and Memory,* Bergson, like his contemporaries James and Freud, broached the subject of what accounts for the inner unity of the person. In opposition to contemporary psychology, Bergson asserted that memory cannot be understood as a simple reservoir of completed experiences, and thereby be reduced to a set of cerebral processes associated with these experiences. Memory, rather, must be approached in its integral relation with the enduring unity and freedom of the self in its full activity.[38]

Bergson's essay, "The Introduction to Metaphysics" (1903), set forth his concept intuition, and marked the passage from a critical to a constructive stage of his philosophy.[39] Here, in opposition to rationalisms and empiricisms, Bergson proposed intuition as a form of knowing which arises out of the deepest part of the self and affords a penetrating grasp of being in time (*durée*). In contrast to Kantianism which, in Bergson's opinion, left the knower uncertain of nature and ultimately the very existence of reality, Bergson proposed "intuition" as a kind of intellectual insight by which the knower can transcend all knowledge based on symbols and "place himself within the object in order to coincide with what is most unique in it and consequently inexpressible."[40] "Metaphysics," so conceived, was "*the science which claims to dispense with symbols*"; "intuition," so defined, became for Bergson a potential vehicle through which he could attempt to extend knowledge to the deepest recesses of the self and the universe.[41]

This movement towards total truth took full form in his next work, *Creative Evolution* (1907).[42] Seeking therein to develop his intuitional metaphysics into a new philosophy of nature, Bergson audaciously argued that the two prevalent views of nature, that is, natural law as formed by Plato and Aristotle, and mechanistic transformism as propounded by Darwin and Spencer, were incorrect. The former erred because it conceived nature exteriorly and statically in terms of a fixed hierarchy of forms and the teleological notion of causation. The latter was equally mistaken because it relied on the abstract and rigid concepts of law and gradualism which could not account for the spontaneous and creative genesis of new forms and levels of existence. Both systems, according to Bergson, remained powerless to comprehend the indwelling spirit (*l'élan vital*), which moves all being dynamically forward and which, in the case of man, has led him from the inferior realms of instinct and intelligence to the higher realms of intuition and spirit—realms in which man can transcend his own determinacy and enter into conscious contact with being itself. Only a philosophy of nature which grasps the radically creative progression of being was for Bergson an adequate philosophy of nature.

With the publication of *Creative Evolution,* which in many ways culminated Bergson's first inquiries of the *Essay on the Immediate Data of Consciousness,* Bergson had arrived by a different path at approximately the same position as the earlier German idealists. In trying to surmount the dichotomies between knower and known, the temporal and eternal, form and change, Bergson, as Maritain later claimed, confused thought and being, being and change, intellect and intuition, and thus carried reason and existence to the edge of irrationality and chaos.[43] From one point of view it is possible to see his philosophy as inspired by a Promethean Romanticism, similar in its vitalism, its dynamism, and its striving after the absolute to the thought of Hegel, Schopenhauer, and Nietzsche.[44]

It was this Promethean and Romantic tendency in Bergson's thought that was cherished for the greatest part by the young men in the most famous lecture hall of all of France. The mystery of their being and selves, freedom from their selves and times, openness to other selves and times, and the heroic pursuit of truth in a new world of concept and action were themes which were all potentially alive for them within this new philosophy. The young men in this lecture hall were inspired by Bergson, their Descartes, to dream their own dreams.

Those who heard Bergson's message cannot, however, be considered simply the young men of the Generation of 1905—students of Péguy, Barrès, and Maurras, who, in the wake of the Dreyfus Affair and amidst the mounting tensions of the coming war, hungered for allegiances and actions.[45] In a large sense, they were part of those successive French generations, composed of such men as Taine and Renan, Romain Rolland, Paul Claudel and Maurice Barrès, Gide and Proust, Jacques Rivière, Alain-Fournier, Henri Massis and Georges Bernanos, whose consciousness had, since 1870, passed at ever-accelerating speeds back and forth between the meanings of France and Germany, philosophy and science, religion and poetry. And in an even larger sense Maritain and his generation were, as later Mounier and his generation would be, members of all those European generations who, since the last decades of the nineteenth century, were driven by two conflicting senses: the absolute decadence of society and culture, and the absolute need for a total regeneration of national life and civilization itself.

Bergson spoke to more than a single generation. He spoke to almost all quarters of French *fin du siècle* culture.[46] The older Sorel, engaged in a revision of Marxian socialism, found in Bergson's thought the potential nucleus of a new social doctrine. Péguy found in Bergson's thought a way to deepen philosophically his attacks on the idealists, sociologists, and historians, and to better set forth what Péguy believed was the mystical unity that existed between the people, nation, and faith in France. Proust heard the philosophical anticipation of what was later to be the essence of his *Recherches des temps perdus*—the voyage across the present memories of youth to the enduring self. As the War drew near, the young men were more and more prone to make Bergson the teacher of a new energy and heroism—the philosopher general who would spiritually defeat Germany.[47]

Among Bergson's most intent followers were Catholics like Edouard le Roy, Charles Du Bos and Etienne Gilson. Both before and after the Great War, Catholic intellectuals were inspired by Bergson. Taught by Brunetière, editor of the *Revue des Deux Mondes* in the 1890s, that science and religion were not in contradiction, young Catholics like Mounier's teacher, Jacques Chevalier, saw Bergson offering them a way beyond contemporary materialism and relativism, and creating the possibility of a new synthesis of faith and science.[48] Influenced by Bourget's religious novels and Maurice Blondel's philosophy, young Catholic intellectuals grew more and more confident in their assertions that humanistic ethics were inadequate to man's ultimate meaning, and they increasingly saw Bergson's philosophy as integral to their final assault against what they considered the self-destructive anthropocentrism of the modern world.[49] Inspired by the conversions of such men as Paul Claudel and Jacques Maritain, and more importantly by the sense that they were part of a true Catholic intellectual renaissance, Catholics before and after the First World War looked to Bergson more than any other as the one who was preparing modern man for his return to faith.

Bergson spoke to many levels of the young Maritain's being. The mobility of Bergson's philosophy corresponded to the young Maritain's fluxing inner world; its movement from the rational to the irrational, the solitary to the communal, the finite to the infinite, corresponded to the ambivalence of the young Maritain's feelings about himself and the world. Clearly, Bergson's philosophy spoke to his divided self by elevating his thoughts to a new level of intensity and abstraction, and by promising that beyond his present condition there existed an absolute truth and meaning. In essence, Bergson's thought transformed, as the following quotation shows, Maritain's "poetry of self" into a "philosophy of existence."

> Upon leaving the surface, he [the philosopher] penetrates in depth—the living and substantial reality astonishes him and seizes him. There everything is reciprocal interpenetration and movement. . . . The further he descends, the more he moves towards a solitude . . . towards the intuition of a *durée* which does not admit separate moments, a *durée* which conserves itself by itself entirely in powerful simplicity and the expansion of its inconceivable unity. He cannot express it, or directly communicate it, but whoever, sufficiently gifted and practiced, will follow the same path, will arrive at the same point. And he will feel himself in the presence . . . of the real itself, which is really imposed and makes itself known by its force, through which it ravishes the spirit, by its absolute nature wherein the most agile rapidities of thought are vainly precipitant. He is like a swimmer, who having left the surface of the sea, plunges to its deeper water, and who feels himself carried by powerful currents, irresistible and warm interior torrents, which ravish his body, and before which all the agility of his body . . . cannot equal their speed or break their cohesiveness. Thus within the violence of the *intuition*, the *durée* is seized by intelligence.
>
> From this first intuition, he will recall, returned to consciousness, but a single truth, and he will say: *I exist in an absolute form*, that is, *je dure*.[50]

Beyond having transformed Maritain's symbolism into a philosophy, Bergson's teaching affected Maritain in several other ways. It gave him a new sense of his meaning, a new confidence in his future. His preoccupation with the inner world of self, so dangerous a phenomenon for young men in particular, was replaced by a vision of a future in which he could grow in truth. Before him now lay the vocation to study a philosophy that he believed would provide him with a real purpose for his life. Equally important to a sensitive youth like Maritain, Bergson gave him the concepts through which he could systematize and explain the senses of alienation he felt from the educational system, the adult world, public life, and his age. Thanks to Bergson, Maritain felt himself able first to refute, and then to transform all those materialists, relativists, and positivists into a single anti-identity: they were collectively the enemies of beauty, mystery, truth and life.[51] They were, in essence, all that youth should battle against.

In more academic terms, Bergson defined Maritain's intellectual career. The first twenty years of Maritain's career as a philosopher were spent correcting Bergson's philosophy in the light of Christianity and Thomism.[52] His Thomism, on one hand, accepts Bergson's criticisms of idealism and materialism, and seeks to be, in its ascent to the unity of truth and being, the realism after which Bergson aspired. Maritain's Thomism, on the other hand, receives its form from its opposition to Bergson's thought. Its epistemological concern for precision in matters of logic, concept, and intelligence constitute an effort to refine Bergson's notion of intuition. Its metaphysical concern for the Aristotelian distinctions of causality and change were written in counterpoint to Bergson's conception of creative evolution. And last, to accent Bergson's abiding influence on Maritain, all Maritain's discussions of pre-philosophical knowledge, mysticism, and aesthetics are derived in critical dialogue with Bergson's notion of intuition.

Bergson, to conclude, was Maritain's first master in philosophy. From the vantage point of many years later, Maritain recognized his indebtedness to Bergson, and evermore, both he and Raïssa saw him in retrospect as the first to respond to the truth they sought—as a Virgil who had led them up to the gates of the Church.

Léon Bloy: Conversion and Manhood

In 1905 Jacques and Raïssa, now married, met Léon Bloy. Within a year, this once atheist and decadent poet, and this now solitary and impoverished religious critic of all things modern, had become their godfather.[53]

Despite their readings of Pascal and the mystics, Plotinus and Ruysbroeck, which were inspired by Bergson, they believed Bloy represented their first real contact with Christianity. Bloy quickly became and thereafter remained for them a true prophet, a "pilgrim of the absolute"—God's special envoy to them and their age.

Bloy did not distinguish his own personal suffering from his apocalyptic view of his times. In contrast to Péguy's vision of Christianity which accented the incarnation and hope, Bloy's Christianity stressed judgment and redemption. Man's need to join his suffering to God and prepare for Christ's imminent return was the heart of Bloy's prophecy.

Influenced earlier in his life by such symbolists as Verlaine and Baudelaire, and now intent on the second coming, Bloy bitterly denounced the entire course of modern history.[54] History from the Renaissance onward was reduced, in Bloy's view, to a single theme, man's revolt against God. The French Revolution witnessed the sons overthrowing the fathers. The Restoration was not a real restoration but the ignominious installation of the bourgeois, whose pettiness, business, and money banished what diabolic but inspired glory Napoleon had given France. The defeat of France in 1870 was not interpreted by Bloy as a political event, it was rather considered the defeat of the New Testament. Leo XIII's rapprochement with democracies was treated by Bloy not as a matter of church-state relations, but was for Bloy the work of the Anti-Christ. The Dreyfus Affair to him was but additional proof that no one in France cared about anything except the city of man. And last, Bloy saw France's refusal to heed what he believed the revelation of the Virgin to two shepherds at Salette in 1846 as proof that Christ's wrath was to be certain and soon. "From 1890 onward," Bloy prophesied, "the table is cleared; there is no intermediary between the world and the wrath of God."[55]

From this reactionary critic of the modern world, the Maritains received their Catholicism. After anguishing for one year over the place of the Jew in the Christian redemption schemes, the failures of contemporary Christians in matters of social justice, and fearing rejection by their families and friends, Jacques and Raïssa were converted. The children of Jaurès and Baudelaire, Péguy and Bergson, the Republic and Abraham, became Catholics.

It is impossible to make a definitive judgment on why Maritain was attracted to the anti-modern Bloy, and the experiences he underwent in the year before his baptism, but a few factors can be set forth: Maritain first was part of a generation that less and less accepted theory as an end in itself and more and more strove to find a heroic vocation in action. His readings in mysticism and poetry, his criticisms of bourgeois culture, and his desire for a personal mission were all factors which could have drawn him to Bloy. Other factors were: the older Bloy was a writer, and a writer rejected by his times; he hated the bourgeois, and their worlds of money and business; he lived in and spoke of poverty; he freely asked for the Maritains' aid and he willingly brought them into the intimacy of his private life. He appeared to write about what he lived, and he did not conceal the conflicts and passions of his life from them.[56] All this must have filled the young Maritain and his wife with the sense that they were in the presence of a man with a "real destiny"—a man who was the antithesis of all things bourgeois.

Christianity itself provided Maritain with a new identity. The feelings and words of his youthful symbolism were translated into Christian prayers and mysteries; his concern for the suffering of the worker and his belief in revolution, the source of his tie to socialism, were superseded and translated into his preoccupation with the passion and redemption of Christ. In terms of Christianity, Maritain found a new identity and mission, poetry, and philosophy—a new set of terms by which he could reinterpret himself, his life, his relations with his wife, his family, other men, and his times. All that he had been, was, and would be, became for him part of the divine mystery of man's relations to God.

In the broadest sense, Maritain had undergone a conversion. That is, he passed through an experience that made him over, made him what he had not been prior to it. This conversion was integral to the dynamic process of his passage from youth to manhood. The conversion experience resolved the identity crisis that had marked his youth from his middle teens onward, and prepared the foundations upon which his manhood thereafter rested.

To define at least generally the type and dimensions of the crisis Maritain was undergoing as a youth, and what thus was his fundamental condition at the time of his conversion, we can rely introductorily on one of Erik Erikson's basic descriptions of the young man's identity crisis: "The major crisis of adolescence [is] the identity crisis; it occurs in that period of the life cycle when each youth must forge for himself some central perspective and direction, some working unity, out of the effective remnants of his childhood and the hopes of his anticipated adulthood; he must detect some meaningful resemblance between what he has come to see in himself and what his sharpened awareness tells him others judge and expect him to be."[57]

The substance of such crises, to rely further on Erikson, goes beyond simply the task of leaving the family house, finding a job, and taking upon oneself a new public identity. First, such crises can, as they so often and tragically do, return the adolescent to the most rudimentary crises of childhood, which are those of trust and security. Second, they can seriously aggravate the problems of early adolescence, the problems of adjusting to one's own body, the concern for friendship, and the anxiety over being both dependent and independent. Third, these crises can open for those undergoing them the most mature, profound, and penetrating questions of man's existence, the questions of the meaning of love, death, God, and life. In substance, hence, the most profound identity crisis can simultaneously open a youth to all crises of the human spirit. For those who have experienced such a crisis to an intensive degree, there is no way back to the shores of the ordinary; for them, almost everything seems to raise the absolute questions of the meaning of life and the integrity of the self. In Erikson's opinion, out of this depth experience *homo religiosus* is born.[58]

Undoubtedly, Maritain from his middle teens on had experienced an identity crisis. Aside from his attempts to identify himself as a socialist with the downtrodden and his early poems which reflected simultaneously radical self-assertion and radical self-denial, there were other signs of the presence of such a crisis in his life. There is the young Maritain of seventeen or eighteen "who rolled on the floor of his room out of despair because *there was no answer* to all the questions."[59] There was the young Maritain's desire to have a perfect union with Raïssa, as if all differences of personality could be banished once and for all. Then there were their reflections, which, in Raïssa's words, led them "to think out the entire universe anew, the meaning of life, the fate of man, the justice and injustice of society"—reflections that once led them to the edge of despair and suicide.[60] Unquestionably, within the young Maritain there was a soul intent on and in quest of itself.

Identity crises, nevertheless, do not exist independent from the epoch and milieu in which they occur.[61] Some periods in history will favor the occurrence of such crises; sometimes these crises will pertain more to one class than another, sometimes it is religion and other times it is politics that nurtures them. On occasion, as the case was in pre-World War France, the culture itself induced such crises.

In many ways, Maritain was but one intellectual among a multitude of intellectuals who experienced, and were taught to experience, such a crisis by a culture occupied with heroisms, mysticisms, vocations, and rebellions. All arenas of French *fin du siècle* intellectual life were filled with young men searching for the meaning of themselves in their times. Perhaps the identity crisis and the search integral to it were the essence of the turn of the century intellectual.[62] Perhaps it was this very crisis and search which provide an overall unity to the young men's socialism, nationalism, and religion, as well as a general explanation for the older Bergson's search for the absolute, Péguy's quest for Joan of Arc, and Bloy's wait upon the Apocalypse.

While no definitive statement can be made on a subject of this sort, the fate of Maritain's closest friend, Ernest Psichari, is suggestive of the important place of identity crisis in any explanation of pre-War French culture.[63] Psichari twice attempted suicide because of a broken love affair with Maritain's sister, Jeanne. Then after a period of self-debauchery, he joined the army to flee the Paris which he could no longer stand. Stationed in the deserts of North Africa, he turned military discipline into a type of religious asceticism, underwent a religious conversion, and wrote a type of symbolist literature which fused together the desert, its peoples, God, and the mystery of faith. Psichari's life, therefore, might be taken as an expression of an age when intellectuals were in crisis and search. Clearly, neither his nor the young Maritain's crisis and conversion were alien to the spirit of the times.

From whatever final perspective one chooses to understand the meaning of Maritain's crisis, what is undeniable is the existence of some such crisis in his life. For only in terms of such a crisis, is it possible to understand how Maritain could have been so totally transformed by a conversion which in effect made him a new person by effecting his passage from youth to manhood, furnishing him with a new source of energy and a new axis for his life, and providing him with a faith in terms of which he could restructure his understanding of himself and his times. Only a self in radical crisis and search could have undergone such a reversal as Maritain experienced in his conversion.

Maritain's conversion, in turn, meant, to paraphrase an idea of William James on conversion, that religious concerns came to occupy the center of his attention and to form the habitual center of his energy.[64] His conversion made it possible for him to alter his understanding of the world around him. His wife, family and friends—the personal world —were viewed as part of God's creation and love. Conversely, most of contemporary thought and society were conceived of as belonging to the secular city of man. The Sorbonne and the Republic, which were the anti-ideals against which Raïssa later developed the history and meaning of their conversions, were seen in the wake of the conversion as expressions of a world without God. The spirit of youth that had rebelled against the Sorbonne and the "bourgeois world" was seen accordingly as nature's impetus to God. The modern world thus became for Maritain the story of man's revolt against God.

From Maritain's baptism until the Great War, he consolidated his personality upon his conversion experience. His voracious reading of all forms of Catholic literature, his daily prayer, meditation and communion, his love of religious art and the Middle Ages were some of the means by which he wove his mind and life into the fabric of the Church. While still unsure of the specific career he would pursue, his vocation as a Catholic lay intellectual was not in doubt. In 1906 he went to Heidelberg to study physiology under the neo-Vitalist Hans Driesch. As a later article proves, Maritain's intent was to provide an alternative science to the mechanistic and materialistic science which he believed were destructively dominating the modern spirit.[65] Returning to France two years later, his new faith having been tested and strengthened by Raïssa's long and grave illness, he took on small posts like compiling an orthographic lexicon and a dictionary of everyday life in order to have as much time as possible for his study of Catholicism. Within a small group of religious intellectuals gathered around Léon Bloy, composed of the geologist Pierre Termier, the painter Roualt, and the Dutch writer Pierre van der Meer de Walcheren and his wife, Maritain found a community to replace the small circle of intellectuals at Péguy's *Cahiers* and a personal buffer against what he believed were the anti-religious forces of the modern world.

In 1908, upon the advice of Bloy, Maritain chose Clerrisac as his spiritual advisor; Clerrisac, in his turn, advised Maritain to read Saint

Thomas. Here Maritain discovered his career and vocation: "Woe to me," he later wrote, "if I do not thomisticize."[66]

Thomas became the language of Maritain's adulthood. For him Thomism provided the highest unity of faith and reason, and the best vehicle for unifying his critique of contemporary thought. In his first writings, which occurred simultaneously with his initial studies in Thomas, Maritain asserted that faith and reason were compatible.[67] As faith, he argued analogically, ends in the person of Christ, the teaching of the Church, and beatific vision, so man's reason comes to know the laws and hierarchies of nature and arrives at certitude about God's existence. The central error of all modern thought was, conversely, having overlooked the unities of faith, reason, nature, and God. To assert the validity and primacy of Thomas was for Maritain a way to serve both God and man.

As the War drew near, Maritain moved closer and closer to the Church and Thomism and further and further away from his first mentors, Péguy and Bergson. Maritain's break with his first mentor Péguy became inevitable. First, there were family reasons. In attempting at Péguy's request to prepare secretly the way for his return to the Church (which was conditional on the consecration of Péguy's marriage and the baptism of his children) Maritain found himself in battle with Péguy's anti-clerical, Republican wife and mother-in-law. Conversely, Péguy revealed to the Republican mother of Maritain his growing ties to Léon Bloy and the Church.[68] In addition to these delicate family matters, Maritain grew impatient with Péguy's failure to profess his faith openly. Péguy, conversely, believed Maritain was succumbing to reactionary clericalism in the hands of Bloy and Clerrisac. In 1912, after a series of misunderstandings from at least 1908 onward, Maritain wrote regarding a *Cahier* containing Benda's *Ordination* that he did not wish future issues if they were as impertinent and badly written as the present one. Péguy's response was to strike Maritain's name from the list of subscribers. Neither cared to face each other again. This last ritual merely enacted what had already become a fact; their friendship was finished. Between them remained no more than a last quarrel over Bergson's works. Maritain took the side of Pius X and the anti-Modernists; Péguy, in his last work, fought his last battle of words against those who had put Bergson on the Index in 1914.[69]

Maritain and Péguy, however, did see each other once again. It was to say farewell. France was in danger. Péguy was on his way to fight and die in the first battles of the First World War.

By the eve of the War, Maritain had completed his passage from youth to manhood. His and Raïssa's family accepted their conversions. Two of Maritain's closest friends, Ernest Psichari and Henri Massis, were converted by his example. As an instructor at the *Institut Catholique* in Paris, Maritain was increasingly known as a strong critic of Bergson and an outstanding Thomist. Already parts of the next generation of young Catholics looked upon Maritain as one of their intellectual leaders and fathers.

Thus, on the eve of the War, ironic as it is, Maritain had found his identity, as Europe prepared to lose hers.

CHAPTER III

MATURITY AND PROPHECY: MARITAIN IN THE 1920s

AS MOUNIER was one of the fathers of Catholic intellectual life in post-Second World War France, so Maritain was one of the fathers of Catholic intellectual life in post-First World War France. Like no other thinker in France in the 1920s, Maritain expressed a Catholic lay understanding of the modern world. In the immediate aftermath of the War, Maritain was the voice of anti-modernity. He spoke of five centuries of Western civilization since the Renaissance as if they were in error, and he left no doubt that he was the defender of a past order of civilization. Yet by 1930, in response to the Vatican's 1926 Condemnation of the *Action Française*, Maritain began to exhort fellow Catholics to prepare the way for a new civilization.

There is much to be learned from this radical transformation of Maritain's world view. It is possible in microcosm to understand one part of twentieth century Catholicism's journey from reaction against the modern world to a cautious rapprochement with it. In turn, it is possible to understand the genesis and development of that intellectual process that eventually made Maritain one of the major voices of Christian democratic liberalism in post-World War II North and South America. Even more to our purposes, it becomes possible in terms of Maritain's evolution from reaction to liberalism to understand how in one sense Mounier's Personalism grew out of Maritain's reappraisal of democracy in the late 1920s and how, in another sense, Mounier's Personalism is not only independent from Maritain's thought but represents one of twentieth century Catholicism's most profound attempts to rethink the present and to create a new future.

Maritain's emergence as a central figure in French intellectual life was simultaneous with the conclusion of the First World War. Unable to perform military service, Maritain continued to teach, and he continued confidently to pursue a Thomistic revival. Conceiving the central drama of modern man to be taking place in the hearts and thoughts of men rather than on the battlefields and at peace tables, Maritain did not critically examine the War—the most tragic, awesome, and encompassing event Europe had undergone at least since the French Revolution.

Part of the reason for Maritain's continued confidence in his intellectual vocation, as well as his failure to examine the War, lay in the character of the War itself. Like all truly profound events, the War was not a singular phenomenon. It was diverse in its causes, acts, and consequences. It was profound in its meaning and experiences. At its end, men were left divided over what had been suffered, what had been gained, what was to be done and what lay ahead. There were no scales for weighing ten million dead and all the economic, spiritual, material, political, and social evils adjoined to this slaughter. The War was too great to be rendered into a single lesson; no pedagogy was strong enough to teach it. The divisions that polarized the schools of European intellectual life before the War were thus heightened and multiplied by the War.

The War and its settlements not only failed to unify European intellectual life; they conferred yet more "prophetic rights" upon the intellectual. With fewer reservations and with larger audiences, intellectuals could preach the most radical doctrines of pre-First World War culture and politics. In addition to the enduring priesthoods of Marx, Nietzsche, and Dostoevsky, there was an ever mounting host of younger prophets: Scheler, Freud, Spengler, Ortega, and Berdyaev. The War and its settlements provided intellectuals with countless facts, ideas, ideologies to explain the present; and even more destructively, the War provided a climate in which almost any rhetoric, propaganda, or irrational theory could take root and be sustained. The War could be taken as proof of nearly anything—of the need for either order or revolution, nationalism or internationalism, collectivism or individualism. In retrospect, it appears as if everything had become suspect, as if everything had become credible. In sum, the War encouraged intellectuals across Europe to be more confident in their prophetic post, more certain in fusing together and popularizing the most radical criticism of nineteenth century bourgeois liberal society.

Maritain was no exception. While not fundamentally altering his vision of himself, mankind and the Church, the War confirmed him in his pre-First World War attacks on bourgeois culture, and permitted him to elaborate and intensify his indictment of the *âge moderne*.[1] Ever more certain that Europe's present condition revealed a divine meaning, and ever more convinced (as was his mentor Bloy) that the walls of the city of man were crumbling, Maritain was yet more ready to attack the doctrine of progress, to argue that man without God, reason without faith, and a civilization without the Church were destined to self-destruction.[2]

Another important element which contributed to Maritain's confidence in his role as a Catholic intellectual was the improved position of Catholicism in post-War France. The enhanced prestige of Catholics because of their war effort, coupled with the general shift of the French political spectrum to the right and the split between Socialists and Communists, were factors which weakened anti-clericalism as an ideology and a political platform and, correspondingly, permitted the Church to strengthen and to revitalize all its political and social activity.[3] The new vitality of both the left and right wings of French Catholicism in the 1920s was respectively shown by the Republic's diplomatic recognition of the Vatican in 1922 and by the articulation of an entire spectrum of Catholic organizations unified in 1931 at the *Action Catholique Française*.[4]

Of yet more direct relevance to Maritain's confidence was the growing vitality associated with French Catholic intellectual life.[5] From Maritain's perspective, many orders of secular modern intellectual life itself were increasingly pointing towards a return to faith. For instance, new physics and biologies steadily abandoned their apriori materialistic assumptions and admitted the limits of their disciplines. Likewise, it appeared to Maritain that the philosophies of Bergson, James, Husserl, Whitehead, and Santayana marked a significant departure from the older materialisms and idealisms, and were, however erringly, groping for a new realism. Even in the distortion and violence of surrealistic and expressionistic art, Maritain caught glimpses of a religious awakening of the human spirit. It was not even beyond Maritain's hope that modern thought, despite itself, was preparing for an eventual acceptance of the Church and Thomism.

While Maritain could only hopefully conjecture about the evolution of the secular mind, he was certain that Catholic intellectual life in France had undergone a true intellectual revival since the turn of the century. The numbers and names of conversion alone could be taken as evidence of this revival. To choose only some of the most illustrious, prior to the War, there were the conversions of Bloy, Huysmans, Bourget, Claudel, and Péguy; in the post-War period, there were the conversions of Cocteau, Sachs, and Marcel. Further evidence of the ongoing intellectual revival in France was a remarkable spiritual topography of individual Catholic thinkers: Thomist Garrigou-Lagrange, royalist historian Jacques Bainville, historian of philosophy Etienne Gilson, editor of the *Nouvelle Revue Française* Jacques Rivière, religious historian and literary critic Henri Brémond, Arabic scholar and missionary Henri Massignon, philosopher Maurice Blondel and his younger followers such as Paul Archambault, continuers of Marc Sangnier such as Francisque Gay, the numerous Catholics who drew inspiration from Bergson such as scientist Edouard Le Roy and philosopher Jacques Chevalier, and the younger novelists François Mauriac and Georges Bernanos.[6] Catholic scholarship also was in the process of regaining its own historical, philosophical, and spiritual sources; and its inquiries into history, monographs on saints and mystics, religious literary criticism, independent philosophy, as well as the diverse influences of Augustine, Thomas and Pascal, De Maistre, Lammenais and Newman, were convincing testimony to Catholics that the Church offered an alternative to the values and goals of contemporary European civilization.

Maritain knew himself to be one of the fathers of contemporary French intellectual life.[7] Along with Proust, Valéry, Gide and Claudel, he was one of the "intellectual rulers" of Paris. His importance in French intellectual life was beyond dispute. He was co-founder and editor of the conservative *Revue Universelle* and co-founder and editor of the series *Rouseau d'Or,* which sought to be a literary rival to the *Nouvelle Revue Française.* His numerous works—*La philosophie bergsonienne* (1913), *Art et scolastique* (1921), *Eléments de philosophie* (1921-1923), *Théonas* (1921), *Antimoderne* (1922), *De la vie d'oraison* (1923), *Réflexions sur l'intelligence et sur sa vie propre* (1924), and *Trois réformateurs* (1925)—attracted wide attention and revealed his wide range of interest. To his home in Meudon came some of the most important Catholic intellectuals: among the elders were Berdyaev, Marcel, Cocteau, Bernanos, Dalbiez, Garrigou-Lagrange; included among the young were Julien Green, Stanislas Fumet, Etienne Borne, Jean de Fabrèques, Yves Simon, and Emmanuel Mounier, who perhaps more than any other among the young understood the full intellectual dimensions of the Catholic revival. Undoubtedly, Maritain had become a nexus of French Catholic intellectual life.

Aware of his important place in French Catholic intellectual life, Maritain conceived it as his mission to transform the spiritual ferment in secular and Catholic thought into an authentic Catholic intellectual renaissance. Maritain's mission had a double character. On one hand, it meant trying to demonstrate to the non-believer the contradictions of his non-belief and the compatibility of Christianity with truth and life. On the other hand, it meant trying to convince fellow Catholics of the superiority of their traditions *vis-à-vis* the secular world and to assure their orthodoxy in matters of Christian thought. Both aspects of Maritain's mission were unified by Thomism.

For Maritain, Thomism was the "philosophy of philosophies."[8] Maritain considered it as the crowning philosophy of man and nature, and the most perfect philosophical expression of the unity that exists between faith and reason. Maritain proposed Thomism to believer and non-believer alike as equally being the perennial philosophy of man, the critical philosophy of human knowledge, and the highest intellectual synthesis so far achieved between classical thought and Christian faith. For Maritain, Thomism offered essential truths about man's nature and human knowledge, while preparing man's spirit for those sacred truths of his creation and redemption. To teach Thomism, for Maritain, was to speak of what was most eternal within man's meaning and destiny.

Maritain's Thomism also had political and temporal dimensions; in fact, Thomism shaped Maritain's philosophy for his times. Resembling, in fact substantially anticipating Mounier's Personalism, Thomism was the center of Maritain's world view. From the perspective of Thomism, Maritain attempted to survey the make-up and the origins of the modern world. As a Thomist, Maritain believed himself able to speak of what was most permanent and worthwhile in man, as well as what was most transitory and aberrant in the world of contemporary man. Serving Maritain as it served the Vatican in the second half of the nineteenth century, Thomism provided him with a measure of theological orthodoxy as well as a counter-world view.[9]

Hence Thomism was for Maritain the basis of his philosophy for his times and the vehicle of his anti-modernity. As a view of man and God, as a truth of reason and the Church, as an activity and identity for his life, Thomism gave the mature Maritain of the 1920s his confidence. It was Thomism which made Maritain one of the influential intellectuals of France in the 1920s, and it was also Thomism which in great part impeded Maritain from fathoming the awesome questions of power and values, events and ideas, which were raised by the First World War.

Three Reformers: Luther, Descartes, Rousseau[10]

Maritain's *Three Reformers* (1925), imbued with confidence in himself, Thomism, and the Church, serves as an excellent point to center an analysis of his philosophy for his times. First, it sets forth many of the major themes which preoccupied him since his first writings. Second, it reveals how Maritain grafted the intellectual traditions and criticisms of the modern world which he had received from Péguy, Bergson, and Bloy into a distinct philosophy of the *"âge moderne."* Third, it provides a source for understanding the later transformations in Maritain's social and political philosophy. Fourth, most importantly, there is already found within the *Three Reformers* many of those fundamental criticisms of the modern world upon which Mounier based his own first critical world view.

In the light of the *Three Reformers,* a work Mounier knew so well, it is possible to see how Personalism's critical analysis of the modern world, especially its criticisms of collectivism and individualism, were derived from a philosophical and religious indictment of the modern world. And it is possible to grasp how Mounier's Personalism, which was predicated on a commitment to understand and serve man in the temporal historical order, had, ironically, its critical roots in a broad anti-modernity which was shared by diverse anti-Catholic and anti-democratic forces across Europe.

At the outset of *Three Reformers,* Maritain described the importance he attributed to Luther, Descartes, and Rousseau:

> Three men, each for very different reasons, dominate the modern world, and govern all the problems which torment it; a reformer of religion, a reformer of philosophy, a reformer of morality—Luther, Descartes, and Rousseau. They are in very truth begetters . . . of modern *consciousness.* I do not speak of Kant, who stands at the meeting of the intellectual streams springing from these three men, and created, so to say, the academic structure of modern thought.[11]

By criticizing their thought, Maritain sought (1) to define what he considered to be the "spiritual essence" of the modern world, (2) to demonstrate that Catholicism was in full accord with man's nature, and (3) to prove that the thought of Thomas provided the most universal basis for the true advancement of mankind.

These goals shaped Maritain's interpretation of the three reformers. Maritain on one hand defended the perennity of Aristotle, Thomas and the Church against all those diverse ideological positions which conceived Western history under the basic theme of the inevitable progress of human knowledge. On the other hand, Maritain battled against such critics as Marx and Weber, Nietzsche and Freud, who made faith, reason, and truth only epiphenomena of the historical struggle of class and power, or simply reflections of man's will and sexuality. Adopting a position held by the majority of twentieth century Catholic thinkers, Maritain believed himself simultaneously a radical critic of the present Western order and a radical defender of the basic Western values. To study Luther, Descartes, and Rousseau was for Maritain to seek to define the philosophy of modern times—to trace the erring journey of modern man towards the contemporary world.

"Luther or the Advent of the Self"[12]

Of the Luther whom Hegel considered the spiritual father of the modern world, Maritain wrote: "What first impresses us in Luther's character is *egocentrism*. Something much subtler, much deeper and much more serious, than egoism: *a metaphysical egoism*. Luther's self became practically the center and gravity of everything."[13] Luther's inner life was for Maritain a microcosm of the evils of the modern soul—the principle of the Reformation which "unbridled the human self in the spiritual and religious order, as the Renaissance, I mean the hidden spirit of the Renaissance, unbridled the human self in the order of the natural and sensible activities."[14]

The young monk Luther, Maritain argued, was unable to break free from his morbid preoccupation with himself and his own salvation, and was equally incapable of curbing his appetites. This, coupled with his drive for perfection, led him, Maritain argued, from anxiety and depression to resignation and despair. To counter the despair which engulfed him, Luther was driven to a radical solution: he abandoned all hope for religious transfiguration, and willfully asserted that he was saved. He made—and this is the essence of his sin for Maritain—the recognition of his sinfulness the source and justification of his faith in Christ.[15]

For Maritain, Luther's leap to faith—the founding act of Protestantism—was suicidal. As a consequence of it, man is denied all natural dignity; original sin is made to vitiate all of his being; and man, so far as he is only human, is defined by his basest drives and most evil intentions. Man, Maritain further contended, was seen in the perspective of

Luther's faith as having no potential whatsoever for self-reform. Human nature is conceived as neither worthy nor capable of participating in creation; man's faculties, in turn, are left useless. Once reason is declared valueless without faith, will and conscience, denied reason, are left without a unity or guide. According to Maritain, Luther ultimately left a vision of man with no potential either to receive or nurture truth and grace.

Maritain chose to call Luther's faith a "Pelagianism of despair." That is, Luther's faith was willful in all ways: it was born out of despair, initiated by a radical assertion of one's worthlessness, and rendered valid by the presumption of God's grace. In turn, it was sustained and made righteous by the repeated affirmation that I am a sinner, Christ saves sinners, and thus I am saved. In Maritain's own words:

> The Pelagianism of despair! In fine, it is for a man himself to work his own redemption by driving himself to a desperate trust in Christ. Human nature will only have to throw off as an empty theological accessory the cloak of a meaningless grace and turn its faith on to itself, and it will become that pleasant liberated beast whose continual and ineffable progress delights the universe today.

"And thus," Maritain continued, "in the person of Luther and his doctrine, we are present . . . at the Advent of the Self."[16] For Maritain individualism, that modern conception of the autonomous self which equally for him and Mounier was the most destructive of all spiritual principles at work in the modern world, took its first full form because of Luther. Tracing the formation and development of individualism from Luther to the present was tantamount to Maritain as it was for Mounier, to tracing the destruction of western culture, society and politics.

In its metaphysical roots, modern individualism errs, in Maritain's view, because it confounds the fact of being separate (the metaphysical principle of individuality which pertains to all material and spiritual being) with the spiritual existence of a distinct person who participates in spiritual and moral orders of existence. In other words, stating an insight that is absolutely fundamental to Mounier's Personalism, Maritain argued that individualism overlooks man's place as a person in the spiritual and human orders of existence, and seeks to define and value man only by his particular individual experience and subjectivity. The historical passage in the Western spirit from the concept of man as person to the concept of man as individual resulted, in Maritain's opinion, in contemporary man's complete alienation from the true sources of his being, and left him an individual who exists only by virtue of his separation, isolation, and finitude. Individualism was for Maritain the destructive essence of modern secular culture:

> But then, surely Luther's case shows us precisely one of the problems against which modern man beats in vain. It is the problem of *individualism and personality*. Look at the Kantian shrivelled up in his autonomy, the Protestant tormented by concern for his inward liberty, the Nietzschean giving himself curvature of the spine in his effort to jump beyond good and evil, the Freudian cultivating his complexes and sublimating his libido, the thinker preparing an unpublished conception of the world for the next philosophical congress, the "surrealist" hero throwing himself into a trance and plunging into the abyss of dreams, the disciple of M. Gide viewing himself with gloomy enthusiasm in the mirror of his freedom; all those unhappy people are looking for their personalities; and, contrary to the Gospel promise, they knock and no man opens to them, they seek and they do not find. [17]

Again, it was individualism, in Maritain's view as well as in the view of Mounier, which accounted for the disintegration of modern society. Once modern man had been denied his universality, he became vulnerable in his solitude to collective identities offered in ever greater degree and number from the French Revolution onward. Having only his individual subjectivity and his own particular traditions for his defense, modern man was unable to resist the emerging collectivizing forces of money, society, state and ideology. Thus, for Maritain, individualism was the cause of collectivism—as it was to be later for Mounier.

Political tyranny in particular, Maritain maintained, was yet another part of Luther's legacy. In agreement with numerous contemporary scholars, Maritain argued that Luther left the individual and the Church defenseless before the state. However, for Maritain, who was intent on discovering the "inner logic" of events that shaped the modern world, the steps did not seem either large or complicated that led from Luther's territorial state and the monarchic tyranny of Hobbes to the democratic tyranny of Rousseau and the providential tyranny of Hegel's state. In sum, Maritain believed that in freeing man from everything but his own subjectivity and will, Luther denied man his nature and reason, and enslaved man to his own passion, politics, history, and immanence.

To conclude, it was almost inevitable that Maritain should have treated Luther as he did. Bergson had shown Maritain the integral relation between Kantianism, idealism, relativism, and positivism; Péguy and

Bloy had taught Maritain that France was the Israel of the New Testament; Pius X declared that modern democracy and Modernism were equally the unwanted consequences of Protestant and secular conceptions of freedom and truth. That Maritain was a member of the nationalistic Generation of 1905 and that France had fought Germany in 1870 and 1914 are but additional reasons why Maritain—French and Catholic—made Luther, the acknowledged spiritual father of German history, the first heresiarch of the modern world.

"Descartes or the Incarnation of the Angel"

Maritain considered Descartes the creator of the myth of progress. Maritain believed that in the name of this myth modern man declared his latest thoughts true, and all past thoughts dead. In the name of progress, modern man learned, according to Maritain, to assume that faith and reason were circumscribed by time and place, and that the Church and Thomas were of interest only to those concerned with the archaeology of the human mind. Accordingly, Maritain's interpretation of Descartes was developed in opposition to all those schools of thought which would make Descartes the founder of a new philosophy that liberated man from past authorities and established human knowledge upon the more certain bases of reason and science.[18]

In Maritain's view, Descartes' fundamental error was the theological "error of angelism."[19] Descartes assumed human knowledge, like that which Thomas attributed to angelic beings, to be intuitive (direct and unmediated in its comprehension), innate (inherent within the thinking subject), and independent (free of the need for and conditions of experience, time, situation, and space). Other errors were intrinsic to this "error of angelism": man's first object of knowledge became his own mind—his own clear and distinct ideas. The mind itself, conceived independent from the body and the senses, was made autonomous; experience, habit, and wisdom, essential to Aristotle's and Thomas' conception of knowledge, were denied their place in the act of knowing. The mind was disembodied from the person; and in turn, the person, valued only in reference to his mind, was disembodied from his life, nature and the human situation.[20] Reason, to further sketch Maritain's analysis, was made the mind's essence. Modeled on the deductive sciences of geometry and mathematics, reason, so understood, was abstracted from man's spiritual and material nature, as well as the perennial truths of philosophy and the sacred truths of theology. The inevitable result of Descartes' errors, Maritain argued, was that man was torn from both the human and divine; and God Himself was reduced to doing no more in the Cartesian universe than assuring the "human angel" of his clear and distinct ideas.

Descartes' "angelism" was, in Maritain's view, the result of the accumulation of mistakes and pride since late medieval thought, a revolution against classical and Christian metaphysics, and the inner driving principle of a profound but self-destructive attack against Western consciousness and civilization.[21] In his words:

> The result of a usurpation of the angelic privileges, that *denaturing* of human reason driven beyond the limits of its species, that lust for pure spirituality, could only go to the infinite: passing beyond the world of created spirits it had to lead us to claim for our intelligence the perfect autonomy and the perfect immanence, the absolute independence, the *aseity* of the uncreated intelligence. Of that claim, Kant was the socialistic formulator, but the origins lie much deeper; and though the world's experience has already been wretched enough and humiliating enough to give it the lie, it remains the secret principle of the breakup of our culture and of the disease of which the apostate West seems determined to die.
>
> Thus the Cartesian reformation is not only at the source of the torrent of illusions and fables which self-styled "immediate clarities" have poured on us for two centuries and a half; it has a heavy weight of responsibility for the immense futility of the modern world and that strange condition in which we see humanity today, as powerful over matter, as informed and cunning to rule the physical universe, as it is weakened and lost in the face of intelligible realities of which the humility of a wisdom subject to being once made it partaker. To fight against bodies it is equipped like a god; to fight against spirits it has lost all its weapons, and the pitiless laws of the metaphysical universe crush it in mockery.[22]

Maritain believed that to understand the interior development of Descartes' own thought was to understand in microcosm the destructive course of modern thought. Maritain believed that it was thereby possible to reconstruct the steps by which modern man was first tempted with total knowledge, and eventually seduced to believe in his own total control.

Descartes, first, led modern man to deify his thought as perfect and to treat his own immanent subjectivity as the center of existence. For Maritain, idealists as well as skeptics, regardless of their specific sect, worshipped the primacy of their own thought—their own *cogito ergo sum*.

Descartes, second, led modern man to conceive of nature as no more than a set of essences which conform to his reason. Creation and the incarnation were banished from the Cartesian kingdom; knowledge gained by experience, analogy, analysis and conceptual development was made superfluous. Modern thought for Maritain was increasingly and narcissistically bound to the power of the single and intuitive glance into being, and mind became a machine which ignored mysteries and hierarchies, and consumed "truths" without participating in reality.

Third, in Maritain's opinion, Descartes created a universe of which God was left only an outer limit. As the Church was now relegated to the role of regularizing the customs and mores of the society in which men lived, God was relegated to the task of systematizing the universe which men knew. Nature was no longer a theophany relfecting God's majesty and power; and grace, revelation, the histories of the Jews and Christians, like the very person of Christ, were no longer pertinent to the philosopher's vision. Meditation upon the divine, like the experience of the holy, were here voided of relevance for the modern intellectual.

Fourth, Maritain argued, Descartes created a world without a place for man in it.[23] Man's mind was contracted to his reason. His body and his senses were consigned to the realms of the mechanical and the realm of shadows. The perennial wisdom of "know thyself" taught by Socrates and Jesus was now understood as a mere matter of past cultures. That is, more formally stated: ethics was jettisoned from the new metaphysics; conscience was divorced from human knowledge.

Once having strayed so far from a true image of man, it was inevitable, Maritain argued, that the Cartesian legacy—"the great French sin in the history of modern thought"—ended in voluntarism.[24] Believing himself capable of infinite knowledge and moved by the desire to expand his own mind without limit, the modern intellectual lived only by declaring his own supremacy and denying all experiences that contradicted it. Knowledge became power; nature was subjugated, and man claimed himself to be both the creator and the end of creation. Individualism was here given its "rationality" and mission.

In essence, Maritain accused Descartes of teaching Western man to choose himself over God. For Maritain, this "anthropocentrism" was the central evil of modern history. In his view, the eighteenth century *philosophes* gave anthropocentrism its full theoretical statement, and in the nineteenth century the revolutionists of different progressive ideologies acted upon it. All conditions of human finitude—time, space, matter, and nature—became enemies of humanity; everything must be brought under man's dominance—society, state, religion, and the future. Bolsheviks and Republicans were in varying degrees one in seeking to erect the city of man, a city in which man, utterly alone, pridefully and unwittingly builds his own hell. This for Maritain was the essence of the Cartesian legacy.

"Rousseau or Nature's Saint"

As might be expected, Maritain considered Rousseau the third destructive spiritual founder of the modern world. At variance with idealists like Windelband, Bosanquet, and Cassirer and such French idealists and Republicans as Levy-Bruhl and Jaurès, Maritain denied that Rousseau in any way marked a positive step in man's progress. Once again Maritain's anti-modernity placed him in conformity with those diverse currents of European criticism which generally charged Rousseau with the ill-consequences of the French Revolution, and which in France since the 1870s and the Dreyfus Affair onward, vilified Rousseau as the father of individualism, collectivism, statist democracy, and all else that was considered detrimental to France, the Church, and Europe.[25]

The spirit in which Maritain transformed his judgments of Rousseau into a philosophy of modern history is revealed in Maritain's preface to Rousseau:

> It is manifestly absurd to show the Renaissance, the Protestant Reformation, the Cartesian Reformation, the Philosophy of Illumination, Rousseauism, as a *unilinear* series ending in the apocalypse of the French Revolution. This systematization, used by rationalist historians hymning the stages of modern emancipation, arbitrarily conceals essential differences and deep oppositions. Yet to refuse to see the final convergence of these same movements would be an equal misconception of reality. We are faced by breaches at different points, and powers, intersecting and entwined, but tending in fact to the destruction of one same order and one same life. They are then one, at least in negation. It is even possible to find common characteristics and principles in these different spiritual currents, so long as we regard them as analogically, not univocally, common. In them there pass before us, in very different proportions and under forms often opposed—naturalism, individualism, idealism, or subjectivism—all the *-isms* which adorn the modern world.[26]

As Luther perverted faith and Descartes reason, so, according to Maritain, Rousseau, the last of the three reformers, destroyed conscience.

For Maritain, Rousseau's life and thought were based upon sickness and error.

Afflicted by neuroses and paranoia, uncertain in his sexuality and manhood, unable to be a father to his own children or to befriend another person, without a home in the world or within himself, and finding no consolation in the philosophers' stoicism or Protestant and Catholic pietisms, Rousseau despaired. Rousseau's response to his despair, like Luther's, was first resignation and then self-acceptance. His self-acceptance, however, unlike Luther's, was devoid of all transcendence. God's power and Christ's mercy, essential to Luther's world view, and "universality" and "truth," essential to Descartes' philosophy, were swept aside by Rousseau's self-acceptance. Neither the absolutes of faith nor the truths of the intellect were even nominally boundaries in Rousseau's cosmos. The self became everything, and everything became the self.

Rousseau, Maritain believed, prepared the way for total egotism. Without the notions of God and faith, person and nature, there was, in Maritain's opinion, no end around which man could order his thought and life. Anything which implied the need for self-reform, that is moral growth and character development, was shunted aside by Rousseau. Inspiration and feeling were given primacy; will and conscience were swamped by impulses, emotions, and desires. Consciousness became formless; life, purposeless. The self became everything and nothing. Out of this conception of the self, according to Maritain, Rousseau formed a religion of the self. Everything that arose from the self was accepted as an authentic expression of being, and good in itself. The intensity and abundance of man's feelings were made the measure of his holiness and sincerity; and holiness and sincerity, in their turn, became the deities of self-worship. This, in Maritain's eyes, was a heresy against faith, reason, conscience, and person, and the essence of the counterfeit religion that Rousseau had founded.

Rousseau's religion of the self marked for Maritain, as it later did for Mounier, another step in the development of modern individualism. Rousseau, in Maritain's opinion, metamorphosed Luther's despairing believer and Descartes' angelic man into a self-believing non-being. In turn, Romanticism, according to Maritain, made Rousseau's subjectivity the essence of man; and German thought, which Maritain depicted as the true heir of Rousseau, equipped this "new" man with a will and a philosophical justification for his egotistic nihilism. For Maritain, such diverse thinkers as Nietzsche, Freud, and Gide were the end product of Rousseau and Romanticism. Their perverse proclivity for the depraved in man was nothing other than an intellectual manifestation of the profound and inevitable errors that accompanied a century of a self-cultivating individualism.

In Maritain's view, Rousseau's errors not only had contaminated modern man's thought about himself, but his tragic mistakes formed the basis of contemporary misconceptions of man in society. Rousseau—whom Maritain depicted as paranoiac and genius, poet and madman—erred, according to Maritain, on the very first premise of his political thought. Believing that mankind's nature and experience were the same as his own, Rousseau fallaciously and egotistically asserted that man as an individual was naturally good, and that society was corrupt. Additionally and mistakenly assuming that there was an absolute correlation between the morality of the individual and society, Rousseau fell victim to a myth common to eighteeenth century *philosophes* and shared by most nineteenth century revolutionaries—the myth that a perfect society would result in a perfect man.

This utopian myth led Rousseau, in Maritain's eyes, to several other myths. First among them, Maritain identified Rousseau's equivocal use of the concept of nature.[27] Wishing to overcome the pessimism inherent within the nominalism and materialism of Hobbes, Spinoza, and Locke, Rousseau was led, on one hand, to employ the classical and scholastic notion of nature which pertains to the essence and end of man's being. On the other hand, Rousseau, devoid of a real metaphysical sense, used the concept of nature in the naturalistic sense which aims at only a description of man's material and historical situation. This equivocal use of the concept of nature, in Maritain's natural law perspective, produced in all of Rousseau's thought those fundamental confusions between metaphysics and naturalism, values and science, which had vitiated all political thought since the Renaissance.[28]

For Maritain, Rousseau's confused use of the concept of nature resulted in his false understanding of the subjects of liberty and equality. Assuming that "nature" ordained liberty and equality, Rousseau mistakenly concluded that all forms of subjugation and inequality should be totally eliminated. Not understanding liberty and equality with reference either to the spiritual and metaphysical orders of creation or the finite conditions and potentials of the human situation, Rousseau transformed liberty and equality into absolute imperatives which should be

totally realized in the social-political order. Thought and reality, desire
and power, were here, in Maritain's opinion, dangerously and mythical-
ly fused together.

From this mythic desire for a perfect city, Maritain believed, Rousseau proceeded to the yet more awesome myths of the social contract
and the general will. Together, the social contract and the general will
were, for Maritain, totalitarian.

In contrast to the ancients who understood the beginnings of society
as the result of an existing consensus among people and man's natural
aspirations as a political being, Rousseau, indebted to a long and corrupted political tradition from Althusius and Grotius, conceived the
beginnings of society as the result of a social contract deliberately
formed by free sovereign individuals. The social contract, so conceived,
Maritain argued, voided Rousseau's political theory of all reference to
God and man's nature and made the act of the contracting parties of
sole importance: "Hence it follows," wrote Maritain, "that the first
author of society is not God, the Author of the natural order, but the
will of man, and that the birth of civil law is the destruction of natural
law."[29]

It was the general will, however, which, in Maritain's opinion, gave
Rousseau's social contract its specific form and his political theory its
unique character. Maritain contended that Rousseau's view was based
on the false assumptions that each individual upon freely entering into
a social contract transfers all his rights to the community, and the community reciprocally restores his rights to him in a higher form. In other
words, Rousseau believed that upon making a covenant a social body
comes into existence which absorbs all men into its more perfect and
universal self; an individual citizen, by obeying the more perfect general
will of the community, conforms himself to the highest good of his
own being. So Rousseau conceived the general will and thought he had
solved the problem of individual and community; so, according to Maritain, Rousseau had created an "immanent social God."

In agreement with other critics of Rousseau, Maritain contended that
Rousseau's general will was totalitarian on several grounds: first, the
inviolability and sacredness of man were not established upon man's
nature and relation to God; and thus the individual person was denied
all rights which transcended his citizenship. Second, institutions and
religion were left without defense against the state. Third, the state,
able to claim itself as the executor of the general will, emerged with

boundless power. Fourth, the state itself became potentially the instrument of tyrannical individuals and shapeless masses.[30]

As Rousseau's individualism translated itself into collectivist political theory, so too modern individualism had prepared a rendezvous with nineteenth and twentieth century collectivism. Again anticipating the essence of Mounier's critical analysis of the modern world, Maritain argued that the relationship between individualism and collectivism constituted the destructive dialectic which had formed the last five centuries of Western history. That is, the individualism which was spiritually created by Luther, Descartes, and Rousseau, destroyed man's natural and spiritual ties with other men, and left him defenseless before the new collectivisms of state, society, economics, and ideology which appeared *en masse* with the French Revolution.

In summary, Maritain's treatment of Rousseau, the last of the three reformers, revealed Maritain's philosophy of his times. Sharing the Vatican's criticisms of liberalism, socialism, and Bolshevism, Maritain was the enemy of all doctrines which proposed the independence of man from the Church. Spiritually born at the turn of the century out of an intellectual revolt against all that was considered part of the *monde bourgeois,* Maritain found little promise in any aspect of contemporary man's secular activity. In many ways, Maritain resembled the nineteenth century reactionaries who saw modern man's intellectual and political attacks against the *ancien régime* not as the beginnings of freedom but as the descent into godlessness and tyranny. In effect, the Maritain who wrote the *Three Reformers* was unquestionably an antimodern and anti-democrat. However, within one year of the publication of the *Three Reformers,* Maritain was forced to reconsider seriously some of the fundamental premises of both his philosophy of his times and his political philosophy. The reason for this was the Church's 1926 Condemnation of the *Action Française.*

Maritain and the Condemnation of the Action Française

In 1926, Pius XI condemned the *Action Française.* In reply its leader, non-believer Charles Maurras, issued his notorious *"Non Possumus."* A parting of the ways had come for many Catholics attached to the *Action Française;* among them was Jacques Maritain.

The Church's Condemnation had been primarily motivated by the conviction that the *Action Française* was annexing the Church to its

political philosophy and was competing with its teaching authority.[31]
That the *Action Française* was making significant inroads into the education of French and Belgian youth, and that the Vatican itself wished
to solidify its improving relations with the Third Republic, were also of
importance in determining the Vatican's decision.

Since the birth of the *Action Française* in 1899, there had been a
growing convergence between it and the conservative and reactionary
sectors of French Catholicism.[32] The *Action Française,* which had its
first roots in a theoretical and aesthetic adherence to royalism, nationalism, and classicism, was born out of the Dreyfus Affair as a unique
proponent of anti-modernity. Placing itself in opposition to Dreyfus
and putting itself at the ideological service of the army and the forces
of reaction and nationalism, the *Action Française* assimilated into itself
the whole spectrum of older and newer right-wing views. At one and
the same time the *Action Française* was, as it remained until the Second
World War, monarchist, decentralist, and traditionalist, as well as nation-
alist and statist.[33]

In the pre-War period, the *Action Française* was far from having
defined itself in terms of a single doctrine, strategy and class of supporters. While unified under such banners as *"politique d'abord"* and *"pays
réel"* over the *"pays légal,"* the *Action Française* contradictorily did
not become a political party, and found its appeal not among peasants
and workers, but among young intellectuals. While on a few occasions
certain of the *Action Française* supporters ventured to form paramilita-
ry groups and take direct part in political action, the *Action Française*'s
continuous concern was intellectually with the immediate and eternal
fate" of a France caught up in domestic conflicts and international
hostilities.

More than any other person, Charles Maurras set the course of the
Action Française. On the one hand, he offered a running commentary
on the state of the nation. It was especially pleasing to much of the
hierarchy and conservative Catholic circles that Maurras not only
proved himself a sharp critic of the Republic but specifically assailed
the anti-clerical legislation of 1905, as well as an enemy of modernism
and the *Sillon* movement, which can be considered an early forerunner
of Christian democracy. On the other hand, Maurras strove to set forth
the guidelines for a national restoration. Out of the works of de Maistre, de Bonald, Comte, Taine, Renan, Fustel-Coulanges, Le Play, La
Tour De Pin, and Barrès, Maurras tried to find an alternative political

philosophy for France.[34] Not precluding alliances with either syndicalism or such maverick intellectuals as Sorel and Péguy, Maurras was as
committed then, as Mounier would be later, to finding a way beyond
bourgeois decadence and the existing contradictions between individual
and society, state and nation, tradition and contemporaneity that
formed bourgeois society.

Even beyond Maurras' expectations, the *Action Française* became
popular in the post-First World War period. Traditionalism and nationalism proved compatible with many sectors of a France that had strug-
gled against a Germany on the battlefields as well as against a Wilson at
Versailles. While the *Action Française* did not capitalize upon its war-
won popularity to form a political party, it took upon itself the significant right of furnishing adult, conservative, religious France with a view
fitting for those who wanted the heroisms of the past remembered and
everything but a select set of conservative, national exigencies forgotten. The message of the *Action Française* was simple: France, past and
present, was the sacred and enduring one to be supported; German and
Bolshevik, parliamentarian, Communist and Jew, were the alien and
hostile many to be resisted. So, despite its continued hold on many
young intellectuals in the post-War period, the *Action Française* progressively passed from youth to maturity, from heroism to comfort,
from a fervent ideology to an intellectual orthodoxy which served an
upper middle class in its belief in France and its distrust of the Republic.

From this general perspective Maritain's rapprochement with *Action
Française* can be understood. Maritain's youthful intellectual passage
from socialism and symbolism to Catholicism and Thomism led him at
ever quickening speeds away from the world views of the Enlightenment and the Revolution, and ever more into the worlds of anti-
modernity. Only a few years after his conversion, Maritain's spiritual
director, Dom Clerrisac, guided Maritain to the *Action Française,* and
by the eve of the First World War, Maritain was sufficiently convinced
of the worth of the *Action Française* that he encouraged his friends
Psichari and Massis to join.[35] By 1918 Maritain saw sufficient unity between his quest for a philosophical renewal and Maurras' desire for national restoration that he was willing to accept Maurras' invitation to
jointly finance the beginnings of the *Revue Universelle.*[36]

As philosophical editor of the *Revue Universelle* (headed by reactionary Jacques Bainville), as member of the *Parti de l'Intelligence* which

called for the continued mobilization of French intellectuals for the spiritual defense of France, as critic of modern thought in general and Gide's *Nouvelle Revue Française* in particular, Maritain's affinity with Maurras and the *Action Française* was undeniable.[37] His view of the modern world converged with that of Maurras on several important points; together Maritain and Maurras (1) affirmed the unity of France, Catholicism, and Western Civilization, (2) proposed in theory a reformation of the entire contemporary order, (3) criticized notions of progress and egalitarian democracy, and (4) identified collectivism and individualism as central problems of modern life. On yet another plane, there was a profound agreement between Maritain's and Maurras' philosophies of their times. Both men, having suffered identity crises in youth, were intent on preserving a vision which offered them order and certainty against a world of change and anarchy.

However, beyond these points of convergence, there remained a deeper source of divergence between Maurras and Maritain. They were men of different spiritual families. Maritain was a son of the Church; Maurras, a son of France. Maritain was a philosopher; Maurras was a man of the political order. Maritain proposed Thomas, while Maurras was of the rationalist lineage of Descartes and Comte. It was the Middle Ages and the teachings of the Church that guided Maritain; for Maurras it was the classical city and the daily affairs of France that mattered. Maurras sought to realize a visible order, and Maritain waited upon the invisible order. All was measured for Maurras in reference to the ideal city. For Maritain, salvation was what mattered primarily. Theologically their division was that of the kingdom of Caesar and the kingdom of Christ. Philosophically, it was the division between the immanent and the transcendent.

When the Church issued its Condemnation in 1926, it was as certain that Maritain would comply with it as that Maurras would issue a *"Non Possumus."* For regardless of the degree to which Maritain had come to share the philosophy of the *Action Française*, his identity as a Christian and philosopher lay with the Church. Conversely, regardless of the degree that Maurras conceived of Catholicism as an essential part of France, he, a non-Christian son of France, would not sacrifice his identity as defender of the real France to the alien city of Rome. What was at stake in the Condemnation for Maritain and Maurras was nothing other than their identities.

Henry Bars adequately summarized Maritain's response to the Condemnation and the closing days of his ties to the *Action Française*:

> It is understandable how the crisis of 1926 . . . caught Maritain off guard.
> . . . In the work, *Une opinion sur Charles Maurras et le devoir des catholiques,*
> he tried to achieve an appeasement by giving the best sense to Maurras' positions and clearly indicating necessary corrections; he wished to make obedience more easy on the one hand and the Condemnation less severe on the other. One can doubt if he satisfied anyone. . . .
>
> *The Primacy of the Spiritual* which appeared later in the year (1927) had a different tone. The *Action Française's* break with Rome was consummated. . . . However, on numerous points, *The Primacy of the Spiritual* is the last testimony to an epoch that had finished. There is found there, in a language as violent as ever, *le procès des 'libertés modernes.'* And far from having joined the revengers, Maritain cast a last look of friendship towards those he had left: "It is with sadness I think of Charles Maurras. . . . My affection for this unconquered heart makes me feel the entire tragedy of his destiny."[38]

The Condemnation of the *Action Française* liberated Maritain to the world around him and the future. Until then Maritain's philosophy of his times was radically confused. He was simultaneously asserting the possibility of the restoration of a traditional social order and the Church's place in it, while prophetically declaring the impending total destruction of the modern world. He simultaneously was assuming that the Church was relevant to modern man and modern civilization, while inferring the need for the complete reversal of five centuries of Western history. In short, apocalyptic, reactionary, and reformist views cohabited within Maritain's philosophy of times. However, with the Condemnation of the *Action Française,* this situation was no longer possible. For the sake of his faith, he was forced to rethink his philosophy of the modern world.

While the Condemnation surely did not free Maritain's thought entirely from all these dilemmas and contradictions, it did compel him, nevertheless, towards a more empirical and less ideological view of his times. And furthermore, while the Condemnation did not of course lead Maritain to alter his judgments on Luther, Descartes, and Rousseau, neither did it cause him to transform the basic intellectual lines of his critique of modernity. It did force him to distinguish what was essential in the Church's teaching from what could be considered negotiable in the contemporary world of politics. In essence, his basic intransigence lost its edge and its unity. By destroying much of the conservative and reactionary underpinning of Maritain's thought, the Condemnation both allowed and forced him to envision more fully the pressing realities of contemporary Europe, and to admit more readily and more humbly the existence of problems and crises in Europe which could not simply be intellectually dispelled. From the Condemnation of the *Action Française,* it is possible to date Maritain's willingness to explore more sympathetically the possibility of a more positive relation between Catholicism and contemporary democracy, and to begin for the first time a sincere exploration of the condition of man in his times. It is this exploration, in turn, that inspired and converged with the younger Mounier's search for a Christian philosophy for his times. As strange as it is, it is necessary to conclude on the ironic note that the particular ecclesiastical matter of the Condemnation of the *Action Française* rather than the awesome tragedy of the First World War started Maritain on a search for a philosophy of our times.

CHAPTER IV

THE EDUCATION OF EMMANUEL MOUNIER

"OUR EDUCATION," wrote Mounier, "is the material which is given to us . . . for our future edification; we can love or detest it, but we cannot elude it."[1] By the time he founded *Esprit* in 1932, Mounier, who was only twenty seven, had completed his first education—the education with which he would have to find the meaning of himself and his times.

From one perspective, there are obvious differences between the youths and educations of Mounier and Maritain. Mounier was born Catholic; his family was middle class, his father a pharmacist. Mounier was brought up in the *provinces*; his first vocational interests were in science and medicine. During his teens, Mounier did not participate in *avant garde* artistic and political movements, but quietly and diligently played the role of student in a stable household and world. Only after studying philosophy at Grenoble and Paris, coming to know the whole breadth of Catholic intellectual life in France and being part of a world that in the years 1929 to 1932 began to have the sense of total crisis, did Mounier complete his first education. Only at this point did he consciously and fully give his life over to joining his fellow man in the active pursuit of a revolution which would, in his own words, end the "established disorder" and do nothing less than "remake the Renaissance."

All this is, of course, in marked contrast to the youth and education of Maritain. Maritain's parents were separated; his mother, a Favre, was a member of one of the most eminent families of the Third Republic. Brought up in Paris, the prodigious young Maritain was at the center of pre-War French culture; from his middle teens onward, he pursued his meaning across socialism and symbolism, philosophy and art, in a world

that took form around the memories of the Dreyfus Affair and the expectations of a coming war. Ultimately, Maritain's first education was
completed—his manhood discovered—through his conversion to the
Church and his commitment to Thomism.

These obvious but profound differences between Mounier's and Maritain's youths and educations explain fundamental differences between
their later intellectual careers. For example, Maritain's primary concern
for truth and orthodoxy, in contrast to Mounier's primary concern for
charity and action, could be seen as testifying to Maritain's need for
security and certainty. Conversely, in contrast to Maritain's desire to
conform to the Vatican, Mounier's persistent effort to identify himself
with the worker, the revolution and the non-believer, even at the risk of
excommunication, could be thought of as his attempt to compensate
for an obvious middle class background. However, from another perspective, these differences between their early lives and thought seem
insignificant when they are measured against the religious, cultural, and
epochal similarities that existed between them.

In one sense, Mounier received the same education after the War as
Maritain had received before the War. Among the most important influences upon Mounier were also the philosophies of Bergson and Péguy;
many of the political, social and cultural forms of pre-War France continued to dominate the climate and milieu of the 1920s. The young
Mounier was taught, as the young Maritain had been taught, two things:
to hate the bourgeois and to believe in the Church. The young Mounier,
too, was an enemy of the bourgeois. That is, he learned to distrust the
Republic's politicians, to despise the rule of money, to denounce the
impersonal life of the city, to refute the bourgeois philosophies of idealism, materialism and positivism, to repudiate the bourgeois for having
banished the heroic from man and the mysterious from life. The young
Mounier, also, was a believer. Every bit as much as Maritain, Mounier
found his identity and his integrity in his service to the faith. He asserted, as Maritain did, the primacy of faith, the existence of a true Catholic revival and the ultimate unities between faith and reason, civilization
and the Church. In essence, the young Mounier's education, if not an
education in anti-modernity, was one that prepared him to challenge
the entire contemporary social, political and cultural order in the name
of his Catholicism, while simultaneously speaking of a new human and
spiritual order. It is not surprising, therefore, that Mounier's life and
thought should have been influenced by and converged with the life

and thought of Maritain in the late 1920s. For, even though Mounier and Maritain were of different temperaments and generations, they were spiritually two nineteenth century Catholics in search of a meaning for themselves and their faith in the twentieth century world.

From another perspective, the perspective which will occupy us most, to understand Mounier's education is to understand the making of Mounier's philosophy of and for his times. Exteriorly described, Mounier's education begins with his arrival at the University of Grenoble in 1924 to study philosophy with Jacques Chevalier; it leads to his fruition as a Catholic intellectual at the Sorbonne and in Paris under the tutelage of Jacques Maritain; and it ends with his decision to found *Esprit* under the inspiration of Charles Péguy. Interiorly understood, Mounier's education is a spiritual voyage; it passes from his first understanding of himself, God, and his times to his established adult identity as a Catholic intellectual who commits his life totally and absolutely to calling man to make a revolution for a new human order. Each step within this voyage marks Mounier's spiritual passage from faith and philosophy to action and revolution. Each step reveals how Mounier synthesized diverse currents within Catholic intellectual life in France into a unique philosophy of and for our times. In effect, to understand Mounier's first education is to understand the genesis of Personalism.

Philosophy with Jacques Chevalier

There is not a complete explanation of why the young Mounier, born in 1905 into a middle class family of Grenoble, abandoned a career in medicine after two years of preparatory study in Paris and returned home to study philosophy at the University of Grenoble with Jacques Chevalier.[2] What is clear, however, is that this choice marked the resolution of a serious personal and vocational choice. Mounier wrote of his decision:

> 1924-1925, I found myself in physics, chemistry and natural history. Despair just to the desire of suicide. To forget I work harder; I prepared a special degree in chemistry at the same time. A third year lost. No reading except that of my first suffering. By March I was no longer eating. Then I went to the first closed retreat of my life. . . . The retreat was enlightening. I saw the writing on the wall; it was time to reverse paths. All this interior opposition had confused my personality a little. I left the retreat as supple as a lamb. Chevalier was at Grenoble; a way to avoid the expenses of Paris; it was seen and decided.[3]

The energy and joy with which he took up the study of philosophy
further suggests that, in choosing philosophy, Mounier had found more
than an alternative course of study; he had decided on the subject to
which he wished to dedicate his life.

The young Mounier found his first mentor in Jacques Chevalier. During the years 1924 to 1927, Chevalier was at the center of Mounier's
life. Mounier attended his courses, participated in his group discussions,
and wrote his thesis under Chevalier. Chevalier, on his part, intent on
forming a Catholic intellectual elite, gave special attention to the promising young student. He asked Mounier to help edit his work on Bergson, shared his thoughts and experiences with him, and did all possible
to help prepare Mounier for his return to Paris.[4]

In the very first article which Mounier ever wrote, he set out to introduce Chevalier to Catholics across France. He wrote:

> Solid secondary studies assured Chevalier a brilliant success in the general
> examinations and led him at eighteen to the *Ecole Normale*. At twenty one he
> graduated a successful doctoral candidate. After two years of research in Eng-
> land, he began his university career at Chateauroux. At Lyon where he had just
> completed his two doctoral theses, *The Notion of Necessity in Aristotle's and
> His Predecessors' Works* and *A Criticism of the Pseudo-Platonic Dialogue, Ax-
> iochos,* the War overtook him. His perfect knowledge of the English language
> and mind made him choose to serve as an interpreter in the British army du-
> ring the War. Upon his release in 1919, he was nominated to a chair at the
> University of Grenoble. In the aftermath of the hecatomb, the task of libera-
> ting our thought from foreign domination and searching within our tradition
> for the seed of its renewal imposed itself on him. He set out in his successful
> winter courses to publicize and make popular "the great masters of French
> thought." His first works grew out of these courses: . . . in 1921, *Descartes;*
> *Pascal* in 1922; . . . . in 1923 his *Essay on the Formation of Nationality and
> the Religious Revival in Gallic Countries* that suggested a new conception of
> history; and in 1925 his edition of the *Pensées* . . .; and within a few weeks his
> *Bergson* . . . will bring to us the echo of a great system by one of the men who
> knows it perhaps as clearly as any man. The strong work of a talented man
> who matures without forcing his growth; work, manifesting the French mind,
> by its realism and its clarity.[5]

Mounier did not conceal his own romanticized and youthful admiration
of Chevalier. As if he were consciously describing Chevalier as France's
second Bergson, Mounier wrote:

> An amphitheatre in the province. Five in the afternoon. In the vast hall of
> fifteen hundred seats, the crowd grows silent. The silence, however, is heavy
> with attention. It seems that out of this dissimilar crowd freed for one hour

from its agitation, there has come into existence a unity of intense souls in a prayer tied to the truth. . . . Down below, the lecturer. His face still lit by youth's glow; the living image of a force in full maturity . . . all his digressions converge towards an end . . . as if a cathedral of ideas were being built before us . . . the dialogue of a musician and his instrument which vibrate sympathetically within us. Thus, at the end, the spontaneous applause of the crowd seems, every bit as much as the words just heard, to reach the intimate harmonies, those ineffable visions that were awakened in the center of every heart.[6]

Leaving no doubts of Chevalier's lasting influence upon him, Mounier wrote to Chevalier two years after having left Grenoble: "It is essential that you do not doubt my friendship, even when it is silent. I am always under your sign and impulse. The spirit which you have breathed into me grows and deepens."[7]

From the year 1929 on, however, the distance between student and teacher rapidly widened. As Chevalier continued to pursue the formulation of a new philosophy within the confines of the university, Mounier, having come progressively under the influence of Maritain and Péguy, abandoned an academic career and increasingly sought a revolution for his times. By the time of the Spanish Civil War, contact between the two had ceased; Chevalier considered Franco as the leader of a crusade against the Communist menace to civilization and Mounier criticized the Church's support of Franco.[8] When Chevalier entered the Vichy government as Minister of Education and Youth and Mounier moved to the side of the Resistance, ten years—in essence, the events and ideologies of the 1930s—divided student and teacher.[9]

The later separation of Mounier and Chevalier should not, however, lead one to underestimate Chevalier's profound influence on Mounier. Chevalier was Mounier's first mentor. He introduced Mounier into Catholic intellectual life in France; and, even more importantly, he introduced him to the beginnings of a Christian philosophy which was integral to his later formation of Personalism. An unpublished piece in Mounier's notebooks which significantly records Chevalier's criticism of Maritain's philosophy serves as an excellent point at which to begin our discussion of Chevalier's influence on Mounier.

Since we had with us Riondet who has visited the Maritains, Chevalier asked him his impressions of Maritain, the man and his work. Our discussion started from this point.

Riondet: "I have the impression of a man who only loves the truth, and with neither *a-priori* idea nor sentiment goes to it by his reason alone."

Chevalier: "With no *a-priori* idea?" But isn't Saint Thomas for him the very expression of the truth?"

Riondet: "The closest expression that is."

Chevalier: "That is not what he says. He wants to make Saint Thomas the unique expression of the truth. . . .It is possible that Saint Thomas is closest of all (that is to be seen). But what I cannot admit, is that Saint Thomas (or Pascal, or Descartes or any other) *encloses* in his system all truth. It is necessary to believe in the truth, and to seek it . . . but those who seek it give different points of view. Each of these formulations translates the truth in a manner, but all of them are inadequate and consequently no single one of them can be imposed upon me in the name of the truth. . . ."

Riondet: "But Maritain admits that Saint Thomas is amendable."

Chevalier, Mounier [and the others]: "On points of detail alone!"

Chevalier: "Maritain has retained the pantheistic mysticism of his first education; there remains in him that intellectual pride that takes this form in his doctrine. . . ."

Riondet: "This is impossible to believe by anyone who knows his ascetic life."

Chevalier: "That doesn't matter at all. . . . As in Spinoza, there exists in Maritain an unconscious and involuntary pride. . . ."

Chevalier: "And further, why condemn Descartes as worse than Luther? Because of what the eighteenth century made his thought? The eighteenth century was only a caricature of Descartes; its reason was only rationalizing, that is, the opposite of a full intuitive and sympathetic reason of Descartes, who was first a realist and second a convinced believer.

"I understand now why the same milieu are faithful to both the *Action Française* and integral orthodoxy. The idea common to both is what is living and solid in Christianity is the Greco-Roman law."[10]

Chevalier and Maritain, both former students of Bergson, had been in public debate since the War.[11] At stake between them (and hence integral to Mounier's training in philosophy) was the nature of Christian philosophy. The question of Christian philosophy, in turn, raised hosts of questions concerning the relation of nature and grace, knowledge, and revelation, as well as questions concerning the proper sources of such a philosophy: reason or faith, Plato or Aristotle, Augustine or Aquinas, Descartes or Pascal.[12] These questions of abiding importance to Catholic thought had received immense attention since the middle of the nineteenth century onward as the Church was forced to clarify its message within and outside itself regarding the democratic, scientific, and historicist revolutions. Within Catholic thought in France it is possible to distinguish three basic schools of philosophy: an orthodox

Thomist position, identified, with Maritain, that conceived human reason as sufficient unto itself to discover basic truths about man, nature, and God independently from faith and revelation; the position of Blondel and his followers, which suggested that a searching inquiry into the human condition will itself demonstrate the need of faith; and, a position, inspired by Bergson and followed by men such as Teilhard de Chardin, LeRoy, and Chevalier, that strove after a new synthesis of faith and science.[13] However, already by the late 1920s it became almost utterly impossible to localize the debate over Christian philosophy to these three positions. For not only were numerous cultural, political, historical, and theological dimensions involved in the discussion of Christian philosophy but also involved were such factors as the increasing diversity of Thomism, the growing influence of such diverse thinkers as Gabriel Marcel, Newman, Maine de Biran, and the Russian Orthodox Berdyaev, the deepening importance of well-known and minor medieval thinkers and sixteenth and seventeenth century Spanish and French mystics, and a growing number of historical inquiries into past systems of Catholic thought.

On the one hand, the debate between Chevalier and Maritain could not be separated from their broad and sweeping disagreements over Catholic philosophy. Most simply, to suggest their differences, Maritain chose to ally himself closely to the Vatican, denied the need for Catholic thought to renovate itself radically because of changes in modern thought, and asserted that Saint Thomas was the first if not the final guide in all matters of epistemology, metaphysics, and ethics. Refusing such a commanding role to Saint Thomas and any other scholastic or Church father, Chevalier believed that modern thought constituted a substantial revolution in human thought and that, in the light of this continuing revolution, there was need for a reassessment and renovation of Catholic philosophy. Obviously, implicit within their debate was the issue of the ancient versus the modern, along with accompanying judgments on the perennial nature of ancient and medieval thought, and the worth of contemporary thought.

On the other hand, this debate between Chevalier and Maritain could be understood in far less general and in far more specific terms. Clearly, their broad disagreement over the nature of Catholic philosophy did not preclude many obvious points of agreement. For instance, they both believed that the Church was a repository of truths that refuted, encompassed, completed and transcended all modern thought; they affirmed the possibility of a new Catholic philosophy which, while based on reason and not in contradiction to the clear truths of modern science, would lead to faith; they both concurred on the ultimate primacy of faith, and they both avowed their willingness to doubt the results of their reason if it came into direct conflict with the teachings of the Church. Why then was their disagreement so deep and so sharp?

Simply put, they disagreed on Bergson—his thought, its worth and its role. Both Chevalier and Maritain, in fact, had their identities as philosophers in terms of their relations with Bergson. Maritain was known as Bergson's foremost critic; Chevalier increasingly came to be known as one of Bergson's foremost proponents. Both contended over Bergson's legacy for Christianity. Maritain cautioned against it because of what he believed to be its irrationalism; Chevalier promoted it as a way to a new Christian philosophy. In debating the value of Bergson's thought, Chevalier and Maritain defined their own philosophies. Hence, to understand Chevalier's use of Bergson, is not only to understand implicitly his disagreement with Maritain, but more importantly to understand Chevalier's influence upon Mounier.

If in any way Chevalier's influence upon Mounier was profound, it was so because Chevalier introduced Mounier to Bergson. In essence, it was Bergson who gave impetus, form and direction to Chevalier's teaching, and in turn, it was Bergson's thought that inspired Mounier's respect, attention, and dedication to Chevalier's teaching. In short, Bergson was the philosophical altar at which teacher and student worshipped; he was the promise of truth and life.

Chevalier's whole career was based upon Bergson. Chevalier believed that he found his vocation in philosophy because of Bergson; in turn, he accepted Bergson as the highest commentator on his works, tied his own academic and scholarly promotion to Bergson, justifiably thought of himself as a lifelong friend of Bergson, and had the satisfaction of believing that in large measure Bergson's final acceptance of Catholicism was due to his activity. That Chevalier left the Vichy Regime because of its failure to give full official recognition to Bergson at his death and that Chevalier was given authority over Bergson's unpublished materials are the last and most convincing signs of Chevalier's ties to Bergson.[14] In sum, it was Bergson's philosophy which (1) gave Chevalier his place among contemporary French intellectuals, (2) formed his basic understanding of modern philosophy and its history, and

(3) determined his own unique philosophical project that so greatly influenced Mounier.

In accord with Bergson's philosophy, Chevalier believed that idealism and materialism were inadequate in their exploration, explanation, and representation of both natural and human realities.[15] They specifically failed as philosophies, according to Chevalier, because they did not grasp, as Bergson's thought did, the unity of being in time (la durée) and the real reciprocity that existed between human consciousness and reality (l'intuition). For Chevalier a true philosophy would not fabricate and codify reality, but would first recognize the singularities and unities of being and then, only after finding their structure and uniqueness, formulate them into a philosophy.[16]

Chevalier believed that it was not only possible to use Bergson's thought to demonstrate the inadequacy of contemporary philosophy and science, but to create a philosophical system which, in absolute contrast to modern secular thought, would admit the limits of its own approach to reality, concede the mysterious character of existence, and prove itself harmonious with a Christian conception of man and reality. Such a system of thought would have for its object a reality made up of change and continuity, universality and uniqueness; and such a system would be based on a progressive knowledge which in its highest intuition would provide a concrete universal knowledge. Its final aim in Chevalier's opinion would be to reverse the entire history of Western thought's dependence on the abstract and the general and to form a new philosophy of the individual.[17]

Chevalier titled his own attempt to create this new Christian philosophy, the science of the individual. For him the science of the individual proved to be the axis of his career.[18] Its primary aims were: (1) to reintroduce all the individuality and personality absent from contemporary thought; (2) to replace the idolatrous search for being itself; and (3) to create a science of the individual and personal, the contingent, free, and miraculous. When completed, Chevalier believed that this science of the individual would (1) offer a comprehensive and hierarchical vision of all natural and human orders; (2) show the primacy of the spiritual realms of freedom, faith, and God; and (3) conceive of reality as the singular and free act of God, as Creator and Father.[19]

Chevalier developed his science of the individual primarily in reference to the history of Western philosophy; therein he also did his most valuable work. The basic perspective from which he wrote his history of philosophy was: all philosophy until Bergson had failed to account fully for the contingent, free, and individual; and, because of this failure, knowledge remained abstract from the known, and the knower from being.

Herein for Chevalier lay the limits of both classical and medieval philosophy. While Socrates gave philosophy a necessary and radical human axis, and Plato and Aristotle justly extended human reason into its exploration of man and nature, classical thought on the whole remained, in Chevalier's opinion, tied to and bounded by the concepts of necessity, universality, and law at the expense of the free, singular and personal.[20] Even Augustine and Aquinas, according to Chevalier, philosophically failed to transcend these limits of classical thought, and thus did not succeed in incorporating the radically new dimensions inherent within Christian theology into their thought.[21]

Chevalier, in contrast to Maritain, chose the side of the moderns. Revealing his ever-present nationalism, he asserted that a new stage of philosophy was reached with Descartes and Pascal.[22] "Descartes and Pascal," he proclaimed, "can be considered the Aristotle and Plato of modern times."[23] While granting, as did Maritain, that there was inherent in Cartesian thought the temptation to substitute geometry for reason, science for philosophy, and thus divorce thought and being, Chevalier maintained that Descartes did not yield to this temptation. Descartes, in fact, properly reestablished philosophy on human reason, and redirected philosophy to matters of nature and existence. In sharp contrast with Maritain, Chevalier believed that Descartes' philosophy counterbalanced Pascal's thought (in particular Pascal's recognition of man's irrationality and need for redemption), and constituted the successful beginnings of the French mind and modern philosophy.[24]

Bergson represented for Chevalier the next momentous step forward in the development of French and modern philosophy. Bergson not only reversed the errors which followed from Descartes and Kant, but opened the possibility of a new Christian philosophy, a science of the individual. It was in terms of philosophy and this new philosophical project that Chevalier taught Mounier.

While Mounier did not carry on this search for a science of the individual with the same intensity and on the same scale as Chevalier, Mounier clearly adopted Chevalier's and Bergson's basic approach to philosophy. That is, Mounier (1) considered idealism, materialism, and positivism inadequate as philosophies; (2) underlined how all rational inquiries in themselves are limited because of the uniqueness of being and the mystery of existence; (3) proposed that reality is first to be explored, experienced internally, and only then formulated as philosophy; (4) asserted that at the center of existence is man's ineffable freedom and God, and, (5) ultimately put philosophy in the service of faith. Without explicitly developing each of these points, a presentation of some of Mounier's early writings and his thesis on Descartes will reveal the distinct formulation Mounier gave to Bergson's and Chevalier's philosophical method.

In his very first writings, Mounier took upon himself the role of teacher and guide.[25] Emulating Chevalier and Bergson, Mounier strove to make his message conform to the philosophical virtues of simplicity and clarity, universality and depth. Mounier's first intention was epistemological; it was to help form a new consciousness on the meaning of "knowing." In turn, going beyond this epistemological concern, Mounier intended that from this new consciousness there might arise a new position towards life.[26]

According to Mounier, three fundamental insights were essential for human knowledge. The first, man alone of the animals lives amidst and within significance; in man alone consciousness passes beyond habit and reflex into the domains of intention and symbols.[27] Human language, the most revelatory of this, shows man exploring and constituting, denying and affirming, proposing and judging needs, relations, and goals. Second, and here Mounier reaffirmed what was central to Bergson's and Chevalier's approach, man must admit how reality eludes and overwhelms his analyses, judgments and systems.[28] On this point Mounier not only calls attention to much of what is incomprehensible in the unities and disunities of thought and reality, but stresses how man encounters the ineffable singularity of being in the form of the individual event, the other person, the specific existent.[29]

The third insight that structured Mounier's epistemology was: all objects of man's knowledge are not exclusively reducible to their causes and effects.[30] Restating the central insight of Bergson's *Time and Free Will*, Mounier argued that, as a single human action ultimately defies a simple reduction of its preparations, context, enactment, and its results, so all objects of human knowledge cannot be totally reduced to manipulative data for analyzing, unifying, and systematizing. Reality—to translate Mounier's concept of it into the language of Karl Jaspers—is fundamentally a *cipher,* a mysterious sign or text. To reduce reality to man's concept of it or the process by which he comes to know it, takes the mystery from life, adventure from knowing, and ultimately leads to blindness to both the self and the world.

These three insights constituted for Mounier the beginnings of a new consciousness for man. Freed from mistaking his thought for its object, man found many of what he once considered irreconcilable contradictions now no more than contrary statements or diverse points of view.[31] The traditional contradiction between the spiritual and material, to use an example favored by Mounier, no longer poses an ultimate yes or no choice over the nature of all existence, but conversely presents man with two alternatives and, in great part, unifiable modes of inquiry into man and nature. The rational and irrational, to take another of Mounier's examples, no longer constitute an irreconcilable opposition, but now become two different paths of investigation into human experience.[32] Thus, for Mounier, what a man once thought to be proof of the radical bifurcation of reality can be transformed into paths of man's continuing search for truth.

At this point it becomes apparent that the young Mounier was already translating Bergson's and Chevalier's philosophical approach from the more formal and traditional inquiries into metaphysics, epistemology, science, and ethics to the realms of man's experience and moral edification. From his perspective, purity, subtlety, friendship and love, and the more existential aspects of life were made part of man's search for truth; and a person's entire life became for Mounier the vaster, more complex, and mysterious path to truth.[33] Experiences and encounters became a series of educations about the self and the world.[34] To live well—to guide life on its proper course and to bring it to its full end——was the ultimate meaning of this search and discovery of the truth. Openness, willingness to change, to think and rethink, became for Mounier the hallmarks of the good life. Chevalier's science of the individual was thus transformed by Mounier into a philosophy for regulating the conduct of life. Already, Personalism had found its existential dimension.

Just as these early writings reveal the young Mounier's conception of philosophy, so his thesis exposes his view of modern philosophy, and the central ideas of his first world view.[35] Its title alone, "The Conflict of Anthropocentrism and Theocentrism in the Philosophy of Descartes," so expressive of Chevalier's and Maritain's concerns, voiced the young Mounier's preoccupation with the relation between modern philosophy and religion, and thus the existing division between a secular and a religious view of man.

Expressing what was a fundamental axis of Maritain's as well as Chevalier's thought, Mounier developed his thesis around the tension between an anthropocentric view and a theocentric view of the world. According to Mounier there were destructive consequences inherent in the full extension of either of these world views. An extreme theocentric view subjugates man to God to the point that man is left utterly worthless.[36] An extreme anthropocentric view, conversely, denies God to the point that man is deprived of any ultimate worth. Each view, Mounier agreed with Chevalier and Maritain, ended against man and reality.

For Mounier, Descartes—"at the middle road between the Middle Ages and the Enlightenment"—was the ideal juncture at which to understand the passage of Western man from God to himself.[37] Agreeing with Chevalier, Mounier presented Descartes as having rescued human reason from the destructive dialectics of Renaissance naturalistic anthropocentrism and Lutheran anti-natural and anti-human theocentrism. In agreement with both Chevalier and Maritain, Mounier believed that the Cartesian legacy was progressively transformed into the willful, rationalistic, and materialistic philosophies of the eighteenth century *philosophes*. More in accord with Maritain than with Chevalier, Mounier found serious error within the Cartesian legacy and within Descartes' very notion of God.

Mounier believed that three basic conceptions of God could be identified: (1) God as pure act; (2) God as all powerful and impersonal; and, (3) God as a loving Father, who created the world out of love. Descartes' God was of the second type—"a sovereign whose action, even if all good, is imposed independent of the individual because between the individual and the creator there is no common measure."[38] While believing there was no science or existence without God, Descartes, nevertheless, conceived God as an inaccessible being who, absolutely separated from His Creation, offered man neither knowledge nor love. As the theoreticians of absolutism separated king from nation, Mounier concluded, Descartes had analogically severed God from nature and man. The Cartesian dichotomies between mind and body, nature and reason, science and faith, were for Mounier the result of this first error of Descartes—the fundamental failure to understand man's relation to God.

On the surface, Mounier's study of Descartes did not seem original. His assumptions about medieval thought as derivative from classical thought, his distinction between an anthropocentric and a theocentric view of man, and his concern for the individual, could be attributed to his mentor Chevalier. His criticisms of the Cartesian legacy, in turn, could be heard to reecho both Chevalier and Maritain, as well as other nineteenth and twentieth century Catholic thinkers, who had concluded that Descartes was, if not antithetical to Christianity, inadequate for the basis of Christian philosophy.

The thesis, however, had resolved one question for Mounier: the question of the purpose of philosophy itself. Rather than stress that Descartes did, or did not, provide the successful beginnings of modern philosophy, Mounier preferred to assert that it was Pascal alone who afforded the beginnings of a Christian life. The difference between them for Mounier was a crucial difference of spirit—the difference between thought and life, security and adventure, age and youth.

> The whole of Descartes' reflection concentrates itself around the idea of order, and the concern, most certainly, to protect the infinite transcendence of God, but that itself is done in order to put man *in his place* and to give him *all of his place* vis-à-vis God. Man's imperfection leaves indefinite progress ahead of him, he does not dream too much of sin, sacrifice or death. Above all else, he wants to feel at home; nothing stops him from doing it, because God assures him, within and without, of a security from which he can contemplate God at his leisure. . . . The whole of Pascal's meditation, conversely, is to show the essential disequilibrium in things of this world. For him, as for Newman, "To be at ease is to be unsafe." The infinite is no longer a serene vision but an abyss within us and a call from on high. . . . For one, Descartes, man . . . is satisfied in the finite . . . for the other, Pascal, man . . . finite by Creation but participating in the Infinite through Redemption, is a perpetual instability.[39]

With his choice of Pascal, the young Mounier, perhaps even beyond his own awareness, had set himself upon a course which led away from the more systematic and academic philosophy of his teacher and towards a more existential concern for man's situation and destiny. Prefigured herein was Mounier's refusal to tie himself to any single philosophical program and his attempt through Personalism to understand and serve man in his present condition. While it is certain that the Mounier who went to Paris in 1927 was a disciple of Bergson and Chevalier, it is equally clear that he was a disciple with his own calling.

CHAPTER V

THE ENCOUNTERS OF THE YOUNG MOUNIER

The Sorbonne Revisited

IN A LETTER of October, 1927, to his sister Madaleine, Mounier expressed his feelings about the first few months of his return to Paris. "Trust that I have not come here with a dark soul, but everything . . . . has totally created within me an atmosphere of sun, to say all a mood of expansiveness despite moments when inevitably separation is felt and loneliness is anguished over."[1] The Mounier who returned to the Sorbonne in the fall of 1928 was filled with confidence about his future and with enthusiasm for the study of philosophy.

Part of Mounier's confidence rested, as Maritain's did in the 1920s, on his identity with what he considered a growing French Catholic intellectual renaissance. His knowledge of its philosophy and its literature, his association with the Society of Saint Vincent de Paul and the newly founded *Association Catholique de la Jeunesse Française,* and his active defense in student circles of the Church's Condemnation of the *Action Française* were all factors that strengthened his ties to the Church and assured him that the Church was in the process of revitalizing itself. Another part of his confidence was a result of the Catholics' changed understanding of the Sorbonne itself. As the Sorbonne once appeared to many Catholics in pre-World War France as the militant arm of atheism and secularism, the Sorbonne increasingly appeared to the young Catholics of Mounier's generation as no more than an official repository of an impotent idealism which was hardly capable of inspiring anyone, much less challenging faith. In short, it seemed to many young Catholics that the Sorbonne and science were becalmed, and the winds of the hour were in the service of faith and religion.

Mounier's confidence explains the spirit in which he set to ordering his life in Paris. Almost immediately upon arrival he set to work for the learned biblicist and teacher of Chevalier, Père Pouget.[2] In time he came to know the makers of twentieth century French Catholicism: among the elders were Jacques Maritain, Louis Massignon, and Charles Du Bos; among his contemporaries were Paul Vignaux, Jean Danielou, and Jean Guitton, another student of Chevalier. Later Mounier wrote some of his first articles for an organization of Catholic instructresses, *Les Davidées*.[3] At the Sorbonne and the *Ecole Normale,* Mounier had the best of French academic life. In philosophy, he had courses from the famous idealist, Léon Brunschvicg and the noted historian of philosophy, Emile Bréhier. In religious studies, Mounier had contact with such prominent Catholic thinkers as medievalist Etienne Gilson, historian and literary critic Henri Bremond, and student of mysticism Jean Baruzi. All of this was the sign of an active and dynamic young French Catholic intellectual. In 1928, when Mounier was second to Raymond Aron in his examinations for the *agrégation* in philosophy, everything indicated that before Mounier lay a promising career as a teacher and a scholar.[4]

Other realities, however, were at work within and upon Mounier. There was within him a sense that had haunted young men in Paris at least since the time of Baudelaire; Paris was *la grand ville indifferente.* There was also within him the equally old but real feeling that his professors were as unaware in thought as Paris was in practice of the meaning and needs of man. "What is especially missing from the assured souls of the professors are the notions of accepted sacrifice and risk, and even the concrete notion of human misery. They only understand the hospital as a place for their hygienic program."[5] The Sorbonne, as it was a generation before for Péguy and Maritain, was an anti-identity for the young Mounier. He expressively wrote to Chevalier in 1928:

> I believe you can now trust me. I believe myself impermeable to the Sorbonne's venom. . . . Decidedly I am incapable of the "objective" attitude of these young men of the Sorbonne who place themselves before problems as before objects of anatomy, and before their careers as before a mechanism through which they ascend to their preregulated end. . . . It is this that the Sorbonne sustains.[6]

As Mounier's examinations drew closer, his criticism of the Sorbonne led him to dissent from the whole academic system itself:

You will laugh if I tell you the ludricous manner in which I foresee my successful candidacy. Neither envy nor fear of the examination itself. . . . I think
of it as an immense package that in the end I will discard. . . . In sum, I don't
give a damn about being a successful candidate for the *doctorate*. To no longer
be a candidate (*agrégatif*), that is what interests me. [7]

Mounier's criticisms of the academic system—so similar to those of
today's students across Europe and the West—could be understood as
simply a repetition of the commonplace *fin du siècle* intellectual rejection of bourgeois life and thought, and a reiteration of feelings shared
probably by most sensitive students on the eve of their examination. In
Mounier's case, however, his criticisms were more than this, for they
were tied to stronger emotions and ideas at work within him. There was
his Pascalian view of the human condition, his belief that modern man
had rejected God, his passionate desire to serve faith and practice charity. In fact, these were the thoughts and feelings which had led Mounier
into a profound crisis of identity in the spring of 1928.

Death of a Friend

This crisis came in January of 1928, when Mounier's closest friend,
Georges Barthélemy, unexpectedly died.

My anguish over Georges gripped me all night. I had just come from seeing
him. It was frightful to find him in such state when having seen him alive fif-
teen days ago. In an absolute coma, his eyes rolled back, he was almost a ca-
daver. He could not see anyone; he recognized vaguely his parents; and then
there were those terrible efforts to talk. . . . Pray a little for him. My friendship for him is the most spontaneous I have ever known. . . . I feel something
of myself is dying with him. These are sad days. [8]

Two weeks after his friend's death, Mounier wrote to his sister:

I find myself before that young life which was put out, before that friendship broken in its bloom. . . . Young, our friendship smiled at the future for it
was rich with promise. I feel again the void of all this, and the bitterness of
being twenty-two and without a friend. [9]

The meaning of this experience for Mounier cannot be located on a
single plane of his life: "You cannot believe what broke down in me
with the disappearance of such a spontaneous friendship." [10] "I hear the
deafening resounding of all my past crisies." "I am remorseful for not
having forced out intimacy a little more." [11] "The more one lives, the

more one lives close to Pascal."[12] How true it is that suffering opens
God's ways."[13] The shock was hard, the pain was not transitory; and it
was, in Mounier's words, a metaphysical drama that little by little
threatened to swallow him.

The crisis was a test of Mounier's faith. He met it as such: "It is still
only suffering," he wrote Chevalier in May of that year, "that recon-
ciles you with things and life itself. This is a truth of Christian experience, the hardest. . . . to understand from the outside. The day of my
friend's death marked the end of my youth, and made first in my mind
the drama of a family, that of a generation and that of humanity."[14]
Mounier's manhood and adult faith was inseparable from this experience.

In retrospect, Mounier saw this experience as "an intellectual and religious reconversion which I had to undergo during the year or two after
Georges' death."[15] Taking upon himself the obligation to live out the
meaning of Georges' life, Mounier's reconversion involved grasping the
mysterious unity of all men in time and eternity—sensing what it means
to participate in life with other men and what it means to give oneself
for them. Clearly, some of the depth premises of Mounier's Personalism
were a result of his response to a friend's death.

After successfully completing his examinations in the summer of
1928, Mounier continued, despite this experience and his criticisms of
the whole academic system, to look forward to a career in university
teaching. Ahead was the immense task of the two theses. Mounier initially projected a major thesis on the sixteenth century Spanish mystic,
Saint Jean d'Anges, and a minor theses on personality. Even though he
went so far as to gather materials in Spain for his study of Saint Jean
d'Anges, Mounier remained uncertain of the order and subjects of his
theses. Finally after much consultation and even considering the possibility of a thesis on sin, he reversed in spring of 1930 the order of his
original choices. St. Jean was to be his minor thesis, and personality his
major thesis. This very reversal reflected a significant alteration of his
goals. In giving prominence to the study of personality, Mounier was
subordinating his commitment to the religious revival in its historical
and scholarly dimensions in favor of what he considered the more immediate and contemporary questions of faith and modern man.[16]

Mounier's discussion of his projected thesis on personality summa-
rizes his growth to this point and anticipates the dominant themes of
his later writings. In a report to the *Fondation Thiers*, which had given

Mounier a scholarship for the years 1928-1930, Mounier set forth its dimensions.[17] At the outset he declared that all serious inquiry, be it that of a Pascal, Comte, or Durkheim, must admit a "hierarchy of urgency." His own task was "to collaborate in the edification of an ethics the absence of which is felt by philosophers and men of action alike . . . " for, "during the last century, ethics has lagged terribly far behind its sister sciences."[18]

Of methodology, Mounier wrote: "I accept as an instrument of work, defined at numerous points by Bergson, the study of lines of facts converging towards a resulting idea, of which the limited results, modestly and progressively will little by little contribute to the building of a synthesis."[19] Of his task's vast and encompassing dimension, Mounier further wrote: "I am taking as materials to study: psychology, law, and more precisely the history of law and customs, the history of cultural sensibility (*l'histoire du sentiment*) and the history of religious thought and linguistics."[20] On no smaller scale, Mounier wrote of its guiding inspiration: "I consider that there is no other definition of morality than the interior and free relation of man to his acts. I was drawn to this paradox: crises of moral thought and the conjoined crises of action come into existence each time that the direction of an epoch aimed at an idealized superior or exterior reality disappears."[21]

In effect, Mounier had chosen to study what he considered the crisis of human consciousness and the breakdown of the value system and structure of the modern world. Restating themes so similar to Maritain's *Three Reformers*, Mounier revealed the philosophy of his times which formed his thesis:

> I addressed myself first . . . to the study of individualism. . . . I considered individualism a position capable of equilibrium. The facts dissuaded me. To choose two examples, I studied the evolution of juridical individualism starting with the Rights of Man and the Napoleonic Code and the development of aesthetic individualism from a Renan and a Barrès to any given literature of the present. On one hand, I saw in jurisprudence and customs the impossibility of establishing, limiting, and maintaining the notion of the individual without appealing to exterior postulates. . . . On the other hand, I saw the exhaustion of the individual as a source even in the hands of those who sought to cultivate it. . . . In reacting against all exteriority they were led even to treat as a restraint that form of harmonious and regulated personality that classical morality proposed as our end. Under the guidance of a psychology developed from a hastily assimilated Freudianism and especially by the internal logic of their attitude, these contemporary moralists . . . have begun to pursue in themselves a shadow without content or form, and have finally, through a practical nihil-

> ism, exhausted the individual into a new conformity of transitory sensations ... which is less developed than the intellectual conformisms against which they battled. ... They have shown us how the collective is insinuating subjectivity into the individual and how the self that is sought in solitude builds itself, despite itself, into an alien soul.[22]

Mounier believed his thesis would cover the following topics: (1) the limits and content of personality on the planes of biology, law, psychology, theology, and Christology; (2) the origins and theories of individualism as expressed by the Reformation, natural law and its later branches, and Rousseau, Kant, modern liberalism and aestheticism; (3) the tie of the individual to religious reality and mysticism. Mounier claimed that the final value and worth of his study would be to show:

> The individual only maintains himself as a fecund source if he can stimulate his effort and renew his inspiration by contact with a superior or simply exterior reality, possesses himself only so far as he sacrifices himself, liberates himself only so far as he builds himself, finds himself only so far as he gives himself.[23]

Mounier had thus brought under this singular thesis project all the knowledge he had gathered to this point and gave a short outline of all his future thought.

A First Meeting with Maritain

Inevitably, in the course of his stay in Paris, Emmanuel Mounier would have come to meet with Jacques Maritain.

Upon the Condemnation of the *Action Française*, Maritain had striven to disassociate Catholicism from the established social political order, and consequently his vocation to his times was progressively extended beyond the promotion of Saint Thomas and the defense of the viability of a Catholic understanding of the world to the search for a new religiously inspired political and social philosophy.[24] In effect, Maritain further opened the doors of his house, his times, and his publications to almost all young and promising Catholics, and in particular to those who were concerned with the role of faith and the Church in the contemporary age. Mounier was among these young Catholics.

To be an educated Catholic was to know of Maritain; to be an educated Catholic in Paris made the pull of Maritain almost irresistible, for he was one sun in the small Parisian universe. Such giants as Marcel, Cocteau, and Berdyaev would meet at the house of this friend of Péguy, godson of Léon Bloy, critic of Bergson and foremost proponent of Saint Thomas. Like no other, Maritain was creating and sustaining the French Catholic intellectual revival.

Despite the fact that Mounier had presumably once adopted Jacques Chevalier's attitudes towards Maritain, Mounier did not long resist Maritain's attraction. In his thesis on Descartes, Mounier had already shown the influence of Maritain's *Three Reformers*; and, as early as the fall of 1927, showing that he was disposed to Maritain on more than an intellectual level, Mounier wrote: "Maritain has said beautifully in his letter to Jean Cocteau: 'It is necessary to have a hard spirit and a soft heart. How many people believing themselves to have a soft heart have only a weak spirit.' "[25]

The extent to which Mounier frequented Maritain's residence from 1928 on was an outward sign of their deepening relationship. Between the years 1928 and 1932, Mounier turned increasingly to Maritain for counsel and advice; first regarding his interest in Péguy and his selection of a thesis topic, and then regarding the publication of his work on Péguy and the mutual conception and planning of *Esprit*.[26] Mounier gradually turned from Chevalier and toward Maritain for guidance. Maritain, for his part, saw in the younger Mounier the promise of a mature young Catholic companion in the search for a new place of faith and the Church in the modern world. By 1932, they had become, as is later shown, friends in thought and colleagues in action.

Maritain, however, never became Mounier's sole mentor. By the time Mounier had entered serious relations with Maritain, he had already found his adult identity; and no single system of ideas—be it Chevalier's science of the individual or Maritain's Thomism—could altogether capture Mounier's being. Even more importantly, by the time Mounier came to know Maritain, he had already come to know a third mentor, Charles Péguy. Of Péguy's and Maritain's mutual importance, for his and his generation's formation, Mounier wrote:

> To what does one owe this renewal of Christian realism if not to those men
> who were at the same time hard and prophetic, Péguy and Maritain, whom the
> young Christian personalists considered as their masters for living and think-
> ing? Who, if not Péguy, directed our bodies and souls to the sense of the incar-
> nation, who, if not Maritain, progressively guided the fervor of our youth
> away from the sin of angelism? [27]

For Mounier, Maritain could only be second to Péguy. Ultimately it was Péguy who gave Mounier the vocation he sought. Péguy's example led Mounier to abandon his thesis, give up an academic career in the university, and commit himself irreversibly to the service of modern man by founding *Esprit*.

Discovery of Péguy

Between the lives and thought of Charles Péguy and Emmanuel Mounier there are obvious similarities.[28] Both renounced university careers and threw themselves into the political and intellectual conflicts of their times. Both unremittingly attacked what they conceived to be the reign of bourgeois society, and were uncompromising in their attacks on contemporary idealisms and pragmatisms. Both approached the present order as if it were in a state of radical crisis, and dedicated themselves to a "revolution" which, in Péguy's words, "would be moral or not at all."

However, to understand fully Péguy's importance for Mounier, it is necessary to go beyond these similarities, and to grasp how Péguy's example permitted Mounier to recenter his consciousness and thereby redirect his life. By starting with the visible signs of Mounier's first interest in Péguy and Péguy's role as an educator of the post-First World War generation of French Catholic intellectuals, and then proceeding to examine Mounier's personal and intellectual tie to Péguy as expressed in his work on Péguy, it will be possible to understand Péguy's part in effecting Mounier's passage from theory to action, from youth to manhood.

While Mounier had known of Péguy since 1925, his first serious interest in Péguy began shortly after his arrival in Paris. At two separate points in his letters, Mounier revealingly wrote of his first serious encounter with Péguy: "Hardly at Paris, in the grips of solitude, I lost the best of my friends. . . . It was the beginning of a great crisis of anguish, and it was Péguy who saved me from it.[29] Again: "Then Péguy intervened. . . . I understood then why I hesitated at the edge of the well-regulated mechanism which led directly from the *Ecole Normale* to teaching in higher education. Péguy crystallized the entire part of my life that lay outside of the university system."[30]

Steadily in the years 1928 and 1929, Péguy eclipsed everything else in Mounier's life. Mounier's dissertation fell to the side along with his hopes for a university career, as he studied Péguy, gave lectures on him in Spain and France, and projected a work on Péguy with Péguy's son, Marcel, and the future co-founder of *Esprit*, Georges Izard. By the time of the publication of *La Pensée de Charles Péguy* in Maritain's editions of *Roseau d'Or* in 1931, Mounier's life had been substantially altered.[31] The early stages of conceiving and planning *Esprit* were under way, and Mounier had dedicated himself to carrying on the "revolution" which he believed Péguy had begun.

Part of Mounier's receptiveness to Péguy can be explained by his membership in the post-War generation of French intellectuals. Their ears were attuned to hear Péguy's attacks on the bourgeois order and mind, and were prepared for his call to a heroic life.[32] They were ready, according to Mounier, to discover in Péguy's work:

> a politics, a style of life, a renewal of their consciousness of France. . . . It was at that moment in the late 1920s and early 1930s when the influence of Péguy began to win over French youth. All those who were unified by a sudden revolutionary awareness of the need to save human values amidst the twentieth century revolution came to group themselves more or less on the points of unity set by the author of *Notre Jeunesse*. . . . Above all others he alone among our contemporary masters pushed so far a radical synthesis of all French traditions; the Christian tradition, the socialist and revolutionary tradition, the Republican and Revolutionary tradition. Beyond this, Péguy, first socialist and humanist, then socialist and Christian, put us at the threshold of that great revolution which is advancing across the world: "The Revolution will be moral or not at all."[33]

Equally relevant to understanding Mounier's and his generation's receptivity to Péguy was the basic continuity between pre- and post-War culture. In professing their sense of alienation from bourgeois politics and culture, Mounier's generation was continuous with Maritain's. In opening their minds to American social novels, Surrealism, Freudianism, and all the diverse faces of the culture of the 1920s, Mounier's generation was simply experiencing the continuing explosion in novelty, irrationality, and fragmentation that characterized pre-War culture. The young intellectuals of the 1920s, like those of the pre-War era, were cast into a world of changing images and causes, and it was for them to find an identity in a world that seemed constant only in its change.

For those who saw no hope in the present social order and found no political party with which they could identify, Péguy was an attractive figure. He spoke of missions and unities of peoples, truths and lives which went beyond the confines of the present bourgeois order and the chaos of modern contemporary life. As *Dreyfusard*, socialist, patriot, peasant, Christian poet, Péguy represented, as much as any other, a life which had a meaning unto itself, a life which appeared above any set orthodoxy.

For Mounier and the Catholics of his generation, there were additional reasons for their attraction to Péguy. Péguy was a great Catholic poet, whose heroic death in the first days of the Great War symbolized the unity of person, faith, and nation. And Péguy offered a way to live with the pressing dilemma of accepting or rejecting the Republic.

The dilemma was this: to deny the Republic and democracy seemed to defy the Vatican's condemnation of the *Action Française*; to accept the Republic and democracy fully (1) seemed to ignore the Papacy's pre-War condemnation of the Christian democratic *Sillon* movement, (2) suggested adherence to the uninspiring rule of bourgeois society and culture, and (3) inferred that Catholicism and the French Catholic revival had no greater end than supporting the Third Republic's defective social and political structure. Thus, defiance of the Republic seemed to imply reaction, acceptance, cowardice. In sum, the young Catholics like Mounier who thought in terms of a much more radical transformation of the present order than then offered by Christian politics and Catholic social action had no political or social philosophy with which they could respond in favor of or in opposition to the Republican democracy. Péguy's appeal was that he seemed both a companion and a guide in this dilemma.

Péguy appealed because he was an individual beyond any fixed political position. He adhered to the Republic as set forth by Michelet, the social revolution as propounded by the young Jaurès, Christianity as lived by Joan of Arc, while denying the vulgar democracy of the contemporary Republic, the socialist parties, and clerical orthodoxy. He was, like many of the young Catholics themselves, a radical critic of the present order but not a promoter of reaction. He, like them, maintained the tensions between faith and nation, past and present, the temporal and the eternal. His faith could be understood as personal and universal; his life, adventuresome and stoic; his mission, to man and God. Unlike any other figure of the times, Péguy mirrored the tensions in the souls, ideals, and lives of the young Catholics who wished to find a mission for themselves in the modern world and a place for the Church in structuring their times. In short, he offered a way around, or perhaps, beyond the political choice of allegiance or dissent to the Republic, and suggested a wanted mission for them as individuals and believers.

Beyond these historical factors of generation which help account for Péguy's influence on Mounier, there lay more individual explanations. Mounier could not have overlooked the coincidence between his views of life and those of Péguy. Both rejected the Sorbonne and the impersonal life of the modern city. Both believed that the ruling powers and ideas of their times were in the process of destroying what was most elemental and sacred about man. Both aspired under the inspiration of Bergson's philosophy after a vision of man which would join his spirit and body.

Furthermore, Mounier's interest in Péguy paralleled and was interrelated to his growing concerns for matters of contemporary society and politics as expressed by some of Mounier's early essays dating from 1919 to 1932. In "Charles Péguy and the Problem of Teaching," Mounier linked education to the task of finding a truly human culture and society.[34] In "How One Conducts One's Life: The Example of Descartes," Mounier sought to establish a view which made life and thought inseparable and provided "the sole means that exist to produce a lasting work; to gather one's actions around a center of unity which steadily differentiates itself from youthful emotions."[35] In "The Event and Us" and "Intellectual Action" Mounier tried to join further a philosophy of knowledge and a philosophy of life. In "The Event and Us," he asserted that to be a Christian was to accept events "as messages from the divine order and the means for reaching greater perfection."[36] In "Intellectual Action," he argued that the intellectual and the Christian were responsible to the realm of human events, and he attacked Gide and Benda for separating thought from action.[37] In "Defense of Civilization," a book review of Duhamel's *The Science of the Future Life,* Mounier agreed that both American capitalistic collectivism and Soviet state collectivism represented a challenge and threat to civilization.[38] Each of these essays had a corresponding part in Mounier's appreciation for Péguy. It was Péguy who sought the ideal city, who refused the separation of life and thought, truth and event; it was Péguy whose faith was one with his concern for man and his times.

Finally, Péguy became the means and model by which Mounier could complete his manhood and his vision of the world, for he gave Mounier in an allegorical sense a bridge from the realm of thought to the realm of action, from the world of the individual self to the world of men. By examining Mounier's first book, *The Thought of Charles Péguy,* it is possible to understand how Péguy aided Mounier in finding his adult understanding of the world.

Mounier introduced Péguy under the rubric of a "Prophet Philosopher."[39] Making Péguy the greatest of Bergson's disciples, Mounier emphasized how Péguy translated Bergson's formal philosophical criticism of contemporary thought to the whole anti-spiritual character of the Third Republic; its bourgeois man, its overriding reduction of life to habits, ideals to interest, the present to money, and the past to lifeless facts. "Péguy," as Mounier later wrote, "carried to the public square a spiritual combat which Bergson due to his academic reserves . . . conducted only against the theories of an opposing general staff."[40] Here for Mounier was a man who "would not have tolerated, in fact, not have understood an effort to separate in himself the thinker and the man; in the same movement he unified the one and the other as two hands joined in prayer."[41]

This unity of thought and person, vocation and destiny, accounted, in Mounier's opinion, for Péguy's remarkable capacity to transcend the false contradictions of individualism and collectivism, materialism and idealism, and romanticism and classicism. It further gave him the ability to align Bergsonian philosophy with an eternal philosophy; to sense human history as rooted in grace and truth; to understand the slavery of the spirit to the worlds of habit and flesh and the deterioration of all worldly things; and to recognize that hope alone affords salvation. Péguy, clearly, was a means for Mounier to discover and forge his own ideal of the good life.

In setting forth his conception of the unity and ideals which were at the center of Péguy's being, Mounier set forth the goals and values which structured his own adult consciousness and formed his guiding vision of life:

> Péguy's whole vision of the world . . . converged on . . . the Incarnation. Reality was an image of this central Christian drama. . . .
>
> The spiritual . . . and the eternal . . . are perpetually exposed by their incarnation to the inquietudes and incertitudes of matter. . . . Jesus came to plant the eternal words, but it depends on us if they are nourished in a living heart. . . .
>
> At twenty Péguy was resolved already: "The first question that is raised when one realizes the world is totally evil in one sense is to know what we can do about it." To save [it] Péguy became a socialist, to save it was still his predominant concern in his second stage as a Christian. . . .

Péguy learned his Christianity from Joan of Arc. She was for him the exclusive model of all saintliness. . . . Bergson, on the other hand, taught him that through the point of action spirit enters matter. . . . These two masters traced the direction, and perhaps also the limits of his spirituality. He seemed always ready to declare the primacy of the temporal. But he did not forget . . . that human action falls quickly into politics if it does not incessantly revivify itself at its sources. . . . To push action out of fidelity to its end, and then let God decide, herein we find Péguy's code of the good battle.

Under the reign of hope, time becomes the song of the eternal Easter. The Christian spirit is a continuous revolution.[42]

With Péguy, Mounier completed his first education, that education which was given to him and which—to use Mounier's words—he could "love or hate but not elude." Because of Péguy, Mounier grasped the role and obligation of a Christian in human history. Because of Péguy, he also found the impetus to carry his training in philosophy and theology to the public square. Because of Péguy, he committed himself to helping make the revolution which would be moral or not at all.

Péguy was Mounier's third conversion. His first had been to philosophy; his second, to life; and his third, to action for the men of his times. Mounier found himself with Péguy. Péguy taught Mounier to trust himself. It was this trust which permitted Mounier to recenter his life during the years 1929 to 1932. It was this trust which gave him the courage to abandon an academic career, the confidence to create *Esprit*, the strength to overcome his hesitations about himself, and to act upon the belief that to lose oneself is to find oneself. Perhaps the simplest statement of Péguy's importance for Mounier is: Péguy was a decisive factor in Mounier's passage from youth to manhood, from philosophy to life, from faith to action.

To conclude: all of Mounier's later thought and action was to be lived under the sign of this first education, and Péguy's completion of it. In effect, Mounier had received a *fin du siècle* understanding of the modern world. That is, as the thought of his mentors—Chevalier and Bergson, Maritain and Péguy—was born of pre-World War I culture, so Mounier's understanding of the modern world (his general indictment of its culture, politics, and society as well as his search for a new unity between individual and society, action and life, religion and culture) had its sources in this same culture. In turn, it was in terms of this first education—an education far more dependent on the spiritual life of Catholicism than on an analysis of the politics and society of nineteenth and twentieth century Europe—that Mounier was to encounter and seek to understand the awesome and tragic events of the 1930s and 1940s.

CHAPTER SIX

A REVOLUTION: TO REMAKE THE RENAISSANCE

UNDERSTANDING a twentieth century intellectual often involves understanding his reactions to the events of the public life. That is, it can mean not only identifying his political stance as well as the larger assumptions that sustain it, but acquainting oneself with those interior resources, tensions, and agonies that make up the spirit of a man who consciously and sensitively experiences a world caught up in diverse, radical, and contradictory change. To react to events—either to seek a science of them or more simply to fear, hope, and live intensively and consciously in relation to them—may indeed be the hallmark of the twentieth century intellectual. Undoubtedly, the way in which intellectuals react to events distinguishes them from one another.

For instance, to listen to American poetess Laura Riding is to hear a voice from the late 1920s expressing the belief that all historic time had effectively come to an end:

> All the Chinese bandits having chopped off all the foreign ears, we have time to consider not only the subject *Atrocity,* but the subject *Bandits,* and the subject *Foreigners,* and the subject *Chinese.* All the politicians who are going to be elected have been elected; and all the artificial excitement in events which no one really regards as either very important or very interesting has been exhausted. All historical events have happened.[1]

Conversely, to listen to Bernard Shaw speaking through one of his characters in *Too True To Be Good* is to hear a man who felt that he could do nothing in the face of a changing world, but nevertheless felt he must do everything, if anything of worth would survive.

> I stand mid-way between youth and age like a man who has missed his train: too late for the last one and too early for the next. . . . 'I have no Bible, no creed: the war has shot both out of my hands. . . . I am ignorant: I have lost

my nerve and am intimidated; all I know is that I must find the way of life for myself and all of us, or we shall surely perish.'[2]

Like almost any sensitive intellectual between the wars, Mounier experienced the stern and agonizing rule of events. He too came to know them as too diverse to be systematized, too profound to be ignored, too ruthless not to be resisted. Some of the most fundamental concepts of his thought testify to the profound seriousness with which Mounier addressed himself to the events of his times. To bear witness (*porter le témoinage*), to be engaged (*être engagé*), to confront (*confronter*)—each of these concepts, so central to Mounier's thought, asserts that man must fully accept his conditions and his finitude in a precarious world, and yet risk everything unto final defeat for the sake of what is best and what could be best among men. Ultimately, even the existential and historicizing character of all of Mounier's thought testifies to the abiding importance he attributed to the realm of events.

Esprit itself was born out of Mounier's reaction to the critical events of 1929 to 1932. In 1941, Mounier wrote of some of the reasons which led him to found *Esprit*: (1) the belief that literary journals like the *Nouvelle Revue Française* and the *Mercure* were dead, and that consequently the young men of his generation were without a vehicle through which they could express themselves; (2) the painful awareness that Christianity was increasingly tying itself to what Mounier later called the "established disorder," and the desire to break Christianity from this order; and, most importantly, (3) the perception that below the growing economic crisis of 1929 and the events associated with it, there existed a total crisis of civilization.[3]

Those who helped found *Esprit*, as well as many of its first contributors, not only shared Mounier's reasons for doing so, but were also motivated as Mounier was by the feeling that civilization was truly in crisis and that they must totally respond to this crisis.[4] While many of the young men first drawn to *Esprit* earnestly sought a synthesis of Bergson and Péguy, Maritain and Berdyaev, Proudhon and De Man, Kierkegaard and Marx, no one of them, including Mounier, had in the planning stage of *Esprit* a developed world view or a consistent approach to the present crisis. In fact, in 1930, when Mounier himself decided in the course of a series of meetings at Maritain's to join three other young intellectuals in founding a new journal, he knew very little about its nature or his future with it. He knew only that a young student of law, Georges Izard, a young librarian at the Sorbonne, André Déléage, and a young student of architecture at the *Ecole des Beaux Arts,* Louis-Emile Galéry, wanted him to be editor of a journal that would transcend what they considered both the worn literary preoccupations of Gide's *Nouvelle Revue Française,* and the journals based on the narrow and rigid political ideologies and categories of the right-wing *Action Française* and the left-wing Communist Party. Beyond this, *Esprit* at this point was for Mounier little more than a set of questions to be debated and answered concerning the nature of the crisis that existed (spiritual or material, political or economic), the form of response to be made to it (intellectual or political, direct or indirect action), the type of contributors to be sought (Catholics or non-believers, Marxists, or members of the *Action Française*), the form the journal should take (intellectual or popular, philosophical guide or party organ).

Maritain himself was crucial in determining the character of *Esprit.*[5] Directly through his weekly meetings at his house at Meudon and indirectly through his prestige, he provided as much as anyone the intellectual milieu in which the young Catholics Mounier, Déléage, and Izard envisioned the purpose of *Esprit.* Beyond this, Maritain lent his support to Mounier and Izard by publishing their work on Péguy, seeing that *Esprit* was given a room at the important Catholic publishers Desclée de Brouwer, and encouraging others to support *Esprit* in all ways possible. Most significantly, not only did Maritain help Mounier in selecting *Esprit*'s collaborators and defining its policy, but Maritain used all his influence to commit *Esprit* to serving that broad Christian intellectual renewal which he identified in the twentieth century.

Ever more in agreement with his friend and contemporary, the Russian emigré Nicolas Berdyaev, that modern man and bourgeois civilization were undergoing a radical and irreversible crisis, Maritain saw *Esprit* as providing a source for a Christian understanding of this crisis.[6] Sharing the Vatican's desire to rethink its social and political policies, Maritain hoped *Esprit* might be a beginning point for a broad inquiry into the Church in his times. Even beyond this, Maritain wanted *Esprit* to be central in developing a new Christendom, a goal which he had already tried to articulate in his *Religion and Culture* (1930):

> It remains essential to work with all our heart towards this realization of a new Christendom no longer according to the medieval idea of the Holy Empire but according to the new and much less unitary ideal where the spiritual and moral action of the Church presides over a temporal order composed of a mul-

titude of culturally and politically heterogeneous people whose religious diversities themselves are not near disappearing.[7]

In almost diametrical opposition to Maritain's conception of *Esprit* as primarily cultural and intellectual, Déléage and Izard wanted it to be political. Izard, who first invited Mounier to join them in founding *Esprit* and who later became its first director, envisioned it as not only providing a new political forum throughout France but as helping generate a new political coalition which would afford an alternative to capitalism and Communism. Thus, in the mind of Izard, *Esprit* was to serve a new popular political movement, a movement which in fact Izard later created under the name of the Third Force.

There were many others who in part gave *Esprit* its character. In contrast to the positions of Izard and Maritain, there was the discussion group *Nouveau Ordre,* which was composed of such young men as Arnaud Dandieu, Robert Aron, René Dupuis, Henri Daniel-Rops, Denis de Rougemont, and Alexandre Marc. In *Esprit* they published their well-thought indictments of the contemporary order along with their plans for a new national and international political, social and economic order.[8]

Among yet other earlier contributors to *Esprit* one should mention the Russian philosopher Nicolas Berdyaev, the French thinker Daniel Halévy; numerous professors such as Etienne Borne, Aldo Dami, Georges Duveau, Olivier Lacombe, André Philip, and some artists like Edmond Humeau and Maximilien Vox.[9] However, what is most important to grasp in any list of *Esprit's* early participants and contributors is that, aside from their diverse ideological backgrounds and their ties to the university, most of them were young men who were beginning their careers, and they were taken with the notion that they must build a new world. For non-believing literary critic Pierre-Aimé Touchard as well as Catholic historian Henri Marrou, *Esprit* respectively meant an opportunity to review literature and music; while other young men, like non-believer André Ulmann, contemporary critic Pierre-Henri Simon, and political thinker Jean Lacroix, did some of their first writings on Europe, politics, political institutions, and decentralization.

Nevertheless, despite the diverse collaborators who were drawn to *Esprit,* and more seriously the divergent philosophy which surrounded its inception, within two years of its publication it was decidedly the work and creation of one person, Emmanuel Mounier. Part of the reason for this was that Mounier alone of the original team remained; another reason was that Mounier alone dedicated himself totally to bringing *Esprit* into existence.

Try as hard as he could, Mounier was not able to find a satisfactory middle path between Maritain's spiritual demands and Izard's political demands. In fact, Maritain's enthusiasm for *Esprit* had waned within a year of its first publication. While continuing until the middle 1930s to treat Mounier as a friend as well as to advise him on religious matters involved with the journal (such as a possible condemnation by the Church in 1936), Maritain believed his worst fears about *Esprit* proved true. Its Catholicism had not been made sufficiently explicit at the outset to avoid the charge of being secretive; and worse, its political affiliation with the Third Force, its flirtation with revolution, in addition to its overall presentism, eclipsed its value as a philosophical inquiry into the contemporary situation.[10] In a word, the older Maritain wanted a journal dedicated to reflection and, from his point of view, the younger Mounier seemed intent on making it a vehicle for action.

For diametrically opposite reasons, Izard separated himself from *Esprit* in 1934. His concern for the immediate issues of French politics led him to resign as director in 1933 in order to dedicate himself full time to forming the Third Force. In 1934 he ceased collaboration with Mounier altogether, when he merged the Third Force into a broad coalition of leftist forces. For Izard, political actions were urgently required; there was no longer time for abstract speculation.

Also in 1934, the young men of *Nouveau Ordre* ceased contributing to *Esprit*. Despite the closeness of *Esprit's* and the *Nouveau Ordre's* plans for a new Europe and France, there were numerous reasons for their separation. *Nouveau Ordre* now had its own journal. Its members were critical of *Esprit's* imprecision and vagueness on social and political matters. In turn, Mounier had publicly attacked them for what he believed was their growing rapprochement with the French right and Hitler.

Thus, by 1934, *Esprit* was Mounier's journal. By then, a migration of those original members who were allied to the *Nouveau Ordre* and the Third Force had occurred, and a new *Esprit* team (which included such young men as Jacques Madaule, Marcel Moré, François Goguel, and Paul-Louis Landsberg) had been formed. Thus, in 1934, it was Mounier alone who had made *Esprit* what it was, and defined what it would be.

He alone had determined that *Esprit* would seek to be a community of believers and non-believers, that it be directed towards the realms of both events and reflection, and that it should, while rejecting any particular political alliances, point towards action. In a word, *Esprit* registered Mounier's pulse beat; it was an aspect of his biography.

Mounier justly wrote at one point in his journal, in May of 1934: "Until now, *Esprit* has been me, my personal history."[11] Its creation not only marked the culmination of Mounier's first education under Chevalier and Bergson, Maritain and Péguy, but it marked the beginning of a second education in which Mounier was challenged to transform the thought of these masters into a veritable education for his times. However, it should not be forgotten that what ignited Mounier, as it did all those who initially supported *Esprit*, were those profoundly dramatic events of the years 1929 to 1932, which seemed to make real for all Europe the talk of new heroisms, and the ends and beginnings of civilizations.

1929 to 1932: The Crisis Years

All orders of European life were involved in the crises of 1929-1932. Hajo Holborn's *Political Collapse* sets the stage for an understanding of the political and international situation during these years:

> By hindsight it is easy to say the years between 1925 and 1930 were the years in which Europe could have been constituted, not as an entirely self-contained political system, but as a strong powerblock in world politics if the beginnings of co-operation between Britain, France, and Germany had been carried to a full understanding on all major issues of Europe. . . . The five years after 1925 gave Europe a last Indian summer before the blizzard of the world economic crisis struck in 1931. Nobody foresaw that Europe, politically and economically, lived on borrowed time. . . .
>
> Once the bubble burst and it dawned upon the world that there had been a general overproduction and overinvestment, the American government preferred virtually to stop all intergovernmental debts, reparations, and inter-Allied obligations in order to save the American private loans that more directly affected the American banking situation. President Hoover proposed in 1931 a holiday of reparation and inter-Allied debt payments. In 1932 at the Conference of Lausanne, reparations were actually buried. But at that time Germany was already determined not only to demand a radical revision of the Paris settlement in her favor but to force a full reversal of the historic decision of World War I.[12]

Pierre Renouvin suggests more specifically some of the political and social dimensions of the world economic crisis:

> By its amplitude and its duration it is without precedent in the contemporary world. . . . The shaking was so grave and so prolonged that the basis of the economic and social order appeared threatened. Individualism, free enterprise, the setting of prices by competition—the foundations of the capitalist system—were in rout. . . . It was not thus only an economic and social crisis, and even a moral crisis; it was a crisis of the collective mind. . . . The *Annus terribilis* which Arnold Toynbee evoked at the beginning of 1932, was not 1914 or 1917, it was 1931.[13]

In the year 1932 France first experienced the Depression and some of its social, political, and international consequences. Chastenet wrote in his *Decline of the Third Republic:*

> The year 1932 is close to its definition: France's painful year. In matters of economics it is clearly touched by the Depression. . . . In matters of finance "Poincaré's prosperity" is only a memory. . . . In matters of politics, the May elections have placed in the Palais-Bourbon a majority whose heterogeneous character meant impotence, while the minority, nursing its bitterness, refused its support to even the government projects which were in accord with its program. In matters of international politics, the failure of the disarmament conference appeared almost certain and France was held abroad as responsible for this failure without having in any corresponding way succeeded in establishing her policy "security first."[14]

In 1932 France thus faced its third challenge of the century. The first challenge, which can be dated from 1905 on, was the challenge of forming a positive government, society, and state which could truly meet the problems of the industrial age and the rapidly changing world power balance which accompanied it. France's second challenge was brought forth by the First World War. It demanded that France not only emerge from Europe's first total war victoriously, but that it emerge from this War that had bled it white with the will to be Europe's first power. The third challenge, which repeated and intensified the first two challenges, arose with the awesome and near simultaneous dawning of the Depression, the breakdown of the international order, and the advent of Nazism.[15] If France were to survive, it was now necessary for it to build (1) an effective government out of its parliamentarian institutions, (2) a dynamic society out of its lethargic bourgeoisie, and (3) a certain and strong foreign policy out of its diverse allies and own ideological families. Inherent within this challenge was the necessity of asserting collec-

· tivism over individualism, change over tradition, security over freedom.
Perhaps France was being asked to become what it was not, if it were to
be at all.

This third challenge surfaced in an age when liberal democracy was in
retreat across Europe, when mass society was in ascent, when the European order had ceased to be anchored in either power or morality, and
war and revolution pervaded nearly all European life. In the deepest
sense, France's third challenge was Europe's and the West's.

As the years 1929 to 1932 were crisis years for Europe and France, so
also were they decisive years for European reflection. Generalizing on
the impact of the events of the 1930s on European intellectual life, H.
S. Hughes wrote:

> As Europe experienced its second great crisis of the century—as depression
> and fascism added their shocks to the psychological damage that the First
> World War and its aftermath had inflicted—people began [like Spengler, Croce,
> Meinecke, Bloch, and Toynbee] to turn towards historical speculation and to
> ask themselves in the broadest terms to what end the modern world was
> moving. This mood of cosmic questioning had already been widespread in the
> post-war years; the experiences of the 1930s revived it and increased its
> range.[16]

This "mood of cosmic questioning," caused in great part by the First
World War and by the events of these years, transformed itself into an
intellectual anxiety over the destiny of man and civilization. The names
of such contemporary thinkers as Husserl, Heidegger, Jaspers, and
Barth, and the names of Malraux, Marcel, Berdyaev, and Shestov in
themselves evince this new note of existential concern and anxiety
about man, culture, and civilization which spread across Europe.[17] The
increasing importance of Freud and Jung for European intellectual life,
no less than the ever-growing number of supporters of Nietzsche and
Kierkegaard, were symptomatic of a culture in crisis. The nature and
destiny of man, the past, the present, and the future, all became con-
testable, sufferable, and inseparable in European thought.

This existential anxiety over man's fate and the West's destiny fused
together, transformed, radicalized, and universalized nineteenth century
criticisms of bourgeois society and politics. No past criticism of European life went unvoiced; no past attack against some aspect of European society or culture was considered entirely without some truth
regarding the contemporary order. De Maistre and Dostoevsky, Proudhon and Marx, Burke and De Tocqueville, Sorel and Péguy were equal-

ly, and often simultaneously, made guides to what was thought to be the present crisis of civilization.

The speculations of two of Maritain's contemporaries, Karl Jaspers and José Ortega y Gasset, demonstrate how European self-reflection was radicalized and universalized in the 1920s and notably during the period 1929 until 1932. The breadth of their visions and the depth of their criticisms of the West not only transcended the synthetic and analytic dimensions of liberal, conservative, and radical understanding of the modern world, but anticipated fully the existential, historical, and civilizational themes of the most profound moral and political speculation of the 1930s and 1940s.

Consciously inspired by Kierkegaard's, Burckhardt's, Nietzsche's, as well as earlier German Romantics' analyses of European civilization, philosopher Karl Jaspers affirmed, as Mounier did, that Western man was experiencing a total spiritual crisis. In his *Man and the Modern Age* (1931), Jaspers specifically argued that Western man's triumph over nature had the result of causing him to lose his sense of the absolute, and consequently, led him to base his understanding of the world on a radical historicism. For Jaspers, this transformation of Western consciousness disastrously and tragically culminated in what he considered the present nihilistic "epochal consciousness":

> Beyond question there is a widespread conviction that human activities are unavailing; everything has become questionable; nothing in human life holds good; that existence is no more than an unceasing maelstrom of reciprocal deception and self-deception by ideologies. Thus the epochal consciousness becomes detached from being, and is concerned only with itself. One who holds such a view cannot but be inspired with itself. One who holds such a view cannot but be inspired with a consciousness of his own nullity. His awareness of the end as annihilation is simultaneously the awareness that his own existence is null. The epochal consciousness has turned a somersault in the void.[18]

Assuming that this alienation of Western consciousness from itself and reality was the central dilemma of his times, Jaspers proceeded to survey contemporary politics, society, culture, and education in terms of what he believed was the second major fact of his times—the destructive leveling of the European "life order" by a new "technical mass order." Finding no immediate political or spiritual force capable of halting or reversing this process of destruction, Jaspers believed that Western man had his only present hope for salvation in an heroic quest after the truth of man's existence and the reality of his present situation.

Spanish philosopher and liberal, Ortega y Gasset, arrived at many of the same pessimistic conclusions. Already in his essays in the early 1920s, Ortega realized that man was inseparably part of his historical conditions, and that man could save himself only by saving his circumstances. To do this, Ortega thought, as did Mounier, that man must find a new philosophy which could transcend the false dichotomies of rationalism and emotionalism, collectivism and individualism, materialism and spiritualism, and traditional conservatisms and liberalisms.[19] Only a philosophy which emerged from a vital conception of man, his reason, and his historical situation would provide in Ortega's eyes a new ideal for Europe.

In his classic work, *The Revolt of the Masses* (1930), Ortega stated that the dominant fact of contemporary European life was the advent of mass man—his accession to "complete social power."[20] Created in numbers by a three-fold demographic growth in nineteenth century Europe, secured in his existence by technology and science, and given his confidence and voice by nineteenth century liberalism, mass man emerged as a collective body of sufficient magnitude to destroy the civilization which brought him into existence.

Without a sense of the fragility of politics and civilization and intent on making his norms the measure of all else, mass man, Ortega believed, presently threatened to destroy the fruits of civilization and unleash the state on the minorities and ideas which were the essence of the West. The United States, Soviet Russia, and Fascist Italy were for Ortega but the most visible signs of this vertical invasion of the masses. As both Mounier and Maritain basically concluded in the course of the 1930s, Ortega believed that Europe's only hope lay in a new federalism that might redirect and spiritualize the dynamic impulses and forces of twentieth century European society and thought.

Taken together, Jaspers and Ortega reflect a new level of global consciousness reached by European self-understanding in the years 1929 to 1932. At this point, the European dialogue shifted its axes from the fundamental nineteenth century questions of progress versus decadence, science versus religion, reform versus order to the yet more universal question of the very survival of Western civilization. While this question had been anticipated on innumerable fronts since the French Revolution, the fate of the West now became a pressing question that seemed to entail for its very understanding a study of all past reality and seemed to demand for an answer an entirely new historical faith and world order. Clearly in the years 1929-1932, it was no longer possible for a serious thinker to discount the First World War, the Russian Revolution, and Italian Fascism as tragic but ultimately only temporary aberrations in the mainstream of Western historical progress. For during these years it became obvious to ever greater numbers of Europeans, confronted by the simultaneous collapse of the social, economic, and political orders, that these events might prove to be the very headwaters of the twentieth century. As painful and as unwanted as such reflections were, sensitive Europeans everywhere came to agonize, and revoice those awesome lines of Paul Valéry: "We later civilizations . . . we too now know that we are mortal."[21]

It was this sense of the mortality of civilization which came to predominate in French thought in the years of 1929 to 1932. While notions of decline and decadence had flowed in French veins since 1870, these notions could no longer be localized to a certain form of cultural rhetoric, to a given event, to a given thinker, and to the ideology of a certain group. The radical disruption of what political and social certitude France had prior to 1930 was now converted on the intellectual plane into the sense of total crisis.

The crisis, in fact, marked the end of abstract and academic theory. Idealism and science, as well as the disinterested aesthetic inquiries into art and the self, were interrupted. Bergson's last major publication, *Two Sources of Religion and Morality* (1932), had symbolically turned to matters of society and change. Its sympathetic development of the notion of open society could be understood at least symbolically as proposing that the hour was at hand for going beyond the closed society of the bourgeois Third Republic. No less significantly, Jacques Maritain, Etienne Gilson, and Maurice Blondel in the same year conducted the last major debate before the Second World War over the nature of Christian philosophy.[22] On most fronts of French intellectual life, there was a recongition that France and Europe had reached a turning point—a time when deed and event were to rule.

And if the intellectuals approached the crisis with anxiety, less certain that older academic theories mattered and more certain that radical action was inevitable, the crisis nevertheless elicited new levels of intellectual activity. New ideas and concepts—better said, a new attitude toward the world—was called forth. Existentialism took hold: Husserl and Heidegger, Scheler and Jaspers were increasingly popular; the two Catholic philosophers Lavelle and Le Senne founded in 1934 the important

series "La Philosophie de l'Esprit"; and Kierkegaard and Nietzsche, Berdyaev, Shestov, and Marcel were increasingly read. A host of journals
were born during these years ". . . each tending towards the construction of a new world destined to replace the world which according to
them was in the process of dying before their eyes: *Les Cahiers, Réaction, La Revue Française, Plans, Mouvements, Esprit, Nouveau Ordre,
La Revue du Siècle, Prélude, Le Front Nationale, Syndicaliste, Les Nouvelles Equipes, L'Homme Réel, Le Club de Février, La Lutte des
Jeunes, Travail et Nation, La Revue du XXᵉ Siècle, La Justice Sociale,
Combat, L'Ordre. . . ."*[23] All this activity was born out of the sense that
man was presently entering a new historical period.

At the center of this activity was Mounier's generation. Having been
brought up on the depth literature of Gide, Nietzsche, and Claudel and
by the inspiration of Maurras, Maritain, and Péguy, they no less than
Maritain's generation on the eve of the First World War were in revolt
against the adult world and in search of a mission which would lead
them beyond the *monde bourgeois.* Every degree as much as the present generation of French university students and young instructors who
caused and shaped *les événements de Mai* (the events of May, 1968),
Mounier's generation was angry about the world—France, its politics,
art, morals, and society. Already before the year 1930, Mounier's generation, composed of such young intellectuals as Raymond Aron, Bertrand de Jouvenel, Jean-Paul Sartre, Simone Weil, and Simone de Beau-
voir, had begun its search for a form of thought and a style of living
which would transcend the confines of bourgeois life.[24] Already before
the year 1930, many of Mounier's generation had already started to
give form to their criticisms of the established order and to draw up
tentative plans for a new society. In 1928 to 1930, Jean-Pierre Maxence
and Robert Francis, of Maurras' imprint, founded the *Cahiers*; young
Marxists Henri Lefebvre and Paul Nizan created *Philosophies*; and Jean
de Fabrèques and René Vincent gave sounding to a new "young right"
with their founding of *Réaction.*[25] Thus, when the full force of the Depression hit France, Mounier's generation was already well prepared to
assert that the bourgeois Republican order was bankrupt and that this
bankruptcy mirrored a crisis of civilizational dimensions.

The young Barthian Denis de Rougemont, collaborator with the *Nouveau Ordre* and *Esprit,* asked rhetorically in 1932 whether it were
possible "to define a common cause of French youth, a community of
essential attitudes." And De Rougement went on to reply that the uni-

ty of his and Mounier's generation did not lie in masters and doctrines, but existed rather in a solidarity that came from their consciousness of the crisis of their times, in their "dissent in the face of the constant misery of an epoch wherein all that a man could love and wish for is cut off at its vital origins, withered, denatured, upside down, botched." "Such groups as *Nouveau Ordre, Combat, Esprit, Plans, Réaction,*" De Rougement further went on to say, "by their declared will of revolt and furthermore by their constructive demands, reveal . . . the first lines of a new French Revolution."[26]

In Jean Lacroix's opinion, it was Mounier who first and foremost in his generation grasped the nature of the present crisis and set the course towards a new French Revolution. "Mounier," Lacroix wrote, "is less the person who articulated an original, new, and technical philosophy and more the person who best grasped in our generation the crisis of civilization and the intellectual, social, and religious conditions of its solution." "He wanted," Lacroix continued, "*Esprit* to be for the twentieth century what the *Encyclopédie* had been for the eighteenth century."[27] Yet even more presumptuously, Mounier wanted *Esprit* to do no less than redirect the course of all modern European history.

"Refaire la Renaissance"

Mounier gave birth to *Esprit* during the years of 1929 to 1932. Inseparable from *Esprit's* creation were: the sense of an age in total crisis, the feeling that a turning point was at hand, and the need and desire to find a way to a new France and a new Europe. *Esprit* was born into an age when consciousness was alert to change and nearly everything seemed possible.

Mounier intended that *Esprit* be the revolutionary voice in a revolutionary age. He titled his lead article (which also was the major address that he delivered at the founding congress of *Esprit* at Font-Romeu) "Refaire la Renaissance."[28] In it, he called for a revolution that would remake all of Europe since the Renaissance.

First, Mounier declared that the revolution must be based upon "the primacy of the spiritual." It must not be considered the "work of biological salvation"; nor should it, in its ultimate human sources and aims, be reduced totally to the immanent domains of politics and society. Furthermore, Mounier contended that the revolution cannot (as happens so often in contemporary theory today) be made identical with the diverse visible disruptions of the world.

Revealing the personalistic tendencies of all his thought, Mounier asserted that revolution is an act of the human spirit. If it is not to be vitiated at its very beginning, it must arise out of a man's willingness to overcome his own insecurity, to forego his own comfort, to accept "life as adventurous and compromised, impoverished and isolated."[29] The revolution has its origin and strength in a man's willingness to risk his life, to bear witness to what he believes to be the truth, even if this means surendering all hopes of success.

Accordingly, in Mounier's view, the first principle of this new revolutionary must be that the spiritual commands all else. Among the revolutionary's first acts must be negations. At the outset, he must avoid what Mounier considered the French temptation to pose all questions as political questions. Equally, the revolutionary must at the outset "disassociate the spiritual from the reactionary." Not to do so is to permit the forces of reaction to continue to identify their cause with God and, correspondingly, to compel the forces of movement to attack the Church and religion, while encouraging them to turn such doctrines as popular sovereignty and democracy into substitute theologies.

In addition to rejecting the primacy of politics and the ideological confusions of both right and left, the revolutionist must initially refuse the prevalent but false choice of either materialism or spiritualism. On the side of spiritualism, Mounier identified the fundamental enemy as idealism. While believing that idealism was justified in many of its first philosophical assumptions, he asserted that idealism deteriorated into useless abstractions because it metaphysically disembodies man and thereby denies his historical existence.

On the side of materialism, Mounier saw Marxism as the most challenging representative. While already revealing his growing appreciation for Marxism by admitting its just accent on the importance of the economic and social orders for human existence, Mounier contended that its ultimate error is its fundamental claim to reduce human consciousness (and thus human value and worth) to no more than a reflection of economic and social relations. Despite the fact that Marxism is a "metaphysical and moral disorder," the revolutionist, in Mounier's opinion, has to admit the essential validity of a Marxist critique of contemporary bourgeois society.

Thus, the initial task of the revolutionist, according to Mounier, is to confront a simultaneous crisis in both man's material and spiritual worlds. To accomplish this task, the moral revolutionist must first make an act of faith in the human spirit. This act alone permits him to escape the despiritualization of materialism and the dematerialization of spiritualism. To assert the primacy of the human spirit does not constitute a vague adherence to ". . . a biological reflex . . . a structural hypothesis, or a vague as if, but a reality . . . which surpasses us, penetrates us, engages us entirely by drawing us beyond ourselves."[30] It is an act of faith that the truth is real and "that the meditation of a single man . . . can move humanity more effectively that do the architects of reform."[31] With this faith the revolutionist must, without confusing the realities of contemplation and action, strive to rejoin the individual and the universal.

The revolutionist, so conceived, resembles both mystic and prophet. He passes beyond himself, through the dark night of the soul, to reach his vocation. "Man does not reconstruct the truth," Mounier declared, "with lies and absolutions"; instead, "man recasts with fire that which has been taken over by lies. A total transfiguration of all values must precede their spiritual reintegration. That is what it means to be a revolutionist."[32] A man becomes a revolutionist, for Mounier, when he is willing to resist the pressing human temptation to surrender to necessities, habits, circumstances—fate—when he is willing to admit fully the rude gravity of the facts and events which make up his world and his responsibility to respond to them. In contrast to those who would make themselves revolutionists simply because of their willingness to use violence, Mounier said that the revolutionist is he who, while admitting his own weakness, honestly and directly confronts a world whose decay is so advanced that collapse of the whole tottering mass seems inevitable.

The revolutionist also exists because he prophetically announces a new order. He asserts that past relations between the spiritual and political must undergo a radical transformation. He professes that it is man's full responsibility to be aware of and participate in the world around him. He furthermore declares that below present crises and dislocations that surround him there exists the possibility of helping man move towards a better order of existence. In a word, the revolutionist believes in the promise of the future.

The revolutionist, Mounier said, begins with the assertion: "The world is broken down; the spirit alone can put the machine on the road again."[33] In contrast to those who accept an inactive and moralizing pacifism, the revolutionist affirms that action is essential for man to

create and govern; and in contrast to those whose action leads to egotism and violence, the revolutionist maintains the values of truth and
freedom. He subordinates the goal of success to the act of bearing
witness. His optimism, thus, does not arise out of a certitude about the
future or an enthusiasm for a utopia but stands fast on a conscious
service to the spirit and the human condition. The revolutionist escapes
the treasons of action and thought by equally rejecting the activist's
impulse to ignore all spiritual boundaries and the idealist's complacency
that denies any real exigency for action. Not without some interest for
us today, Mounier described the latter at one point in "Refaire la
Renaissance" as "those intrepid friends who oppose us because we are
not anxious over the degrees of existence, when men die from hunger,
when the planes of civilization bombard Vietnamese villages."[34]

The revolution itself, in Mounier's view, has to be shaped by two fundamental ends. First, it is necessary to achieve an intellectual "rehabilitation of the material world."[35] To do this, nature first must be reinter-
preted. As Christianity once freed man's understanding of nature from
a cruel and blind concept of fate, so today's revolutionist must drive
the modern gods of mind and will out of our concept of nature if man
is to appreciate again his real place in existence. In turn, in order to
rehabilitate the material, it is equally essential to banish modern individualism which separates man from man and man from nature, as well
as an intellectual dualism which divides man into two alien parts, the
material and spiritual. The material can no longer be denigrated as being
solely a member of the lower realms of the body, the mortal, the base,
and the earthly, any more than it can be elevated into the sole source of
human identity, purpose, worth, and definition.

"The body, love, art and industry—money," Mounier wrote, "has de-
voured all matter. Elusive and impersonal, it has succeeded in realizing
what neither power nor adventure has; it has installed in the heart of
man the older dream of the beast, the irresistible and boundless savage
possession of matter as slave, as indefinitely expandable upon desire."[36]
The revolution must restore matter as part of God's creation and man's
ally in being.

The second aim of the revolution is the "rehabilitation of community."[37] Agreeing completely with what Maritain had written in his *Three
Reformers,* Mounier placed the conflict of individualism and collectivism at the center of the crisis of civilization. On one side, he distinguished an individualism born out of Renaissance humanism which,
more than a morality and ethics, is "a metaphysics of integral solitude,

the only metaphysics which remains for us when we have lost the truth, the world and the community of men."[38] On the other side, he distinguished a collectivism which arose in the nineteenth century to avenge the lost universality of man. This collectivism, which first received a limited and abstract form with Comte and Durkheim and an organic and personal form with Fournier, Proudhon, and Saint Simon, was converted into an immanent and total metaphysics of man in society by Marx, and became a "second humanism" with the Russian Revolution. The drama and challenge of the times lay in overcoming both individualism and collectivism, in reversing four centuries of egotistic will and abused power, of averting imminent collectivist forces which would further subjugate man to the tyrannies of class and state. In essence, the rehabilitation of the human community depended on the defining of a third humanism which would rebuild the human order.

It was to these ends that Mounier believed the revolution must be guided. By affirming the primacy of the spiritual, acknowledging the totality of the crisis, offering a new understanding of man in nature and man among men, Mounier aimed the revolution at nothing less than the remaking of five centuries of European history.

A Revolution?

"Refaire la Renaissance," then, was basically a revolutionary document. It had its sources in a man willing to sacrifice his life for his vision and times. It aimed at a radical transformation of man's consciousness, the overthrow of the middle class and the destruction of Republican France. It denied the nation-state and nationalism, individualism and collectivism. It sought to do no less than reverse what can be considered some of the most significant results of the French Revolution and the Industrial Revolution.

From another point of view, however, "Refaire la Renaissance" was not a revolutionary document. It did not assert the primacy of society and economics, propose an ideology and coalition essential for the total transformation of society, unify consciousness and historical perspective into a global perspective and *praxis*.[39] In effect, as an analysis, doctrine, and form of action it was insufficient to affect a real revolution in the structure of men's lives and consciousnesses.

To this Marxian denial of the revolutionary character of "Refaire la Renaissance," other denials could be added. First, it could be contended that its accent on the primacy of consciousness, and the moral, religious, and metaphysical, made it a-historical, a-political, and a-social. Second, it could be argued that its basic critique of individualism and collectivism, in addition to its general critique of *le monde bourgeois,* was simply a reiteration of commonplace criticisms equally found in religious and aesthetic, as well as conservative and anarchist, repudiations of the modern world. Third, it could be argued that "Refaire la Renaissance" was, above all else, a revolt of conscience. It did not, that is, originate from a true historical and political analysis of the French and Industrial Revolutions; nor did it propose, as would be demanded of any revolutionary doctrine, a path which led beyond the political and economic individualism and statist and societal collectivisms that had stalemated man in the aftermath of the First World War. A summary of these statements into a single attack against the revolutionary credentials of Mounier's "Refaire la Renaissance," would indicate that the document was: (1) an expression of young intellectuals, like Mounier, who could not find a role in mass industrial society; (2) a reiteration of what had become by the 1920s commonplace repudiations of bourgeois life, materialism, and mass culture; (3) a restatement of various economic and political decentralizing federalisms which prevailed notably among pre-1848 conservatisms and utopian socialisms.

Rather than trying to decide immediately and explicitly whether "Refaire la Renaissance" is revolutionary (for after all this might amount to little more than a question of *a priori* philosophies, favored political positions, and arbitrary definitions), a better approach is to examine the ways in which it reveals France's, French youth's, and the Church's situations in the inter-war period and to point out the ways in which it reveals Mounier's response to these situations. In believing that France was threatened by liberal economics, statism, and collectivism, Mounier showed, in "Refaire la Renaissance," what can be considered the "intellectual's" proclivity for the grandiose themes of the movements of civilizations in preference to the "hard" analyses of France's capacity as a modern nation-state to survive politically, economically, socially, and militarily in an age of international violence. In assuming that a spiritual and moral revolution was to have precedence over a political and material revolution, it could further be argued that Mounier overlooked the actual conditions of European power. Such a "realist critique" could additionally suggest that "Refaire la Renaissance" simultaneously mirrored the desperation of France's geopolitical situation, and the French intellectuals' now long standing search for "une réforme intellectuelle."

On other levels it could be maintained that "Refaire la Renaissance" was revolutionary to the degree that educated French youth had come since the turn of the century to experience a sense of alienation from contemporary politics and society. Perhaps what really was at stake for Mounier and the young men of *Esprit* was not the making of a revolution but the finding of an identity. So understood, "Refaire la Renaissance" was one of the many youthful voices that had learned also to speak of the Republic's errors. From this point of view it was not revolutionary; rather it was a result of the Republic's own failure to politicize its extreme rights and lefts, to dispel the mounting and converging attacks against Republican life, and to prove its own strength and determination at home and abroad.[40]

A yet more pertinent line of explanation, in my opinion, would view "Refaire la Renaissance" as primarily an expression of Mounier's and *Esprit's* young Catholics' rebellion against a world which afforded faith neither place nor security. This rebellion could be seen as an attack against: (1) the liberal idea of the separation of state and church and the conception of religion as solely a private affair, (2) a civilization which in the name of its own rational and scientific progress sought to be free from the Church, (3) a civilization which, despite these aspirations for human progress and autonomy, had turned its science to war, its groups into warring classes, and its ideas into propaganda, (4) a civilization which since the First World War had given birth to the Russian Revolution, Communism, Fascism, Nazism, and the dread of yet another war.[41]

One of the most fundamental dilemmas of Catholics in the twentieth century was well expressed by Luigi Sturzo:

> The idea of any Church outside politics, that is, separated from life as we live it, with its struggles, its crises, its disappointments, its tragedies, would be neither historically conceivable nor spiritually possible. Today more than in the past, the States have monopolized almost the whole of social life and a great part of individual life, they have laid hold of the direction of the trends of thought and orientation of their countries, passing from the plane of politics as a technique of government to that of politics as a conception of the life of the world, a *Weltanschauung*. The churches either resign themselves to existing on the margins of society, as the spiritual comfort of a few faithful, undisturbed because they have placed themselves outside all real activity, or else, wishing to remain at the center of the cultural and moral life of society, they must take part, on the religious plane, in all the enterprises and all the conflicts of the dynamism of the age. And since politics are saturated with all political values, it is to politics (not to the technique of politics, nor to the

earthly interests that politics contain, but taken as one of all-absorbing expressions of social life) that the churches must draw near, facing, at the right moment and with spiritual vision, the titanic struggles before them.[42]

In these years part of Catholic consciousness took form around two realities. First, the Church found on the contemporary landscape no government or society which it could trust. Second, it saw within the face of contemporary events neither possibility of retreating to a past order nor the certain signs of an emerging new order. These recognitions, which had both progressively and cataclysmically come forth in the course of the nineteenth century, were now certitudes for those who wanted the Church to have sufficient independence to inform men's conscience and institutions.

In this light more than any other, Mounier's message in "Refaire la Renaissance" can be understood as revolutionary. It arose out of a refusal to accept the Church's subservience to secular states and societies. It had its roots in a situation that had left the Vatican without certain allies and Catholics with incertitude of their present and future goals. It had its ends in the search for a new Christian civilization.

"Refaire la Renaissance" was, in essence, Mounier's proclamation that faith again would have its place in the lives and thought of men. To this end, he called for a revolution that would immediately free Christianity from the "established disorder" of bourgeois rule and establish the spiritual route to a new Christian order. In depth, he sought no less than resacralizing the temporal order.

This drive to resacralize the world was the central impulse of Mounier's revolutionary doctrine. His education had given this impulse its form. Péguy had taught him that the modern world was without mystery. Chevalier and Bergson had shown him that the modern world was without a metaphysic. Maritain convinced him that the logic of ideas and forces that shaped his times was a logic of destruction. His generation had encouraged him to affirm that contemporary bourgeois life was without value and against being. The awesome realities exposed by the events of the years 1929-1932 gave a final certitude to Mounier's belief that the modern world was spiritually bankrupt, that he and his generation were witnessing the fall of one civilization, that they were truly responsible for the creation of new civilization. So Mounier came to believe that if man and civilization were to be restored, all must be rethought and refounded. At the heart of his revolt there was thus nothing other than the desire to make the profane sacred.

CHAPTER VII

PERSONALISM: A NEW HISTORICAL IDEAL

1932 to 1938: The Confirming Years

THE EVENTS of the early and mid-1930s and the continuing economic, social, political and international crises that they revealed further convinced Mounier that civilization had reached a turning point. The failure of France and Europe to respond to these crises made Mounier certain that only a revolution based on a new philosophy of man and society could serve manking in its present historical situation.

While not occupying himself with the daily intricacies of French parliamentarian practice, Mounier shared the common belief that neither needed nor significant changes could be accomplished in the political arena. The erratic changing of governments, the frequent oscillations in domestic and foreign policy, as well as the abiding presence of self-serving political groups and practices were all evidence for Mounier of the impotence of contemporary Republican government and the need for a whole new order. Mounier's reactions to the Stavisky Affair and the Popular Front Government are two examples of how France's political life encouraged Mounier to think in the grandiose terms of total revolutions and new civilizations.

Reminiscent of the late nineteenth century Panama Affair, the Stavisky Affair of January and February 1934 first broke the surface as a financial swindle. It carried with it signs of complicity by high members of Daladier's ruling radical government. After a series of "fruitless" investigations, the "opportune" suicide of the swindler Stavisky himself, and the brutal murder of one of the government's perhaps too-knowledgeable attorneys, the right-wing press turned the mounting incident into a full-blown affair. On the night of February 6, crowds formed in Paris. Leavened, but not led, by newly formed right-wing leagues, the crowds fell into brutal and extensive conflict with the police. Least importantly, the outcome of the night's conflict was the fall of another moderate radical government. Most tragically, the Stavisky Affair, like the Dreyfus Affair, set loose an open ideological battle between the forces of the right and left which continually heightened throughout the 1930s.[1]

Mounier saw the seriousness of the Affair in the massive proliferation of exaggerations, distorted interpretations and deliberate lies which it produced.[2] Among them, he listed the Radicals' concern for the honor of the party, the moderates' accusation of the Radicals' corruption and, more seriously, the left's myth that February 6 was the work of bands of fascists and the right's counterclaim that the tumult of the people in the wake of the Affair constituted popular support for them. These myths further convinced Mounier that any immediate political strategy could not escape the contradictions which, he thought, vitiated all of French politics. Indeed, Mounier saw no chance of, in fact not even a choice between, revolution on either the right or left. The Communist's avowed concern for human misery and his revolutionary vigor meant adherence to atheism and materialism; the fascist's avowed concern for heroism and values demanded acceptance of "hypocritical capitalism," warlike politics, and the uninspiring dictatorship of the self-interested. In brief, expressing what he had learned from the Stavisky Affair, Mounier wrote: "If the revolution is for tomorrow it is not ours. . . . If the revolution is for later, our work in depth will have time to develop a political force which will not betray our work."[3]

In effect, Mounier wanted changes that he believed too radical to flow in the veins of contemporary French politics. Thus, in 1936, when the Socialist Léon Blum led a coalition of Socialists and Radicals (with Communist support) into office as the Popular Front Government, Mounier could do no more than extend *Esprit's* best wishes for its success. For, despite his growing sympathy for the left, and *Esprit's* former director Izard's efforts in creating a broad coalition of the left, Mounier could muster little hope in the Popular Front.[4]

Mounier soon found his initial doubts about the strength of its coalition justified. Almost immediately upon taking office, the Blum Government was met domestically by serious strikes, and internationally by the outbreak of the Spanish Civil War. After some success in matters of social legislation, the government, harassed by growing criticism of right and left radicals, faltered before a host of pressing national tasks. Its dissolution in June 1937 deepened Mounier's belief that Republican politics were incapable of escaping the inherent contradictions of bourgeois society.[5] Those, Mounier believed, who wanted real reform had to continue to look to the more global question of forming a new consciousness of man and society.

As French political life convinced Mounier that there was need for a thoroughgoing transformation of French life, so the international realities of the early and mid-1930s further convinced him that there was a need for remaking all orders of all European life. Since *Esprit's* beginnings, Mounier had interpreted the anarchy of the international order as a symptom of Europe's sickness. He saw the proposed international "cures" of diplomacy, armaments, and pacifism as no more beneficial for the body of Europe than were Republican remedies for France's ills.

Mounier's treatment of peace reveals the perspective from which he approached international affairs.[6] Peace, first, he believed, could not be conceived as an absolute in itself, but had to be treated as subordinate to the values of truth and justice. Second, any real peace, unlike that of Versailles, could not be established upon the principles of nationalism and the social order of bourgeois capitalism. Third, peace was not to be had by continuing armaments, military alliances, secret treaties, or naive pacifisms. Mounier made peace, as he did all international affairs, secondary and contingent upon the building of a new order of civilization.

It is clear, therefore, why the accession of Hitler (January 1933), Italy's attack on Abyssinia (September 1935), and the remilitarization of the Rhineland (March 1936) appeared to Mounier more as the signs of a collapsing civilization, rather than ineluctable steps towards war. In 1935, along with several of France's leading intellectuals, Mounier signed a manifesto which revealed his vision of Europe at that time.[7] The Manifesto asserted that the greatest danger of the times lay in the elevation of the state beyond all else. It denounced, on one hand, all unilateral violations of treaties and condemned the militarization of national life, while, on the other hand, it declared pacifism as the last refuge for the fearful. It called for an international body having sovereignty over nation-states for the sake of distributive justice, and it concluded that, given the absence of such an international body, national defense was a necessary measure but should not serve as a disguise for an immoral nationalism.

This basic position of Mounier, which developed more out of a concern with paths to total peace than the realities of preparing for and fighting specific wars, was not altered by the Spanish Civil War. In spite of his initial sympathies for the Republican cause, his disgust with Franco's use of the Church, and the Church's use of anti-Communism, Mounier, like Maritain, did not openly enroll himself on the Republican side.[8] In fact, Mounier did not confront the War as demanding a response to an absolute set of either-or choices which, in the words of Robert Graves, were posed between "Fascism versus Communism, or Totalitarianism versus Democracy, or Italy and Germany versus England and France, or Force versus Liberty, or Rebels versus Constitutional Government, or Barbarism versus Culture, or Catholicism versus Atheism, or the Upper Classes versus the Lower, or Order versus Anarchy."[9] Increasingly, as Mounier viewed the mounting and senseless atrocities committed by both sides, and the hateful lies that accompanied them, he chose to speak of the War as a tragedy that encompassed Spain, the West, and the innocent rather than a problem that could be solved by specific diplomatic moves or additional military power. Once again, Mounier was proving himself quicker to perceive the signs of an entire civilization's collapse rather than the specific aspects of nations at war.

Only in the wake of Munich (September 1938) did Mounier fully confront the problem of power—the inevitable choices and necessities which accompany preparation for war with a dictator whom Mounier now recognized to have "no limits." By then, however, there was no time for the independent party *Esprit* projected; by then, there was only time for taking up arms.

War had not been at the center of Mounier's attention in the 1930s. There are profound reasons for this. Mounier's first education had prepared him to think of the modern world in terms of philosophy, religion, and culture, not of states, diplomacies and armies. Mounier's second education, which began with the founding of *Esprit* in 1932, taught him to think and speak of the events that overwhelmed European and French public lives in terms of a crisis of civilization, not in terms of the empirical specifics of various national lives. The events from 1932 until 1938 did not reverse the premises of these first educations; in fact, these years, which witnessed the articulation of his full doctrine of Personalism, can justly be considered confirming years.

Personalism: A World View

Personalism represented Mounier's response to what he believed to be the needs of mankind in the 1930s. While historically inseparable from the decade of the 1930s, Personalism was, nevertheless, a distinct philosophy of man in the modern world. It was at one and the same time a critique of an age and a program for its reformation. In the *Personalist Manifesto* (1936), which crowned *Esprit's* doctrinal period of development, Mounier set forth his Personalism in its fullest dimensions.[10]

As a critique, Personalism had its origins and form in Mounier's concept of bourgeois civilization. With the use of this concept, Mounier unified (as once the young Marx and Kierkegaard had) his philosophical, aesthetic, and social criticisms of the modern world into a critical system of understanding. In terms of this concept, bourgeois civilization, Mounier did what is essential for any comprehensive analysis of an age: he offered a global description of his times, depicted its guiding spirit *(zeitgeist)*, offered a historical and dialectical notion of its development, and characterized the present stage of civilization which had to be overcome.

At the heart of Mounier's general critical notion of bourgeois civilization was his moral indictment of the age. Beyond any specific economic or class connotations, the concept "bourgeois" was used by Mounier to evoke a soulless world that refused youth's hopes, that denied the poor's needs, and even resisted acknowledging life's mystery.[11] It was used by Mounier as a way to describe the spirit of indifference which, for him, pervaded the modern world and threatened the very spiritual roots of truth and faith. In accord with the writings of the young Marx, Mounier conceived the bourgeois as alienated and alienator.[12] Even more in accord with the spirit of Péguy, Bloy, and Maritain, he depicted the bourgeois as being devoid of real passion, and deprived of all ideals and values. In sum, the concept bourgeois registered at the deepest levels of Mounier's feelings, evoking for him the essence of the individual, class, society—an age that found no divinity in creation, no humanity in life.

> We are far indeed from the hero. The rich man of the classical period is himself fast disappearing. On the altar of this sad world there is but one god, smiling and hideous; the Bourgeois. He has lost the true sense of being, he moves only amongst things, and things that are practical and that have been denuded of their mystery. He is a man without love, a Christian without conscience, an unbeliever without passion. He has deflected the universe of virtues from its supposedly senseless course towards the infinite and made it center about a petty system of social and psychological tranquility. For him there is only prosperity, health, common sense, balance, sweetness of life, comfort. Comfort is to the bourgeois world what heroism was to the Renaissance and sanctity to mediaeval Christianity—the ultimate value, the ultimate motive for all action.[13]

Mounier converted this moral criticism into a global and historical criticism of the modern age by making individualism the principle of all alienation (be it religious, philosophical, or social) and the commanding idea of bourgeois civilization. It is, thus, understandable how Mounier held individualism accountable for the worst evils of the present: it destroyed culture by separating ideas from truth, art from universals, truth from politics; it negated the possibility of a human economy by establishing the dominance of the market, profit, and production at the expense of worker and society; it corrupted the public life by making self-interest, free-enterprise, and class concerns the measure of all human activity.

Mounier also gave a historical dimension to his criticism of the modern world by suggesting that individualism has caused Western man to lose contact with God, nature, and mankind. In a section titled "The Decadence of the Individual: From Hero to Bourgeois," Mounier sketched briefly what he believed was Western man's descending path from medieval sanctity to twentieth century mediocrity.[14] In a following section titled the "Disembodied Spirit," he (equally predictably) described how Cartesian dualism drove a mortal wedge into the medieval conception of man, leaving man divided between mind and body, spirit and matter, truth and action.[15]

In a third section, titled the "Disruption of the Community," Mounier critically examined the social and political consequences of this individualism.[16] Assuming that liberalism was in essence a continuation and a political expression of the larger metaphysical individualism which he had traced from the Renaissance on, he contended: "It is precisely because liberal individualism cut man off from his spiritual attachments and material necessities that it also disrupted natural communities."[17] Not entertaining even the possibility that liberalism had done any good or carried within it any spiritual potential for the creation of new institutions and human relations, he judged liberalism as anarchic and destructive.[18] He accused it of philosophically and legally creating sovereign individuals, whom he depicted as "primitive and solitary, without ancestry or flesh, endowed with an undirected and inefficacious freedom."[19] He denounced liberalism for having sanctioned the most destructive social-economic forces of the nineteenth century: uncontrolled *laissez-faire* economics; abstract and contractual notions of government; the primacy of "law," money, and production.

By further postulating that all contemporary collectivisms were born, both in theory and fact, out of their opposition to the destructive principles and processes of liberal individualism, Mounier transformed his criticism of bourgeois civilization into a dialectical critique. That is, in making collectivism the dialectical antithesis of bourgeois individualism, he sought to explain not only the existence of both individualistic and collectivist elements that permeated all aspects of contemporary life, but to depict the central drama of the nineteenth century as the dynamic and intensifying struggle between these two faces of bourgeois civilization. He further believed, in conformity with this dialectical mode of analysis, that the present generation was witnessing nothing other than the final struggle between individualism and collectivism.

On this basis, it is easy to see how Mounier interpreted Fascism, National Socialism, and Communism as the latest and most awesomely advanced expressions of collectivism. Each of them for Mounier was born out of its opposition to the most serious ravages of individualism; each proposed a "total solution"—an "inverted theocracy"—which was intent on subjugating free men and free institutions to a monolithic and centralized power which would leave no area of human activity outside its control. Taken together, Fascism, National Socialism, and Communism constituted on the side of collectivism, as did bourgeois and capitalist France, England, and America on the side of individualism, certain proof for Mounier of the nearing end of the present civilization.

While Mounier recognized that, in its strictest sense, Fascism designated only the regime that arose in Italy in 1922, he also recognized that in a wider sense Fascism could be used to describe an immense post-War historical phenomenon which occurred throughout Europe.

> In an exhausted and disillusioned country, which in every case is possessed of a strong sense of inferiority, a collusion takes place between a proletariat that is in despair economically and ideologically, and a middle class that is fearful of being proletarianized (for them the equivalent of communism). An ideology takes form under the intuitive power of a leader. It plays at once upon a whole historical arsenal of forgotten virtues: honesty, national reconciliation, patriotism, sacrifice for a cause, loyalty to a leader. It insists at the same time on the necessity of revolution, thereby capturing the youngest and the most extreme elements. As a tempering influence, it evolves a program which is essentially petty bourgeois: national prestige, social restorations (of land, the crafts, the guilds or corporations, the historic past), cult of the saviour, love of order, and respect for authority. In so far as it is more or less conservative, even though only provisionally and in so far as it is national, the movement willy-nilly rallies to its standard various allied forces; the old nationalisms, the armies, the money powers. . . .
>
> The fascist systems originated in various countries whose historical situations were quite similar. But it was only after their arrival in power that they organ-

ized and developed their doctrines, which are gradually becoming more and more systematized in our day. They define a type of society, a type of man and type of life that are incontestably similar in spite of different national temperaments. It is this fact which today allows us to speak of fascism in a wide sense.[20]

Italian Fascism and National Socialism had for Mounier even more awesome unities once in power. One with its Caesarism and the other with its racism denied all transcendence.[21] One with its activism and philosophy of the total state and the other with its *Volkish* myths and its aspirations for a new *Reich* conferred total sovereignty on the collective nation. Despite what he considered valid in their concerns for a restatement of the spiritual community in the modern world, Mounier described their attempts to build alternative societies with such words as hateful, fanatical, exploitative, tyrannical, dictatorial, intoxicated and violent. Ultimately they were, for Mounier, enemies of the truth, the person, and mankind.

For Mounier the Soviet Union also testified to the final stages of bourgeois civilization. Neither its worker ideology nor its promised future vindicated, in Mounier's opinion, its retrogressive and dehumanizing totalitarianism.[22] Rather than pointing the way towards a better future, he believed that the Soviet Union was not only born out of individualism's destructiveness, but that its very hopes to be more rational, productive, and autonomous as a society threatened to create a world that was against man.

While not identifying Marxism as a theory with Soviet practice, Mounier believed it also threatened to enchain man to bourgeois myths.[23] Marxism asserted the older and more aggressive myths of heroic and rationalistic bourgeois civilization. While it also denied transcendence to human consciousness and creativity, it found its inspiration in a rational and optimistic view of man's power. In accord with its eighteenth century forerunners, Marxism, in Mounier's opinion, never profoundly wrestled with the problems of good and evil and the inevitable spiritual conflicts between man's public and private lives. Instead it assumed that man's knowledge and will were adequate to his dreams. It gave the revolutionist the malignant notion of total conquest, it offered the oppressed a place amidst bourgeois comfort and security and, as a new ideal, it promised in a new form the bourgeois myth of human dominance and control.

Mounier believed that Marxism's narrow rationalism and the specific milieu in which it took form condemned it to a view of man and socie-

ty "*à la* 1880"; that is, it was damned to have the markings of a historical era which lived and produced under a "physico-mathematical"
world view. While acknowledging that, in the hands of its most recent
interpreters, Marxism escaped being a vulgar and mechanistic materialism and asserted the worth of action and the concrete man against
Hegelian idealism, Mounier insisted that Marxism, nevertheless, was a
"truncated realism." Its ultimate denial of the realms of freedom and
intelligence, destroyed it as an ethic and metaphysic.

Nevertheless, Marxism leveled an incisive and comprehensive criticism
of bourgeois individualism. Borrowing a phrase from Maritain, Mounier
spoke of Marxism's "avenging recognition of material causality." He
attributed worth to Marxism on other important matters: (1) it contributed significantly to an understanding and improvement of society;
(2) it grasped the historical importance of the proletarian movement
and gave it its first general justification; (3) it exposed many of the interests and practices which were concealed within bourgeois spirituality
and ideology; (4) it correctly called attention to the formation of ideologies and modern man's alienation from his own work and being.

Not only did Mounier steadily incorporate these insights into his Personalism in the 1930s, but he admitted that Marxism alone at the moment voiced the legitimate needs and hopes of the oppressed. In fact,
he faced Marxism as integrally part of Personalism's greatest test which,
in his words, was to effect "the separation of true values from the established disorder of our day and the separation of Marxism from the
revolution that is imperative."[24] Within this test he found an ultimate
challenge to Personalism, for its outcome would determine nothing other than whether Personalism would be able not only to offer a global
and historical criticism of bourgeois civilization, but to transform itself
into a living doctrine for the building of a new historical order.

In the introduction to the *Manifesto*, Mounier wrote of the challenge:

> Historically the crisis that presses upon us is more than a simple political
> crisis or even a profound economic crisis. We are witnessing the cave-in of a
> whole area of civilization, one that was born towards the end of the Middle
> Ages, was consolidated and at the same time threatened by the industrial age,
> is capitalistic in its structure, liberal in its ideology, bourgeois in its ethics. We
> are taking part in the birth of a new civilization whose characteristics and be-
> liefs are still confused, mixed with the decadent forms or the convulsive prod-
> ucts of the civilization that is disappearing. Any program of action that does
> not attain the dimensions of this historical fact, is nothing but servile and emp-
> ty work. Five centuries of history are in the balance, five centuries of history
> are undoubtedly beginning to crystallize.[25]

To respond to this dramatic situation, Personalism must become a new "historical ideal."[26] Personalism, that is, must spiritually guide the building of a new human order; it must make the essential moral revolution so that a new city is perceived and sought. To do this Personalism must disassociate the Church from the reactionary vestiges of the past, integrate into itself what is most valid in the new collectivism, and set the guidelines for a new economics, society, politics, and culture. But the cornerstone of Personalism as a historical ideal must be a new humanism; for only by offering a new vision of man can Personalism make what Mounier considered the historically necessary "metaphysical response to a metaphysical call." Mounier wrote:

> A new civilization, a new man. We risk more by restricting ambitions than by seeking to reach out a bit beyond our grasp. We know well enough that no age will realize a quite human project without having given ear to the superhuman call of history. Our ultimate goal is the same that we put forth in 1932; patiently, cooperatively to *remake the Renaissance* after four centuries of errors.[27]

At the heart of Personalism was Mounier's declaration of the primacy of the person. In agreement with Kant's categorical imperative, Mounier declared: "No other person . . . no collective whole, no organism can utilize the person as an end."[28] The person, Mounier suggests, is before all else, a free being that adopts, assimilates, lives and affirms values which constitute his uniqueness, authenticate his worth, and make him an absolute in comparison with any other material or social reality.[29] The very worth of Personalism as an historical idea depended for Mounier on its capacity to defend man against all that was antihuman in the modern world.

As Mounier made the concept *person* the antithesis of the modern individual, so he made the concept *community* the antithesis of modern society.[30] Broadly defined as those relations in which men treat each other as persons, the concept community—second in importance in Mounier's Personalism only to the concept person itself—provided him with a bridge from the world of the self to the world of other men. In terms of community, he could define all human relationships from those beginning with the family and those ending with the state in the light of their destruction or perfection of human persons.

The family, in Personalist thought, was considered the first and most natural community of the person.[31] While criticizing its dehumanizing abuses in moralistic and Marxian language, Mounier believed that the family should be a spiritual and biological nucleus which prepared men for the larger community of mankind. In no case, he argued, should the family subjugate the individual member's basic humanity to its needs, and in no case whatsoever should this first community of communities be allowed to fall under the control and rule of the state.

From this treatment of the family, Mounier's conception of education follows.[32] He first identified the two extremes to be avoided. The child cannot be allowed to be formed solely by the state. Conversely, the child cannot be deprived of a full and effective education for the sake of the defense of retrograde or egocentric local and family interests. Mounier denounced neutralism as an equivocal response to this dilemma, for while in theory it falsely restricts itself to the dissemination of information, it in fact propagates the false values of the ruling society. Mounier's response to this dilemma was a pluralist education. This form of education, denying the state a monopoly in education, would nevertheless encourage the state to give each distinct "spiritual family" aid while fostering cooperation among these various families. The formation of communities would be promoted at all levels among teachers and parents by both public and private education.

Of course, Mounier recognized that a solution to the problems of education was contingent upon solutions to larger cultural problems.[33] He cast the question of a Personalist culture in terms of Personalism's rejection of contemporary individualisms and collectivisms. On the side of individualism, there existed a culture in complete deterioration. Its signs were: an audience that thought only of self and property; artists who, if they did not succumb to the forces of money, sex, and leisure, most often gravitated towards realms of the dream, the perverse, the abstract, and other antihuman forms arising from a disordered imagination which had lost all contact with both the universal and the commonplace. On the side of collectivism, there existed the planned cultures of the Communists, Fascists and Nazis which sought to make culture serve their regimes and thereby denied culture the very freedom and transcendence upon which it is dependent.

Aware of the need and urgency to elevate the image of man, and equally aware of the contradictions surrounding contemporary culture, Mounier prescribed three formulas for a Personalist reform of culture: (1) a constant return to the people who were yet free of bourgeois values, (2) a series of separate communities of free artists, and (3) the acceptance of the notion that "there is no culture which is not metaphysical and personal."[34] Mounier knew that, below the help these formulas could provide, there lurked a yet deeper question: how is it possible to bring into existence a culture which rests on universal hierarchies of understanding and value and at the same time offers the freedom and spontaneity of creation essential for any authentic art and culture? The question of a Personalist culture, as is the question of all cultures, was found by Mounier to be inextricably bound to questions of the economic, social, political and international orders.

For Mounier, the contemporary economic order was created and formed by capitalism. At the heart of capitalism he found a destructive belief in "the primacy of economics."[35] Since the eighteenth century this belief has progressively fettered man's basic needs and political rights to the mechanisms of market, production, and profit, and it has come to taint "the whole organism of the person and society so thoroughly that all forms of disorder, even the spiritual, have in them a component or even a dominant element that is economic."[36]

Drawing on a Marxist critique of capitalism, Mounier claimed that capitalism alienates man from his activity and freedom since it deprives man of his social, spiritual, and political rights, and gives the benefits of human work and industry to the few. Furthermore, capitalism's inherent tendency "to ignore the person and to organize itself for a single quantitative and impersonal goal, profit," led to other equal dehumanizing processes: money is made the criterion of service, contracts and goods; money's use, which is inseparably tied to speculation, usurious credit, and other manipulative devices, creates an autonomous economic world which operates regardless of human values and needs. The proprietors of this world, the capitalists, in turn subdue the government, make the worker "a raw material to be bought at the lowest price" and the consumer *one of the coordinates of the profit curve.*[37]

To overthrow capitalism, Mounier insisted that it is essential to achieve first a radical change in man's thought and institutions. The very scale of revision *per se* denies the proposals of those reactionary anti-capitalist forces that would return man to the idealized structure of medieval economy; the modifications of those "little capitalists" who wanted rules more conducive for their competition with the "big capitalists"; the revolution of the social-democrats which "would simply change the personnel of the bourgeois world of comfort, wealth, and respectability"; and the Communists' plans which perpetrate "the whole heritage of the capitalistic disorder: intensive centralization, scientific rationalism, over-industrialization, plus a whole array of new disorders."[38]

For the beginnings of any real Personalist economics, it is essential to subordinate economics to the needs and potentials of men as laborers, consumers, and persons. These needs, in turn, must determine the contours of economic production and exchange. While freedom in economic activity should be given as much latitude as possible, capital and its anonymity must be suppressed; and, even more importantly, labor must be recognized as the one agent that is properly personal and productive in economic activity. While work,, in contradistinction to the ideas of Ford and Stalin, should not be made the exclusive definition of man, it must be recognized as an essential and vital human activity that partly completes and satisfies man. Accordingly, for Mounier, work is a universal obligation, an inalienable right, and a personal value.[39]

Mounier conjectured that establishing a Personalist economic system would entail at the outset reliance on the state because of the resistance that would be offered by powerful vested economic forces. In taking up this task, the state would initially have to avoid the specious reform of the technocrats and the pseudocorporatism of the traditionalists, for the former are prone to tyranny, while the latter often reinstitutionalize capitalistic competition and engage in totalitarian manipulation. Once having initially subjugated the centrifugal forces of capitalism, the state then would have to strain towards a free, decentralized, and man-centered economics.[40] Mounier was aware, of course, that the path necessary here was precarious; for states, once given power, rarely return it.

The question of a Personalist economics consequently opened for Mounier the larger question of a Personalist politics. "From the personalist point of view," Mounier wrote, "there is no difference between the German primacy of the nation, the Italian primacy of the state, liberal statism 'at the service of' the nation and the political dictatorship of the proletariat 'at the service' of the proletarian-nation."[41] They were all variants of the same malignant reality": "the cancerous development of the state in all modern nations, no matter what may be their political form."[42] Sounding like a proponent of the anarchist tradition, Mounier went on to say that it was the state which had "annexed all economic life" and constituted "the most formidable menace which personalism had to encounter in the political arena."[43]

Against this "gnawing statism" Mounier posited a pluralist state.[44] Re-echoing older traditions of nineteenth century conservative and anarchist thought, he proposed a state based upon and derivative from inter-personal, regional, and national communities. This state's justification would be its service to persons and communities. Its power and sovereignty would, in turn, be limited by divesting it of all spiritual authority, affirming the absolute rights of persons and communities, and opposing it with a free government and various independent bodies and customary and natural rights. The sovereignty of the state would thereby be lost "in the immense sea of particular sovereignties."

However, reflecting his rejection of what he believed was the impotence of the Third Republic, Mounier charged the state with sufficient authority and strength to carry out essential social reform and maintain rights. Thereby he gave it the right to arbitrate disputes between various social and economic orders, and the right, when arbitration failed, to coerce individuals and social bodies that threatened the material or spiritual independence of persons composing the community. Mounier also charged the Personalist state with the no less sensitive tasks of defending persons and diverse spiritual families while encouraging various types of social cooperation and initiative.

The pluralist state found its final end in the pursuit of a Personalist democracy.[45] The Personalist democracy should, in Mounier's opinion, avoid anarchic individualism and Jacobin statism. While not based doctrinally on absolute individualism or popular sovereignty, it should not, nevertheless, practice selective disenfranchisement by denying voters' eligibility or by interest-controlled representation. Instead, a Personalist democracy must be based on a small or decentralized state. Established upon the recognition of autonomous bodies in matters of education and economics, it would exist within the framework of universal suffrage, referendum and juridical checks and balances. It would entrust its leadership to a spiritual elite. Together, these elements would constitute a Personalist democracy that could pursue what Mounier considered the highest end of the state, society, and politics: "the unlimited personalization of humanity."[46]

Again at the level of international politics, Mounier had to confront the question of the state, which he considered to be at the center of the tragedy of contemporary civilization.[47] Without establishing his criticism by either a broad or thorough historical approach, he suggested that states had achieved their political and ideological aggrandizement by using nationalism to exploit a natural and limited patriotism "precisely as capitalism makes use of the natural sentiment of personal property, for the purpose of giving both sentimental nourishment and moral justification to a system of interests or to collective egotisms."[48] If, in opposition to the present rule and practice of the nation-states, a new world order is to be achieved, present approaches to international affairs have to be discarded. Pacifism was inadequate because it rested on a naive and abstract "bourgeois optimism" that ignored the fact that even war might be essential to defend more important values of freedom and justice.[49] Arms races and diplomacy, the most accepted means of international affairs, only further propagated a system of violence and lies which inescapably were weaving men and societies into the fabric of war. Of the League of Nations and the internationalism which surrounded it, Mounier bitterly remarked: "We are now witnessing on all sides the breakdown of the last worm-eaten vestiges of a pseudo 'democracy' and a pseudo 'League of Nations' in a Europe that has resigned itself to its fate."[50]

Believing that neither a reform of the League of Nations nor a reform of state nor a balance between a just nationalism and a just internationalism could deliver Europe from the violence that was engulfing it, Mounier held several steps essential to cure the international disorder at its vital center: first, he called for "*the disappearance of the nationalistic state* under whatever form, whether it be fascist, communist, or supposedly democratic." It must be undermined both from without and within its political and economic enterprises. Second, it was essential to make "*the dissociation of peace and of the institutions of peace from the entire disorder of modern civilization*—from the disorder of capitalism, from treaties of war, from secret alliances." Third, he recommended "*a general and controlled disarmament along with the progressive elimination of conscription*"; and fourth, "*the gradual establishment of a juridical society of nations endowed with an organism capable of adaptation and revision in place of the present league.*"[51]

Anticipating the federalism that inspired so many European thinkers in the aftermath of the Second World War, Mounier hoped that each of these measures would bring into existence a new Europe. This new Europe would be based not on sovereign states but on living communities of persons represented directly outside, as well as along with, states. International law would thereby be brought into the highest service of a Personalist world and civilization by having the defense of persons as its highest goal.

Personalism expressed nothing less than Mounier's effort to create a new Europe. His aspirations, however incomplete in their historical and theoretical development, reveal, nevertheless, an effort to make Personalism a new historical idea. He proposed: (1) a culture that would rejoin art and artist, universality and individuality in a new consciousness of man and his experience; (2) an economic order that would replace five centuries of the principles and practices of Western economics; (3) a pluralistic society that would necessitate a reordering of public and private orders, state and society relations. In its ultimate political goals, Personalism voiced Mounier's desire to found a state which would be decentralized, bound by law, subjected to the rights and needs of persons and communities, and committed to the service of mankind.

In light of these aspirations, Mounier's Personalism can be understood in two ways. Positively, it is possible to argue that Personalism is both an accurate perception of the fundamental problems afflicting Europe in the 1930s and an authentic program for any real reconstruction of contemporary man and civilization. Negatively, it is possible to argue— as we first do—that Mounier's Personalism was utopian, and is best understood today as an historical document from a past epoch rather than a living doctrine for contemporary man.

Living in a world that had undergone the shattering experiences of the periods from 1914 to 1919 and 1929 to 1932 and afterwards, Mounier's interior sense of crisis was of such total dimensions that he was driven to formulate his understanding of the present with such a sweeping and imprecise metaphor as the rise and fall of civilizations. Once having given himself over to this apocalyptic notion of the end of civilization, he did not hesitate to postulate the end of all that he spiritually opposed—the idealisms and materialisms challenged by Bergson and Chevalier, the bourgeois spirit detested by Péguy and Bloy, and all the insecurities, uncertainties and inhumanities seen, suffered, and dramatized by his generation. Nor did he hesitate to suggest that at the heart of the modern world's tragedy was man's rejection of God. This religious and apocalyptic aspect of Mounier's thought is further revealed by his failure to give adequate attention to the perennial, if not total, rule of those hard, irrational, mute forces of human history (population, technology, statecraft, etc.) as well as by his equally serious failure to grasp the historical continuity of Personalism with many of the problems and aspirations of nineteenth century liberalism and socialism.

However, perhaps even more important than the apocalyptic and religious aspect of Mounier's Personalism, are the utopian elements which support it. What other term than utopian so adequately describes Mounier's belief that those fundamental and enduring dilemmas of individual and group, society and state, state and church could not only be beneficially reordered for man, but even essentially transcended in order to create an entirely new human order? On this point, Mounier was assenting to nothing other than the proposition that man's knowledge and will—not events and forces—could establish a new order of human existence.

Conversely, it might be maintained in a positive rather than a negative sense, that Mounier is utopian only to the degree that anyone must be who is truly committed to what man is today and what man can be tomorrow. If, in other words, Personalism is utopian, it is utopian because it arose from Mounier's authentic effort to meet and resolve the tragedies that have encompassed the West and the world since 1914. From this point of view, Personalism is considered both apocalyptic and utopian simply because all serious human thought, when reflecting on where man is in history and where he will be, must by the nature of its subject run the circle of beginnings and ends, ends and beginnings.

Personalism, when considered in this broad perspective, can be either negated or affirmed on the basis of its apocalyptic and utopian elements. What is essential for a judgment of Personalism, however, is not a war of words nor a confrontation of opposites as ideal and real, but instead a determination of Personalism's claim to offer Western man a new historical ideal. While, of course, no discussion will resolve the matter decisively, a further discussion of Mounier's Personalism in relation to Maritain's Integral Humanism and the events of the years 1938 to 1940—which I now proceed to—might offer further help in historically and culturally delineating the boundaries of the question of Personalism as a new historical ideal.

A New Historical Ideal?

In the 1930s there was a profound unity between Maritain's and Mounier's thought. Both were convinced that contemporary civilization was in crisis and a new humanism was necessary. Together they shared Ber-Berdyaev's hope for a new Christian order of civilization.[52]

Maritain's *Integral Humanism,* published in 1936, reveals the unity that existed between the older Thomist's and the younger activist's search for a new historical ideal.[53] Having already admitted the impossibility of reestablishing a past historical order of human existence, and willing now to acknowledge at least the theoretical compatibility be-

tween democratic and cultural pluralism and Christianity, Maritain
made in his *Integral Humanism* his first full effort to define the nature
and form of a new civilization.[54]

While more explicit in his Christian concerns than Mounier, Maritain
also believed that a new humanism was the key to a new civilization.
For Maritain, this new humanism must be predicated on man's ability
and desire to go beyond himself and the collective doctrines and realities, bodies of race, class, and nation. And here again, as found in Mounier's Personalism, it must have as its end the love of persons and the
willingness to sacrifice oneself to "the concrete good of the community
of persons."

A new Christian humanism's first challenge was, in Maritain's opinion,
to respond to an age suffering unto death because it had lost a true
vision of man. Its first task was to refute the man-centered humanism
which had proposed that man was everything, and had left him nothing.
"[This] kind of humanism believes," Maritain wrote of what he titled
anthropocentric humanism, "that man is the center of man, and therefore of all things. It implies a naturalistic conception of man and freedom. . . . [It] merits the name of inhuman humanism and its dialectic
must be regarded as the *tragedy* of humanism."[55]

In terms of his opposition to this "anthropocentric humanism,"
which he had already attacked in *Three Reformers,* Maritain found the
essence of the modern crisis. To trace the destructive development of
this humanism was tantamount to giving a history, explanation, and critique of his times.

First, Maritain asserted that Renaissance naturalism conceived man independently from Christian revelation; second, Reformation theology
conceptually divorced faith, grace and salvation from human reason and
freedom; last, in the eighteenth and nineteenth centuries, "an absolute
humanist theology," fathered by Descartes and the *philosophes,* recast
the image of man in accord with the distorted visions of Rousseau,
Kant, Comte, and Hegel.[56] Man was declared respectively by them to be
naturally good, the end of knowledge, the measure of being and the
purpose of all past and future existence. But, in fact, the outcome of
this "anti-human humanism" was devastating for man: man lost his vision of himself, his nature, reason, and God; he had been led on a destructive spiritual journey, which began by announcing him to be a sovereign and autonomous entity, and ended, in the hands of Darwin and
Freud, by claiming that he was no more than an immanent part of a

biological process and a conscious point of intersection between the demands of the sexual libido and the death instinct.[57]

Maritain believed that, after "all dissociations and dualisms" caused by this anthropocentric humanism, his age was "witnessing a dispersion, a final decomposition." "Individual man," Maritain prophesied, "is ripe for abdication. . . . He is ripe to abdicate in favor of collective man."[58] The emergence of collectivism and the bankruptcy of bourgeois liberalism made clear for Maritain, as they did for Mounier, the historical and spiritual drama of choosing between a new order of Christian civilization and annihilation.

Marxism, for Maritain, most profoundly declared the reality of collectivism in the twentieth century.[59] On one hand, it announced the certain end of the bourgeois order. Its vengeful perception of the material world, its irrefutable exposure of the anti-human character of capitalism, and its zeal to transform society were challenges that excelled the spiritual reserves of bourgeois civilization. On the other hand, Maritain interpreted Communism's messianic drive to liberate man from all limits and to install him in a self-sufficing secular kingdom as the most vengeful face of an anthropocentrism that would acknowledge no material, natural, or spiritual boundaries in its drive for total power.

Catholicism alone, Maritain assumed, could respond to Marxism and the emerging totalitarianisms by furnishing Western man with a "new historical ideal." For Catholicism to build a new civilizational order it is necessary, according to Maritain, to establish a conception of a "new Christendom."[60] This Christendom, unlike that of the Middle Ages, would not be conceived as sacral but as "secular and lay." Correspondingly, the temporal order, while ultimately subordinate to the spiritual, must be admitted as constituting an immediate end, to use Maritain's more precise expression, "an infravalent end." In fine, Maritain proposed that man's political, social, economic, and cultural activity be considered a distinct realm with its own important and unique ends.

Having once admitted the partial independence of the secular order, Maritain addressed himself to the question of a Christian philosophy of society and politics. In agreement with Mounier's Personalism, he articulated his philosophy in opposition to individualism and collectivism. Opposed to various expressions of bourgeois social, economic, cultural, and political individualism, he postulated Thomas' notion of the common good as describing a reality higher than the sum of individual ends and interests and pertaining to the material and spiritual welfare of mankind at large. In specific opposition to collectivism, and obviously again drawing on Thomistic and Christian thought, he asserted that every individual has a spirit and a personal destiny which joins him to an order infinitely higher than any immanent political and social order.

On the basis of these two principles, the common good and the spiritual value of the individual person, Maritain developed the framework of a new humanistic economics, society, and politics. Virtually point by point, Maritain's framework corresponded with and anticipated that of Mounier's *Manifesto*. The state was given sufficient strength to curb the anarchisms of capitalism, "liberal parliamentarian politics," and juridical bourgeois law. Conversely, the state's authority and the collectivisms of society were counterbalanced by a defense of the private life, family, and culture as domains of freedom, and by federalist, corporate, and pluralist conceptions of society and politics. In essence, Maritain also aspired to a "pluralist democracy."[61]

Maritain believed that this political and social philosophy, in conjunction with the more important notions of a new humanism and a new Christendom, constituted the basis for a "new *concrete historical ideal*." The "concrete historical ideal"—a concept borrowed by Mounier—was, according to Maritain, at variance with the utopian constructs of such thinkers as More, Fénelon, and Saint Simon, because it was not "isolated from existence," nor did it seek to express an *absolute maximum* of social and political perfection.[62] The concrete historical ideal was, in his own words:

> An ideal essence which is realizable. . . . Realizable not as something made, but as something on the way to being made, an essence capable of existing and calling for existence in a given historical climate, and as a result corresponding to a *relative* maximum of social and political perfection, a maximum relative to that historical climate; and precisely because this essence implies a real relating to concrete existence, it merely presents a framework and a rough draft which may later be determinative of a future reality. . . . I feel, nevertheless, that the notion of concrete historical ideal and a just use of the notion would enable a Christian philosophy of culture to prepare future temporal realizations by exempting it from the need to pass through a utopian phase or to have recourse to any utopia.[63]

Maritain believed that his Christian humanism was a concrete historical ideal for several reasons. It was a call to human freedom. It provided a "prospective image" around which men could unify their reasons and wills. It offered, as liberalism and socialism once had, a long-range goal that (1) demanded the transfiguration of its enactors, that (2) gave a distinct and developing understanding of the world, and (3) set forth an outline of the visions which would command the social, economic, political and cultural reordering of civilization. Maritain hoped that he too was bearing witness to the demise of one civilization and preparing the formation of another.

Taken together, Maritain's humanism and Mounier's Personalism are questionable as "a new historical ideal." As theories, they appear to reflect rather than transcend the tensions and dilemmas of their epoch. Their thought does not appear to be pointing in any tangible way towards a "realizable order," but instead appears to be illuminating, by its own tensions, dilemmas, and agonies, the insoluble and awesome relations that had come to exist between war and revolution, nations and ideologies, since the First World War. The massive disruptions of European life since 1914—Russian Communism, Fascist Italy, the Great Depression and Nazi Germany—did not lead Mounier and Maritain to make an empirical historical exploration in depth of the unities and disunities between nineteenth and twentieth century European experience, but encouraged them instead to think in terms of reversing centuries of history and building new world orders. When one thinks of their attempts to transcend the state, capitalism and individualism, they appear to have returned to the Europe of the period of 1815 to 1848, where one hears of plans for abolishing the state, forming new communities and establishing man in new orders of civilization.[64]

On another plane of historical analysis, Mounier's Personalism and Maritain's humanism retrospectively voice Catholicism's position in the modern world far more clearly than they suggest a new historical order. For instance, their mutual search for an alternative to individualism and collectivism takes up in its own way what, since the French Revolution, had increasingly become the Vatican's burden: the necessity of finding a political doctrine which, while freeing the Church from the older abuses of statisms (Gallicanism and Josephism), would enable the Church to contend ideologically and institutionally with the theory and practice of liberalism and socialism.[65] In their defense of the person, the family and pluralism and in their aspirations to serve the worker and destroy the greatest abuses of capitalism, Mounier's and Maritain's social and political thought can be read as supporting commentaries on the social encyclicals of Pius IX, Leo XIII, Pius X, and Pius XI. In this perspective, the mixture of apocalyptical and eschatological tones of Mounier's and Maritain's considerations of the modern world reflect the Church's painful uncertainty about its security in the modern world and the equally strong certainty that it has and will again be able to win the hearts of men and help them build their civilizations.

Ultimately, it can be said that Mounier's and Maritain's views of their age were not first formed around the questions of peace and war or freedom and equality. Instead, their views were, like those of Bloy and Péguy, a projection of their hopes for a world wherein the sacral and religious would infuse and enlighten the material, the political and the social; a world wherein men in all their thoughts and activities would measure themselves against the eternal verities of faith. Beyond what seemed to them the crumbling of one civilization, there appeared the possibility—the hope for a "New Middle Ages."

While Maritain and Mounier repudiated a reactionary return to the past, their hope for a new historical order, a new Middle Ages, carried within it many undifferentiated dreams. The sacral would reconfigure the profane; the spiritual would touch the material; faith and reason, philosophy and science, contemplation and work, charity and society would be rejoined. Rising out of the new ideal city of different families, cultures, and religions, near the horizons of Maritain's and Mounier's view of a new world, the spires of the medieval cathedral could be seen —the medieval synthesis was being resighted.

The events of the late 1930s and 1940s, however, stripped their dreams of much of their content. From the Spanish Civil War on, it became clear that Pius XI's call to aid the workers in *Quadragesimo Anno* (1931) as well as the Church's effort to free itself from being a captive of either the political right or the left did not mean that the Vatican and great numbers of Catholics were unwilling to aid Franco or make anti-Communism a justification for defense of the established order. Perhaps what had been clear to Mounier and Maritain at the time of *Esprit's* founding in 1932, now became painfully certain: the Church would react to the modern world rather than lead in the creation of another.

In addition to this, there no longer seemed to be any hope in a coalition which reached beyond or was conceived independently from the contemporary terrain of French and European politics. Steadily since the Stavisky Affair of 1934, the young men of Mounier's generation specifically, and almost all Frenchmen in general, were confronted with the immediate and empirical choices of contemporary politics. Choices over domestic legislation and foreign policy, armaments, and conscription, were conducted evermore in the language of pro-Communist and pro-Nazi and in terms of the larger questions of French restoration and French survival. The number, the diversity, and the urgency of these choices turned the young men's heads away from the larger civilizational concerns of the 1929 to 1933 period, and made all coalitions that were conceived outside or beyond the coming test of force appear less and less real.

The sense of the coming of a war and the felt urgency of action took hold of the young men of *Esprit* and Mounier. Hitler and Germany crowded the horizon. The project of the long range revolution was steadily eclipsed by the speed and scope of daily events. After Munich in 1938, Mounier and the members of *Esprit* acknowledged that war was inevitable and soon on its way. Events, and the choices that go with them, were again proving themselves more real than theory.

Foremost among these choices was that of defending one part of bourgeois civilization against another. On what grounds was France to be defended against Germany? What of individualistic England? Collectivist Russia? Capitalist America? War meant mobilization. War meant nationalism—bourgeois and worker, Christian and Communist filling the same regiments. It meant that the world was to be reordered once again not by the spirit but the deed, not by ideals and revolutions, but tanks and planes.

The War came before theory could meet the choices. In the most awesome way, power, for the second time in the century, was posing the most profound questions of values and civilizations in the form of nations and armies. War, in its devastating and catastrophic course, was to dictate; Mounier and Maritain could only respond. Without the anticipation and verve that marked Péguy's long and expectant preparation for the First World War, Mounier and Maritain left the confines of the ideal city and enrolled themselves on the side of Republican France. Both were again to rethink the world in which they lived and hoped to change.

CONCLUSION

MID-CENTURY: THE END OF ONE APOSTOLATE AND THE BEGINNING OF ANOTHER

IN 1950, EMMANUEL MOUNIER died. He was struck down by a second heart attack in the prime of his life. As continuing editor of *Esprit* and proponent of Personalism, Mounier pursued up to his death a revolution to establish a new civilization. In 1951, Maritain published his *Man and State*. This work crowned the second and last stage of Maritain's intellectual development, which was the search for a new Christian social and political philosophy. At mid-century, Mounier through death and Maritain through age reached the limits of their efforts to understand and change their times.

In one sense, the declaring, the waging, and the ending of the century's second world war did not alter the deepest premises of their thought. As men of the twentieth century, they were too well acquainted with the cataclysmic and tragic ruptures of the contemporary world to be internally devastated or intellectually routed by the panorama of violence and destruction which accompanied the Second World War. Since their earliest writings, both of them had prophesied about the "logics of destruction" operative within the modern world. Each of them, to speak hypothetically, could have nodded affirmatively to those other post-War French thinkers who also spoke of the "logics of destruction": Bertrand de Jouvenel's understanding of the geometric growth in power since the French Revolution, Simone Weil's logic of the totalitarian state, Albert Camus' analysis of the genesis of metaphysical revolution in our times, and Raymond Aron's conception of the twentieth century as "the century of total war."[1] Each of their analyses of the West in all their variations could have been understood by Maritain and Mounier as sharing part of what was the heart of their critique of the modern world—that is, man and civilization had lost all

- 148 -

sense of the human and divine, that there were no longer any boundaries or measures in man's world.

Likewise existentialism, which became so popular in the post-War era, did not present itself as anything radically new to them.[2] Through the 1930s they had, in calling for a new form of heroic Catholic action and in underlining the social implications of the doctrine of the Incarnation, already affirmed that man must be understood in his situation.[3] That man was alone, an idea and a feeling which existentialism voiced in various ways, could be heard by them to be on one hand the reiteration of an obvious truth, and on the other hand a more dramatic restatement of the bourgeois individualism of the 1920s. That the forces of irrationality are ever present in the human situation spoke to them ambivalently of both the truths that they had learned from the mystics and Pascal, and of the errors which they denounced in Freudianism, Fascism, and Nazism. In short, Mounier and Maritain had come to know the thought of Kierkegaard, Nietzsche, Blondel, Berdyaev, Marcel, and Malraux, as well as Scheler, Heidegger, and Husserl before the Second World War.

Alterations of French and European political life also in one sense did not challenge the most fundamental premises of their political and social thought. The defeat of France—that "strange defeat of France" in the words of the distinguished French historian, Marc Bloch—was certain proof for Mounier and Maritain of the bankruptcy of bourgeois parliamentarian rule and the need for a whole new political order.[4] Vichy was interpreted by them to prove that the older political and religious forces no longer had a living political doctrine for the modern world and that clearly some form of democracy must now represent the political ideal of the future.[5] In turn, Mounier and Maritain idealized the Resistance as the beginnings of a spiritual and social regroupment of forces which would build a new future human community.[6]

The post-War French political situation itself also confronted Mounier and Maritain with little that caused them to question the root assumptions of their political judgments. The Christian Democratic Party (*Mouvement Républicain Populaire*), which was the most unusual political expression of the post-War period and which with no exaggeration can be said to be in great part an indirect result of their intellectual activity in the 1930s, was in their eyes still bound to the bourgeois order.[7]

It was seen especially by Mounier as incapable of the task of making the revolution that was necessary, and destined to further tie Christianity to those social classes and political forces and processes that resisted all and any significant change. The Communist Party likewise had not fundamentally changed for Mounier and Maritain. Despite the massive Communist gains in the immediate post-War era because of the Party's important role in the Resistance, they continued to see the Communists as mistaken in their ultimate philosophy of man and society, and in their allegiance to Moscow.[8] The Fourth Republic itself appeared to Mounier as the tragic reenactment of the Third Republic. The phoenix that had arisen from the ashes was weak in vision and strength, and still caught within the forest of party interests.[9]

The fate of Europe and the world during and after the War also in good measure convinced Mounier and Maritain of the validity of their pre-War understanding of their times.[10] Almost needless to say, the horrors of Nazism, the ultimate violences of anti-Semitism and nuclear weapons, as well as all other tragic revelations that came forth from a world in total war, were taken as proof of the end of one order of civilization. The various proposals for a new human order, such as world and regional federalisms, more developed charters of human rights and pronounced concerns for pluralistic solutions, revoiced for them aspects of their new historical ideals.

Thus, in one sense, the years of the 1940s were like the years of the 1930s—confirming years. As 1914 to 1918 had confirmed for Maritain the authenticity of his earlier prophecies about the destructiveness of the modern world, and as the years 1929 to 1932 and after had confirmed for both Mounier and Maritain the "truth" of their sense that the world was in total crisis, so, it might be said, the 1940s strengthened Mounier's and Maritain's convictions that there was need for a new civilization.

Specifically in the case of Maritain, it is clear that on one level the War substantiated his view of the modern world. While the First World War had had no great effect on the roots of Maritain's thought because of his preoccupation with matters of faith and the certitude of his apocalyptic vision of all things modern, the Second World War came when Maritain was too old, it would seem, and too experienced a public combatant to go through one of those radical crises of understanding which are most often reserved for younger men.

From young manhood on, Maritain had been in the thick of many of the major battles of French intellectual life. First, he participated in the ideological struggles and the passions of pre-First World War French culture: there were his first attacks against positivism and materialism, clericalism and the bourgeois; and then, after his conversion, there were his battles against secularism and modernity, Bergsonism and Modernism. Then in 1926-1929, there were the painful religious, political, and personal battles involved in his separation from the reactionary *Action Française*. Then there was the search for a new social and political philosophy from the late 1920s onward. With this search came the tensions involved in helping found Catholic radical journals like *Esprit* and *Sept*, the opprobrium and hostility of being considered a Communist and, above all else, the agitation and passions of the "era of Manifestos" during which Maritain, along with fellow Catholics of "the left," publicly censored the acts of Italy and Germany and called for the reform of nations. Then he experienced the Spanish Civil War which, like no other tragic event, had brutally prepared the imaginations of men of good will for the Second World War.

On the eve of the Second World War, it is hence not surprising that Maritain was speaking of the "twilight of civilization."[11] Behind him lay forty years of criticizing the *monde moderne,* twenty-five years of witnessing unprecedented violence and anarchy. Ahead there lay events of which only the most naive could be without premonition: "Europe," Maritain said, "can no longer be considered isolated: it is not Europe alone, it is the world, it is the whole world which must now resolve the problems of civilization. It is too late for the Europe of yesterday. For the crucified Europe of today it is not too late."[12]

When the War did come in 1940, Maritain was on his annual lecture tour in the United States. He remained there during the War, doing all that he could to serve France by broadcasting weekly talks to France, lecturing on war and peace, seeking to win American support for France, and helping to found the *Ecole Libre des Hautes Etudes* in New York. However, below this heightened activity, the War did not seem to have altered Maritain's assumptions about and judgments of his age. He saw the fall of France as the expression of evils he had already diagnosed in the Third Republic. Among these evils he listed the betrayal of France by a bourgeois elite, the undermining of the body and ideas of the French worker by capitalism and the doctrine of class warfare, the disruption of French political life caused by the Russians' Machiavellian manipulation of the Popular Front.[13] The attack of Germany, needless to say, was viewed by Maritain as the nearly inevitable act of the most spiritually irrational of twentieth century collective states.

Instead of empiricizing and politicizing his analyses of the modern world, the War, especially in its initial stages, imparted a new energy and confidence to Maritain's concern for themes on the rise and fall of civilizations. "The present war," he declared, "is not a simple national war, nor a policing action, nor a holy war, nor an ideological war, it is a war of civilization."[14] With this dramatic theme at his command, Maritain could reiterate the essence of his world view in the 1930s: "What was collapsing was the long tottering structure of the French bourgeois."[15] What was dying was what Péguy "calls the modern world, roughly speaking a four century block of history."[16] And if one civilization were in reality perishing, then there was the possible emergence of a new civilization, one that was perhaps depicted in *Integral Humanism*. The War and all its disasters therefore could possibly be seen as announcing the coming end of such older foes as secularism, materialism, individualism, and idealism and the beginnings of a "new heroic humanism."

The central challenge of this new order demanded that the evils of Locke's individualism and Rousseau's collectivism be transcended and that a new society, Christian in inspiration, be built to assure mankind of freedom and justice. "The France of tomorrow" would be, Maritain hoped, "Christian and liberal."[17] The French who suffered today like the Jew and Pole, could be tomorrow the leader of Europe and the world.[18] Out from the tunnel of war at the edge of the horizon, Maritain believed it was possible that the lion of power and the lamb of faith could lie down together. The Second World War had made him stronger in his condemnation of the past, more fervent in his hope for tomorrow.

Even more so did the War appear to strengthen Mounier's world view of the 1930s. With Munich, Mounier had hastily begun to prepare himself and the readers of *Esprit* for the possibility of and even the moral necessity for war. There was, in his opinion, no time to rethink Versailles; power, he had come to believe, was the only language Hitler understood. This new position, which placed Mounier squarely on the side of France, did not mean, however, that he intended to suspend his criticisms of the Republic and bourgeois life. France and England were not perfect; the choice was still not simply yes or no to 1789; to go to war was not to defend France's and Europe's decadence but to defend the value of their traditions and potentials against the tyranny of Hitler.[19]

Consequently, when France fell so quickly, Mounier found a "clear explanation" for that "strange defeat." Again fault was assigned to the political life of the Third Republic and the effects of its bourgeois individualism. In fact, Mounier's temporary indecision over what position to take regarding the newly formed Vichy regime—which his old mentor Chevalier had entered as Minister of Youth and Education—was in no way due to Mounier's sympathy for Vichy's ideas and leaders, but stemmed from what can be called no less than his hatred of the bourgeois Republic.[20]

Neither France's defeat nor the formation of the Vichy government deflected *Esprit* from what Mounier considered its essential goal. In January 1940, he wrote: "The essential goal of *Esprit, which events have in no way altered,* is to rethink a civilization at its turning point."[21] In the same issue, in an article titled "Gardons-nous de notre ennemi, l'Ennemi," Mounier also declared that the victory of *Esprit* could be achieved only through its fidelity to a single task: "Refaire la France avec l'Europe."[22] Thus, in 1940, Mounier revoiced the basic message upon which he had founded *Esprit* in 1932—"Refaire la Renaissance."

After the suppression of *Esprit* in August 1941 by the Vichy government, for its "subversive character," and after having been briefly (correctly or incorrectly) jailed in 1942 for being a leader of *Combat,* Mounier resumed his essential work—the preparation of a new civilization.[23] As his works from this period show, Mounier's efforts continued to be inspired by the goals upon which he had created *Esprit* and formed his Personalism. In the *Affrontement chrétien* (1944), he once again and more fervently called on Christians to disassociate themselves from the corrupt spirit of bourgeois life and thought. In his *Treatise on Character,* written in 1944, as he did later in his *Introduction to Existentialisms* (1946), *What is Personalism?* (1947), and *Personalism* (1949), Mounier sought to clarify and strengthen the anthropology upon which his Personalism was based. In the last years of the War, his thought turned evermore towards the task of building a whole new society. To this end he projected the creation of a Personalist college and sought to transform *Esprit* into a community dedicated to the total service of human society.[24]

The War, consequently, did not interrupt Mounier's basic views of the 1930s. Instead, it convinced him of the essential validity of his thought. His reasons for refounding *Esprit* after the War were in fact nearly identical to those which had led him to found it in 1932. There was, in his opinion, a total crisis in civilization; there was a need for a total response to it; and only a total revolution was adequate as a response. So the *Esprit* which reappeared in 1945 was reborn out of the same consciousness which had brought it to birth over a decade before.

In 1945, when Mounier resumed the publication of *Esprit* and Maritain took the post of French ambassador to the Vatican, it would seem that War had not altered their basic view of the modern world. It would also seem that Valery's awesome phrase—"Everything is threatened by the magnitude of the event," which "witnesses the powerlessness of the ideas men have trusted in"—did not apply to Maritain and Mounier in the face of the Second World War.[25] The Second World War had supported rather than disrupted, strengthened rather than refuted, their view of the modern world.

Yet a truth of this sort, on a matter of this magnitude, does not constitute an absolute; nor does it altogether exclude its opposite. That is, to accent only the way in which the War confirmed Maritain and Mounier in their world views would be not only to overlook the profound ways in which the War fundamentally altered their criticisms of and ideals for their times, but the way in which the War in one sense irreparably shattered Mounier's Personalism and Maritain's integral humanism as comprehensive world views.

Above all else, Europe and the world in the post-War period had become too complicated to analyze simply in terms of the dialectics of bourgeois individualism and collectivism. For this notion, and the concepts associated with it, were no longer adequate for the articulation of a comprehensive description of the present. Furthermore, the situation of post-war Europe and France dispelled some of the apocalyptic and utopian ideas which had accompanied their earlier notions of a "new historical ideal" and a "new historical order." It taught them that the world of events does not follow *per se* the logic of ideas, that the making of a new civilization would be, as the present situation was, inseparable from the specific actions of states and statesmen. This is to say that, in varying degree, their understandings of their times as well as the philosophies, metaphors, and mythologies which formed them, had been tempered by events, by a truer awareness of how unpredictable and precarious the public life is; and that, thereafter, both Mounier and Maritain were to be more cautious in their sweeping indictments of past orders of civilization and less bold in their talk of new orders of civilization.

In more precise historical terms, the world of post-1945 was no longer as simple as the world of the late 1930s. The United States versus Russia, Western Europe versus Eastern Europe, the developed world versus the underdeveloped world—these were some of the new and complex axes around which a valid epochal consciousness had to take form. The destinies of France and Germany could no longer be viewed, as they were in the 1930s, as the key to all world historical change. Beyond this, there was the singular reality of nuclear weapons which might cut short all prophecy, except that of annihilation. Thus, in post-War Europe, the art of declaring definite certitudes about the present and the future was practiced only by the most insensitive and the most dogmatic.

Equally important in changing Mounier's and Maritain's consciousness was the way in which the War from its outset had imposed decisive choices upon them. Foremost among these choices was that of being for or against France. While their response was never in doubt, the implications of having to make this choice were immense: in choosing France, they admitted that values existed within France's national life which justified the fighting of a world war; in siding with France, Maritain and Mounier found themselves defending, in great part, the very liberal bourgeois civilization which they had previously condemned. Also implicit within their defense of France were new-found sympathies for both bourgeois England and America, as well as collectivist Russia. In sum, the War caused Mounier and Maritain to rethink their view of Europe and the world, and the results of this rethinking, as we now go on to see, led Maritain in the direction of American liberalism, and Mounier in the direction of European humanist socialism.

The feelings and beliefs of Bloy and Péguy for France—France, "the Israel of the New Testament," *la France éternelle*—were never really distant from the mind and spirit of Maritain. Maritain would not accept the defeat of France as the defeat of the French spirit. He would not admit that the French people, even though admittedly "politically demoralized," were "morally demoralized."[26] For below the fraudulent values of the bourgeois elite which had led France to the disaster of defeat and the dishonor of the Vichy regime, there existed for Maritain a French nation which was an incarnate repository of values. "Liberty," Maritain said, "flowed in its veins."[27] Its role once again, Maritain prophesied, would be to serve as the center of European consciousness and conscience; its mission would be to bring a new accord between liberty and Christianity.

As the War developed, Maritain became increasingly generous in his treatment of the United States. The once "capitalistic United States" became the America which represented ever more an approximation of his historical ideal for a new Christendom. He later wrote in his *Reflections on America* (1957): "While at the time of writing *Integral Humanism* [1934] my perspective was definitely European. . . . I gradually became aware of the kind of congeniality which existed between what is going on in this country and a number of views I had expressed in *Integral Humanism.*"[28] While, he continued, a concrete historical ideal is far distant from any present reality, there exists a unity between it and "the direction of certain characteristics of American civilization." Among these characteristics, Maritain noted that the United States is a classless society in the social sense and is not *embourgeoisée.* It is going beyond capitalism towards a society of communities and persons. Its separation of state and society, its juridical and political assurance of separate bodies approximate a "pluralist ideal." It is a religious society, thanks to a state that affirms the person, freedom, law, and the rights and diversity of religions. In addition, "The United States is . . . the only country of the West in which society is conceived as being basically a religious society." Nor is it likely to lose this characteristic: "It is unlikely that, however powerful it may be, the antagonistic trend towards secularism will ever be able to tear away from *American civilization . . . . [its] religious inspiration.*"[29] Maritain was willing even to extend this immediate interpretation into a far-ranging "history" of the United States' origin and meaning: "Far beyond the influences received either from Locke or the eighteenth century Enlightenment, the American Constitution . . . is deep rooted in the age old heritage of Christian thought and civilization."[30] From this point of view, Maritain was ready to promote "American civilization" as the soil for a new Christendom, as "the focus towards which all really progressive energies at work in history since the disintegration of the Middle Ages have been tending."[31] America had thus become for Maritain "crucially important for the hopes of mankind and the future of civilization."[32]

It was this belief in the United States and its institutions—as exaggerated as it was—that brought Maritain fully into the mainstream of contemporary liberal political theory, and culminated a political evolution which led from the *Action Française* to the pluralism of his Integral Humanism of the 1930s, and then to American liberal democracy. In sum, it was the support which Maritain gave France and the United States during and immediately after the Second World War that baptized him as a liberal and made him indisputably an adherent to the tenets of freedom, brotherhood and social justice.[33]

In terms of this vision, which we have taken the liberty to call "American liberalism," Maritain as never before was willing in the post-War period to sympathize with the liberal hopes of his contemporaries and ready to admit the diverse forms of actions required of men in different situations, if they were to test their reason and will against the demons of power and the hard complexities which go with any authentic search for peace and justice.[34] Much of what had been negative and hostile to the modern world in Maritain's thought of the 1920s and 1930s was cast aside, and much of what had been positive and constructive in his earlier thoughts was brought forth. For instance, in *Education at the Crossroads* (1943), Maritain, under the influence of Adler and Hutchinson, spoke of an education that was not only preparatory for theological and philosophical wisdom but would prepare all citizens for the task of building a good society.[35] Of all his works, however, it is *Man and State* (1951) that culminates the second and last significant stage of Maritain's thought and offers his most positive counsel to his times.

Man and State was intentionally written as a work in political philosophy. In its deepest aspiration, the work was indeed revolutionary; its primary goal was to deny totally the validity of the notion of sovereignty. In doing this, Maritain undertook two projects. First, he criticized the entire concept of modern sovereignty as it grew out of the works of Machiavelli, Bodin, and Hobbes, and sought to demonstrate how the progressive equating of nation, body politic, and state bred the modern totalitarian state. Second, against the concept of the sovereign state and the naturalism upon which it is based, he attempted on the basis of natural law to show the primacy of the person and the communities which form the body politic, and the need for a body politic wherein power is divided, rights are assured, and full participation is possible.

Beyond these goals, Maritain further proposed societies committed to a true democratic charter which would recognize the freedom, rights, and traditions of its citizens and would rest on a mutual cooperation between families and society, Church, and state. On the world level, he advocated that men direct their reason and good faith into the building not only of a legal world government but a true world political society which would be freely conceived in its origin, pluralist and democratic in its form, and fraternal and cooperative in its essence.

Maritain thus came to advocate a type of liberalism. While still fearing the "democracies" inspired by Locke, Rousseau, and Hegel and while still convinced that Christianity alone was the source of a real personalist democracy, Maritain was now willing to stress the importance of the human city, the need for free institutions within it, and the broader need for a just and humane democratic order. In fact, it might reasonably be concluded that, by mid-century, Maritain was willing to take the modern world seriously. It was no longer simply an ample target for his philosophical derision, nor a useful vehicle for articulating his religious apologetics; rather the modern world had become for him an undeniable situation in which man found himself and was forced to seek to build a just and free human order. In a sense, Maritain's political evolution from the Condemnation of the *Action Française* in 1926 to the period of post-World War II had led him not only forward in time towards a rapprochement with the assumptions and practices of contemporary American democracy but backwards in time to the liberalism of Woodrow Wilson. As many discovered the absolute need for a democratic world during and in the aftermath of the First World War, so Maritain made this discovery in the course and aftermath of the Second World War.

As the War had led Maritain further in the direction of what can be called the "liberalism of Woodrow Wilson," so it led Mounier towards what might equally boldly be called the "socialism of Jean Jaurès." After the War, Mounier never demobilized. In fact, he cautioned against it. His attacks on the bourgeois and bourgeois liberalism were not softened. While admitting that *Esprit* had erred in the past by being too a-political, Mounier continued to seek a revolution too radical to be realized in the confines of the Republic's political life.[36] Neither the newly created Christian Democratic Party nor the revitalized Socialist Party of Léon Blum held any attraction for Mounier. They were considered by him to be trapped within the spirit and practice of the bourgeois world. The Radicals were summarily dismissed by Mounier as fragments of the Third Republic's archaeology; and Mounier could not help but see De Gaulle as a fascist leader *malgré lui-même*. Thus, aside from making one brief and abortive effort, along with Sartre and other left-wing French intellectuals, to form an independent radical party in

1947, Mounier continued his combat for a new world outside the political arena.[37]

One major part of Mounier's combat was for a France and a Europe freed from both American and Soviet domination. He specifically feared that the entire West would be transformed into a fortress to defend capitalism, leaving Europe's sole meaning a sterile and retrograde anti-Communism. Even more deeply, he feared what he saw prefigured in the Marshall Plan and the Atlantic Pact: the inevitable polarization of Eastern and Western Europe and then the equally inevitable preparation for a war that no system of justice could exonerate, no civilization sustain.[38] Hence, the revolution that Mounier once declared essential for France and Western Europe now had to be fought for on a truly global scale.

Increasingly in the post-War period, Mounier defined this revolution in terms of a real socialism—"*un veritable socialisme.*"[39] Increasingly, he came to underline the compatibilities that he believed to exist between socialism and his Personalism, and more and more to interpret the past and present aims of *Esprit* in reference to a search for a true socialism. Significantly, Mounier transformed Péguy's phrase that the revolution will be moral if it will be at all to read that the revolution also will be social if it will be at all. Thus, Mounier defined the revolution ever more in terms of the worker and the city, and as he realized the irreversible character of industrialization and urbanization for the fate of underdeveloped peoples as well as for the future of mankind, it was inevitable that Mounier's long standing discussion with the Marxist would be expanded and intensified.

Marxism appealed to Mounier for several reasons. Like no other doctrine, Marxism spoke out against the exploiter on behalf of the exploited. In the course of less than a century it had won the workers to its side and just recently it had filled the ranks of the Resistance. Like no other doctrine, Marxism, in Mounier's opinion, had a claim not only to the legacy of 1789, but to the possibility of a second French Revolution. At one and the same time, Marxism seemed to Mounier, as it did to much of the French Left, capable in great part of describing realistically the present conditions of man without sacrificing its capacity to call man to a better future. While, of course, critical of Marxism's philosophical assumptions and the French Communist Party's subservience to Moscow, Mounier nevertheless believed that the Communist Party currently carried within itself a real and needed revolutionary potential and that Marxism as a doctrine set forth the material and social goals that must be met by mankind.[40]

In fact, Mounier's socialism in great measure arose out of his attempt to integrate the truths he found in Marxism and the Communist Party with his Personalism. In turn, his conception of socialism was indistinguishable, except in its more pronounced Christian and existential accents, from the broad tenets of humanistic socialism which resurfaced in post-War Europe. Already sharing in large measure its critique of capitalism and its sympathy for the worker, Mounier further assimilated to himself its belief in freedom, equality, and justice, as well as its desire to participate in and lead the material and spiritual advance of all mankind. It was to this conception of humanistic socialism, a socialism that Péguy and Maritain had first shared with Jaurès over a half century ago, that Mounier came more and more to pay allegiance in the post-War period.

It was this humanistic socialism that also ultimately denied in advance Mounier's attempts to carry on a successful dialogue with the Communists after the War. For, in addition to the inescapable metaphysical contradictions between Christian and materialist and the unavoidable conflicts between Church and Party, there was another reason why agreement between Mounier and the Communists was not possible. That is, Mounier ultimately was a son of Jaurès, and not of Lenin. Tactics, class warfare, state centralism, party discipline, and much else that is inseparable from the reality and doctrine of twentieth century Communism, were radically antithetical to Mounier's unvarying faith in reason, freedom, and brotherhood.

What Mounier had come to strive after in the post-War period was a world of freedom, equality, and justice—a world in which the political and economic benefits of the two greatest nineteenth century revolutions, the French and the Industrial, would be shared by all men. Increasingly, before his death, Mounier treated his Personalism less and less as a fixed and pure doctrine, and more and more as a state of spirit, in which mankind could travel in its attempt to rejoin and reshape the highest hopes of the nineteenth and twentieth century forces of hope. When, in fact, death overtook Mounier in his forty-fifth year, at mid-century, he was still *en route* towards a better understanding of the past and towards a fuller commitment to man's temporal future. In one way, he was simultaneously in the process of finding his way back to Péguy's and Maritain's first teacher, Jean Jaurès, while seeking to move forward towards a full spiritual and material philosophy of our times that would incorporate into itself all that was positive in conservatism, liberalism, and especially socialism. In yet another way, perhaps more simply said, Mounier was becoming less and less the prophet of ends, less and less the utopian of beginnings, and more and more simply a Christian humanist committed to serving his times.

****

What then had been the meaning of the War and its aftermath for the evolution of Mounier's view of the modern world? First, the realities, complexities, and problems that arose out of the War and its solutions forced him to transform his world view of the 1930s. His Personalism, like Maritain's Integral Humanism, clearly was not adequate as either a criticism of the modern world or as a new historical ideal for contemporary Europe and the world. The criticism that he had leveled against contemporary "bourgeois civilization" and the last five centuries of European history no longer clearly applied to the present conditions of man and the world. His criticisms had to be rethought. In rethinking them, it was impossible for Mounier to continue to treat Europe since the Renaissance, and particularly since the French Revolution, simply under the rubric of the rise and fall of bourgeois civilization. And thereby, much of what he had inherited from the turn-of-the-century religious, aesthetic, and philosophical critiques of the *monde moderne* had to be discarded; and many of the socialists' hopes, which he had once dismissed as naive, had to be readopted and reintegrated into his world views.

As his criticisms were deprived in great part of their assumed universality regarding Europe and the world, he was driven, as was Maritain, to revise his notion of a new "historical ideal." It became clearer to Mounier that the values of freedom, equality, and fraternity were far more contingent on specific institutions, traditions and national lives, and hence were tied far more closely to the immediate landscape of the empirical choices of economics and politics. Talk of the destruction and creation of civilizations became more distant for him as the realities and dilemmas of the post-War world became more pressing and encompassing. Although neither Mounier nor Maritain abandoned his criticisms of individualism and collectivism or forsook his hopes for a new spiritual and social order for man, both were led to internalize, empiricize, and limit these notions as total world views. Mounier's Personalism, like Maritain's humanism, passed more and more from being total philosophies of man and society, and more and more became interior dispositions towards modern man and his conditions.

Both Mounier and Maritain had to supplement their philosophies of their times if they were to be made applicable to the world of 1945. To accomplish this, both had to look elsewhere for allies. Mounier, who was always far less explicit in his philosophical and religious positions and far more explicit in his political and revolutionary positions, returned to Jaurèsian socialism so that he could more fully enter into the world of worker and social revolution. Maritain, who in the course of the War had developed a deep respect for the United States and its liberalism, returned to the world of Wilson, to the world of World War One, to the world he had not understood the first time he experienced it—in order to find a doctrine which gave man's freedom and dignity and the Church's truth and faith a hope of better days.

The differences between the younger Mounier and the older Maritain in one sense had become profound in the post-War era. One had chosen the world of freedom and law; the other, the world of justice and equality. One continued to pursue primarily a philosophical renaissance, the other aspired after a social revolution. The profundity of these differences between Mounier's socialism and Maritain's liberalism was mirrored in the simple fact that in the post-War period they had found separate vocations. Maritain became French ambassador to the Vatican of Pius XII, and in 1948 returned to teach in the United States where he remained until his retirement in 1960. Mounier stayed on at *Esprit* in France, looking for the revolution that would be both social and moral. Yet another reflection of the profound differences that came to exist between them is the fact that Maritain's thought continued well into the 1960s to appeal to Christian liberal forces of North and South America, whereas Mounier's influence conversely still has its appeal primarily in various radical quarters in both West and East Europe.

As is shown by his last major work, *The Peasant of Garonne* (1966)—a work Maritain wrote in a monastery in France where he had taken refuge the last decade of his life—Maritain had been, as he always was, more committed to the apostolate of the intellect and truth.[41] Mounier, conversely, was more of the apostolate of action and charity. In fact, the analogy is tempting to see Maritain pointing by his more explicit concern for doctrine, truth, and the institutional Church to

Pius XII, and Mounier in his openness, trust, and action pointing to Pope John, and what some call his revolution. Let it be said more simply that while neither Mounier nor Maritain fully anticipated Pope John in his remarkable willingness to call attention to what is good in a world that has known violence and anarchy since 1914, together they aided in further taking the Church from the modern world into the contemporary world.

Of yet equal importance, Mounier and Maritain can be considered similar by their humanism. In the post-War years, both remained friends of reason, freedom, and justice. They refused to despair of a better civilization and equally refused to repudiate what they considered of worth in the past. In a word, they are to be numbered among those who in the twentieth century constitute the party of humanity. That is, in the largest traditions of Western rationalism and humanism, they continued to believe in the ultimate worth of each person, and continued to assert the urgency of finding an education for man in these times.

Of the two men, however, it is Mounier who most fully speaks to, and is an example for man today. Far more than Maritain, Mounier knew and taught the fact that man is a historical creature, subjected to the domain of radical change, forced to experience yesterday's thoughts falling short of today's happenings. In effect, Mounier knew best that man has no certain science, no fixed ethic, no comprehensive morality—no education to guide himself and his times on a certain course.

However, the worth of Mounier lay not in what he acknowledged regarding man's limits, but in what he hoped for in terms of man's potentials. Confronting not only those abiding dilemmas found in man's temporality but also those immediate agonies of a world caught up in the anarchy of power, Mounier persisted in his search for a philosophy of and for our times. Recognizing man's historicity, he taught men to be responsible for one another, to resist a world that was turned against man, to live beyond the realities of sterile sciences and egotisms, degrading politics and ideologies. He taught men further to live for those things that matter most—truth, love, friendship, conscience—those things alone that give man a final dignity when events have cast his clearest calculations aside, when force has undone his best works, when power has made his ideals seem but abstractions. While this in itself may not constitute a needed philosophy of and for our times, herein does lie an invitation for men and women to become more than what the powers and anarchy of their times would make them.

NOTES

INTRODUCTION

1. Under the revealing title *The Obstructed Path: French Social Thought in the Years of Desperation* (New York, 1968), H. S. Hughes has sought through a series of essays to fathom the dilemmas and paths that French intellectual life has pursued in search of a meaningful understanding of the twentieth century. See esp. his treatment of Maritain and Marcel in Chapter Three, "The Catholics and the Human Condition," 65-101.

2. Taken from the text of Emmanuel Mounier, "Jacques Maritain," radio broadcast for the *Service des Emissions vers l'Etranger de la Radiodiffusion Française,* January 22, 1945, 1.

3. For a work that treats the passage of the French Catholic Church from reaction to rapprochement during the 1920s and 1930s, see Harry W. Paul's *The Second Ralliement: The Rapprochement between Church and State in France in the Twentieth Century* (Washington, D.C., 1967).

CHAPTER I

1. Jean Lacroix, "Mounier éducateur," *Esprit*, No. 174 (December, 1950), 839.

2. Paul Ricoeur, "Une philosophie personnaliste," *ibid.,* 861.

3. The standard biography of Mounier is Candide Moix, *La pensée d'Emmanuel Mounier* (Paris, 1960); some shorter studies are Jean Conilh, *Emmanuel Mounier* (Paris, 1966), Lucien Guissard, *Emmanuel Mounier* (Paris, 1962), and Giorgio Campanini, *La rivoluzione cristiana. Il pensiero politico di Emmanuel Mounier* (Brescia, 1968).

4. Emmanuel Mounier, "Refaire la renaissance," *Esprit,* No. 1 (October, 1932), 5-51. This article, like almost all of Mounier's significant works, is found in *Oeuvres de Mounier* (4 vols., Paris, 1961-1963), which in turn is described in the bibliography.

5. Emmanuel Mounier, *Manifeste au service du personnalisme* (Paris, 1936). The English translation of this and other works of Mounier are given in the bibliography.

6. Emmanuel Mounier, *La petite peur du XXe siècle* (Paris, 1948).

7. Emmanuel Mounier, *Affrontement chrétien* (Neuchâtel, 1945).

8. Emmanuel Mounier, *Introduction aux existentialismes* (Paris, 1946). Emman-

9. Emmanuel Mounier, *Qu'est-ce que le personnalisme?* (Paris, 1947) and *Le personnalisme* (Paris, 1949).

10. Almost all Mounier's works return to the theme of the destructive nature and relations of individualism and collectivism in contemporary civilization. For example, see the sections "Le personnalisme et la révolution du XXe siècle" in Mounier's *Personnalisme, Oeuvres de Mounier*, III, 507-525, and "La crise du XXe siècle," *Qu'est-ce que le personnalisme? ibid.*, 203-207.

11. *Ibid.*, 179.

12. Emmanuel Mounier, *Traité du caractère, Oeuvres de Mounier*, II, 7.

13. Henri Marrou, "Un homme dans l'église," *Esprit*, No. 174 (December, 1950), 888.

14. In the *Traité du caractère*, Mounier initially discusses the uses and limits of the concept character (Chapter One "Les approches du mystère personnel," 9-71) and man's basic environments of body, energy, family, peers, etc. (Chapter Two "L'ambiance collective," 72-113), (Chapter Three and Four "L'ambiance corpo- relle," 114-165, 166-224). Then after a discussion of man's emotions ("Les puis- sances d'ébranlement," 225-256) and the various determinants of man's percep- tion of the world ("L'acceuil vital," 257-326), which constituted his fifth and sixth chapters, Mounier arrives at his primary concern: how one becomes a per- son. There he examines the self and its relation to reality ("La lutte pour le réel," 327-394), the formation of the self and action ("La maîtrise de l'action," 395-467), the development of the person in relation to others ("Le moi parmi les autres," 468-522), and in relation to his own self-affirmation ("L'affirmation du moi," 523-600). Mounier concludes in his eleventh and twelfth chapters with the highest activities of the person, the intellect and action ("L'intelligence de l'ac- tion," 601-679) and life and spirit ("La vie spirituelle dans les limites du carac- tère," 680-750). From the beginning to the end of the *Traité*, Mounier is con- cerned about the conditions and struggles that man must undergo to reach is full personhood.

15. Mounier said this in an interview on the *Treatise* in 1946. It is found in *Bulletin d'Emmanuel Mounier*, No. 15 (March, 1960), 8.

16. For one brief critical historical discussion of psychological analyses of the crises of modern times, see the Introduction of Armando Catemario's *La società malata. Saggio sulla filosofia di Fromm* (Napoli, 1962), 1-22.

17. For Mounier's briefest and clearest view of the historical development of bourgeois civilization and the twentieth century bourgeois, see his section "Le monde moderne contre la personne," and the chapter included within it titled "La civilisation bourgeoise et individualiste," in his *Manifeste au service du per- sonnalisme, Oeuvres*, I, 489-542, 491-498.

18. *Ibid.*, 492-496.

19. Great parts of Mounier's writings can be read as a commentary on the ques- tions of what is the intellectual. For Mounier's examination of the intellectual and in particular his concern for the alienation of the bourgeois intellectual, see his

earliest comments on Gide, Benda and others (*Mounier et sa génération, Oeuvres,* IV, 432, 487) and his later analyses of Malraux, Sartre, and others (*Introduction aux existentialismes, Oeuvres,* III, 69-175). For his psychological analysis of types of intellectuals (Rousseau, Stendhal, Goethe and others), see *Traité,* 548-565, *passim.*

20. Emmanuel Mounier, *Qu'est-ce que le personnalisme, Oeuvres,* III, 208.

21. Each subject within the *Traité* is based upon the assumption that to deny the existence of reality or any part of it is destructive. By making his central assumption that the human person achieves his full form only in conformity with his nature and through the acceptance of the reality of the self, the other and the world, Mounier found a principle that allowed him to explain: (1) most psychological aberrations and maladies, like mania, paranoia, schizophrenia, avarice, etc.; (2) different personality types like introvert, extrovert, etc.; (3) the unities of the self and various forms of the self's experience of the world, such as family, work, class, group, etc.; (4) the various stages of personality growth, infancy, puberty, etc.; and (5) the various assumptions, perspectives and results of various schools of psychology represented by Freud, Adler, Jung, Janet, etc. Obviously from this broad perspective of the self and the world—the interior and exterior world, the material and spiritual world—Mounier could join his psychology to his philosophy, theology, ethics, and politics.

22. *Traité,* 523.

23. For these definitions of the self, see *ibid.,* 523-525.

24. *Ibid.,* 524-525.

25. On a less theoretical level, seeking a bridge between the metaphysical unities of man as a being and the empirical unities between types of men, Mounier, as the title *Treatise on Character* suggests, relied on the concept of character. While not conceding an absolute validity to characteriology, Mounier did believe that men conform to basic patterns in terms of their proclivity towards or away from emotions and action, reflection and force; and a description of these patterns does constitute a general global description of a given man's character. Thus, Mounier believed that, by the heuristic adoption of a characteriology, he could explore and compare the similarities and differences that exist between individual selves. For Mounier's use of character and characteriology, see Chapter One, "Les approches du mystère personnel," and Chapter Twelve, "La vie spirituelle dans les limites du caractère," *Traité,* 9-71, 680-749.

26. Mounier, *Le personnalisme, Oeuvres,* III, 486.

27. *Ibid.,* 486.

28. *Traité,* 573.

29. Mounier, *Personnalisme, Oeuvres,* III, 489. Underlining in the original is Mounier's.

30. *Ibid.,* 455.

31. With no intention of being inclusive, Mounier mentions here the names of Kierkegaard, Scheler, Marcel, Berdyaev and Nédoncelle as examples of personalist philosophers, *Qu'est-ce que le personnalisme, ibid.,* 208-209.

32. For the central place of action in Mounier's thought, see for example "La maîtrise de l'action," and "L'intelligence à l'action," which form the eighth and twelfth chapters of the *Traité,* 395-467 and 601-679, as well as a section titled "L'engagement," *Personnalisme, Oeuvres,* III, 498-506.

33. *Ibid.*, 503-506.

34. For Mounier's concept *optimisme tragique*, see *ibid.*, 450. For a work which almost in its entirety is developed around this concept, see his *La petite peur du XXe siècle, Oeuvres de Mounier*, III, 341-425.

35. Mounier, *Le personnalisme, Oeuvres*, III, 450.

36. In the course of the 1940s, Mounier came to see a compatability between his Personalism and Chardin's guiding notion that all existence is the movement towards greater consciousness and spirituality. For various aspects of their personal and intellectual relationship, see *Qu'est-ce que le personnalisme, Oeuvres*, III, 210-211, and "Lettres de Teilhard de Chardin à Mounier," *Bulletin des Amis d'Emmanuel Mounier*, No. 27 (January, 1966), 29-32, as well as Madeleine Barthélemy-Madaule, *La personne et le drame humain chez Teilhard de Chardin* (Paris, 1967), esp. 302-322, and André Ligneul, *Teilhard and Personalism* (New York, 1968), esp. 1-6, 77-82.

37. Matt. 10:39.

38. This quotation from Mounier's *Affrontement chrétien* was cited in *Esprit*, No. 174 (December, 1950), 776.

39. Mounier, *Traité*, 676-677.

CHAPTER II

1. The two basic sources for a study of the young Maritain are Raïssa Maritain, *The Memoirs of Raïssa Maritain: We Have Been Friends Together and Adventure in Grace*, trans. Julie Kernan (Garden City, New York, 1961), and Jacques Maritain, *Carnet de Notes* (Paris, 1965)

2. Jacques Maritain, *Carnets*, 16-17.

3. *Ibid.*

4. Joel Colton, *Léon Blum: Humanist in Politics* (New York, 1966), 18-19.

5. Eugen Weber, "The Secret World of Jean Barois: Notes on the Portrait of an age," *The Origins of Modern Consciousness*, ed. John Weiss (Detroit, 1965), 107. For a radically different interpretation of Jaurès and his socialism, *cf.* Harvey Goldberg, *The Life of Jean Jaurès* (Madison, 1968), esp. 77-93.

6. For an excellent introduction to these three men and their times, see Michael Curtis, *Three Against the Republic: Sorel, Barrès and Maurras* (Princeton, New Jersey, 1959).

7. Jacques Maritain, *Carnets* 24. According to Wallace Fowlie, Maritain's earliest poems also show the influence of Verlaine and Mallarmé, *Ernest Psichari: A Study of Religious Conversion* (New York, 1939), 46, 151. For mention of the influences of Tolstoy, Nietzsche, and Spinoza upon Maritain, see Raïssa, *Memoirs*, 42, 63.

8. For the way in which symbolism became a means to poetize all of one's existence, see Edmund Wilson's classic *Axel's Castle* (New York, 1959), esp. 18-22. Wilson views symbolism as a second wave of romanticism. As romanticism reacted against the rationalistic and mechanistic thought of the eighteenth century by asserting the primacy of the mysterious over the rational and the poetic correspondence of the soul to all realities of man and nature, so symbolism, its heir, goes on to refuse the mounting naturalism of nineteenth century thought, the historicist conception of man as a product of his environment, and literary natu-

ralism expressed by the Parnasse, Flaubert, and Zola. Within the writings of the radical romantic Gérard de Nerval (1805-1855), in Baudelaire's first reading of Poe in 1847, the lives of Rimbaud (1854-1891) and Verlaine (1844-1896), and within the confines of the circle of France's Coleridge, Stephane Mallarmé (1842-1898), to which came Huysmans and Claudel, converts to Catholicism, Whistler, Degas, Moréas, Paul Valéry, Rémy de Gourmont, André Gide, Oscar Wilde, and W. B. Yeats, we see various steps in the articulation of symbolism as both a poetry and an entire philosophy of existence.

9. Jacques Maritain, *Carnets*, 18-19.

10. *Ibid.*, 24-25.

11. According to Roger Shattuck, symbolism, which was integral to that permanent explosion in all theatres of artistic activity from the 1880s onward, constituted a profound attack against Christian and Enlightenment philosophy, psychology, and morals as expressed by its reverence for the child, concern for the dream, and its cultivation of the ironic and the ambiguous, *The Banquet Years: The Origins of the Avant-Garde, 1885 to World War One* (Garden City, New York, 1961), esp. 30-43.

12. *The Social and Political Philosophy of Jacques Maritain*, eds. Joseph Evans and Leo Ward (Garden City, New York, 1965), 319.

13. Raïssa, *Memoirs*, 39.

14. Péguy was not the sole critic of the Sorbonne. For many quarters of the Generation of 1905, in particular for those who, like Georges Bernanos, returned to religion and joined the nationalistic revival, the Sorbonne became a favorite symbol of the loss of France's spiritual values and national strengths. For a general statement of this generation's attack on the Sobronne, see Agathon [Henri Massis] *Enquête des jeunes gens d'aujourdhui* (Paris, 1913). For a dissenting view from this generation, and one that is critical of Péguy's attacks on the Sorbonne, see the semi-autobiographical work, Etienne Gilson, *Philosopher and Theology*, trans. Cécile Gilson (New York, 1962), 21-41.

15. See, for example, his "Durkheim's 'Le suicide,' étude de sociologie," *La Revue Socialiste*, XXVI (1898), 186-190, and "Un economiste socialiste, M. Léon Walras," *ibid.*, XXV (1897), 174-186; and see his "De la situation faite à l'histoire et la sociologie dans les temps modernes," (1906) Charles Péguy, *Oeuvres en prose, 1898-1908* (Paris, 1959-1961), 991-1030, "De la situation faite au parti intellectuel dans le monde moderne," (1906) *ibid.*, 1031-1078, and "De la situation faite au parti intellectuel dans le monde moderne devant les accidents dans la gloire temporelle," (1907) *ibid.*, 1115-1214.

16. For one recent well-done biography of Péguy, see Hans Schmitt, *Charles Péguy: Decline of an Idealist* (Baton Rouge, 1966). For some of the works of Péguy's contemporaries and friends, see Romain Rolland, *Péguy* (2 vols., Paris, 1944), Félicien Challaye, *Péguy socialiste* (Paris, 1954), and Daniel Halévy, *Péguy et les Cahiers de la Quinzaine* (Paris, 1941).

17. Charles Péguy, "Notre patrie" (1905), Péguy, *Oeuvres en prose, 1898-1908*, 801-853.

18. Raïssa Maritain, *Memoirs*, 52-53.

19. Péguy's *Jeanne d'Arc, Oeuvres poétiques complètes* (Paris, 1957), 23-362; *De la cité socialiste, Oeuvres en prose, 1898-1908*, 3-10; *Marcel. Premier dialogue de la cité harmonieuse, ibid.*, 11-86.

20. While one cannot exclude from Péguy's socialism the possible influences of utopians Comte, Saint-Simon, Fourier, and Proudhon, as well as the anarchists Grave and Bakunin, Péguy was tied closely to Herr and Jaurès during the years 1897-1900. For these influences and ties, see Schmitt, *Péguy*, 71-73, 83, Challaye, *Péguy*, 90-106, Rolland, *Péguy*, I, 74-104.

21. Péguy, *Marcel, Oeuvres en prose, 1898-1908*, 11-12.

22. The debates of the Dreyfus Affair fully anticipate the ideological character of the twentieth century. For an excellent discussion of the Dreyfus Affair and the modern intellectual, see Victor Brombert, *The Intellectual Hero: Studies in the French Novel, 1880-1955* (Philadelphia, 1961), 2-34. For a recent interpretation of the Affair and the intellectual, an interpretation not without similarities to Péguy's own position, see Hannah Arendt, *The Origins of Totalitarianism* (Cleveland, 1958), 89-120.

23. The earliest and best expression of Péguy's sense of France's self-betrayal is his essay, "Le ravage et la réparation," *La Revue Blanche*, Vol. XX (1899), 417-432. As late as 1909 in his "A nos amis à nos abonnées" (*Oeuvres en prose, 1898-1908*, 1-52), Péguy considered the Dreyfus Affair an heroic test that only a few individuals had passed.

24. See Charles Péguy, "La crise du parti socialiste et l'Affaire Dreyfus," *La Revue Blanche*, XIX (1899), 626-632; "La crise et le parti socialiste," *ibid.*, 462-468; "L'Affaire Dreyfus et la crise du parti socialiste," *ibid.*, XX (1899), 127-139.

25. For varying accounts of what was involved in Péguy's split with Herr, and the personal and legal altercations involving their publishing house, La Librairie Georges Bellais, *cf.* Challaye, *Péguy socialiste*, esp. 97-106; Rolland, *Péguy*, esp. I, 76-80; Halévy, *Péguy et les Cahiers de la Quinzaine*, 74-81; Schmitt, *Péguy*, 12-15.

26. In fact, Péguy's break with Daniel Halévy in 1910 and Georges Sorel in 1911 was not divorced from Péguy's belief that they were willing retrospectively to compromise the principles and issues involved in the Affair.

27. H. Stuart Hughes, *Consciousness and Society: The Reconstruction of European Social Thought, 1890-1930* (New York, 1961), 347.

28. Charles Péguy, *Basic Verities*, trans. Anne and Julien Green (New York, 1943), 103 and 105.

29. Charles Péguy "De la grippe," *Oeuvres en prose, 1898-1908*, 123-138; "Encore la grippe," *ibid.*, 139-171; "Toujours de la grippe," *ibid.*, 172-204.

30. Sorel made himself completely at home at the office of Péguy's *Cahier's* shop from approximately 1901 until 1909. While the intellectual substance of their relation remains in large part a matter of conjecture, Schmitt, synthesizing what is known about Péguy's relation to Sorel, wrote: "Of humble petty-bourgeois origins, both men had had uncertain and traumatic collisions with socialism. . . . Both were weighted down by an oppressive certainty that French society was decadent and corrupt. Both advocated moral revolution. Time tightened the bonds of common aversions." Schmitt goes on to list among their specific agreements: their recognitions of the "disintegration" of parliamentary life, "decay" of bourgeois conventions, and "bankruptcy" of political socialism; the love of antiquity, which embodied their purist and moralistic conceptions of the ideal city; and contempt for hypocrisy, materialism, and intellectualism, which they identified as bourgeois. Schmitt concludes, as Raïssa infers, that the older Sorel probably only reconfirmed and strengthened the younger Péguy's views, *Péguy*, 113.

31. Raïssa Maritain, *Memoirs,* 64-69.

32. *Ibid.,* 69.

33. For a description of Bergson's lectures, the courses the Maritains took from him and his influence upon them, see *ibid.,* 72-86. For an introduction to Péguy and Bergson, see André Henry, *Bergson, Maître de Péguy* (Paris, 1948) and Emmanuel Mounier, "Péguy, médiateur de Bergson," *Bulletin des Amis d'Emmanuel Mounier,* No. 20 (July, 1963), 3-11.

34. For the best introduction to Bergson, see Jacques Chevalier, *Henri Bergson,* trans. Lilian A. Clare (New York, 1928). For a series of diverse essays on Bergson by some of the masters of French thought and particularly the men of *Esprit* (e.g. Mounier, Béguin, Lacroix, and Davenson [pseud. for Henri Marrou]) see the commemorative work, *Henri Bergson: Essais et témoignages recueillis,* ed. Albert Béguin and Pierre Thévanez (Neuchâtel, 1943).

35. Jacques Chevalier, "Henri Bergson," Vol. I: *Portraits,* found in *Les grands courants de la pensée mondiale contemporaine,* ed. M. F. Sciacca (6 vols., Milan, 1958-1964), 124-125.

36. Henri Bergson, *Time and Free Will: An Essay on the Immediate Data of Consciousness,* trans. F. L. Pogson (New York, 1960), 113-114.

37. In *Time and Free Will,* see esp. Chapter Three, "The Organization of Conscious States, Free Will," 140-221.

38. In *Matter and Memory,* trans. Nancy Paul and W. Scott Palmer (Garden City, New York, 1959), see esp. 233-246.

39. Henri Bergson, *An Introduction to Metaphysics,* trans. T. E. Hulme (revised edition, New York, 1912).

40. *Ibid.,* 81-92.

41. *Ibid.*

42. Henri Bergson, *Creative Evolution,* trans. Arthur Mitchell (New York, 1944); for the overall goal and design of the work, see esp. 204-205.

43. See the entirety of Maritain's important essays, *Bergsonian Philosophy and Thomism,* trans. Mabelle L. Andison (New York, 1955).

44. W. T. Jones, for instance, believes that Bergson's thought was Romantic "in its emphasis on dynamism and continuity, in its denial of the capacity of reason to know the inner nature of reality, and its assertion that reality can nonetheless be known—in intuition," *A History of Western Philosophy* (2 vols., New York, 1952), II, 938.

45. For this construct of the Generation of 1905, see H. S. Hughes, *Consciousness and Society,* 336-344, *passim.* In contrast to the Generation of 1890 (Weber, Freud, Durkheim, Mosca, Croce), which in Hughes' opinion was fundamentally intent on rational theory and the building of social sciences, the Generation of 1905 is depicted by Hughes as irrational activists born out of the atmosphere of impending war. While there is truth in this description, it does overlook the presence of irrationalism, vitalism, and spiritualism in France from the 1880s onward, as well as the sense of despair and the concern for the fragility of civilization that progressively had come to shape European intellectual life since the Franco-Prussian War of 1870. For two broad studies of the theme of decadence and civilization in French thought in this period, see Claude Digeon, *La crise allemande de la pensée française* (Paris, 1959) and Konrad Swart, *The Sense of Decadence in Nineteenth Century French Thought* (The Hague, 1964), esp. 192-212.

46. For Bergson's general influence on French thought, see Romeo Arbour, *Henri Bergson et les lettres françaises* (Paris, 1955), and Georges Fonsegrive, *L'évolution des idées dans la France contemporaine* (Paris, 1920).

47. For this patriotic abuse of Bergson, see the entirety of Agathon [Henri Massi] *Enquête sur les jeunes gens d'aujourd'hui*, as well as Phyllis H. Stock, "Students versus the University in Pre-World War I Paris," *French Historical Studies*, VII, no. 1 (Spring, 1971), 93-110.

48. See Ferdinand Brunetière, *La science et la religion* (2nd ed., Paris, 1906).

49. Anticipating Raïssa's *Memoirs* by a half century, Bourget's major novel, *Le Disciple* (1889), fundamentally argued that secular and relativist values lead to destruction and suicide. Blondel's *L'Action* (1893), an influential philosophical work, argued that choosing and living inescapably raise the questions of freedom, values, and faith. For a work that describes the turn of the century Catholic literary reaction against the modern world and its secularism, see the entirety of Richard Griffiths, *The Reactionary Revolution: The Catholic Revival in French Literature, 1870-1914* (New York, 1965). In turn, for a work that helps make it clear that Catholic intellectuals were in the process of establishing a set of images that could counter the secular thinkers' images of the cleric, the Church, etc., see Joseph N. Moody, *The Church as Enemy: Anticlericalism in Nineteenth Century French Literature* (Washington, 1970).

50. Jacques Maritain, *Carnets* 42-43.

51. Rhetorically anticipating what she will describe as the ultimate importance of Bergson for their discovery of the "truth," Raïssa significantly wrote (*Memoirs*, 69): "We had just made an accounting of all that our professors had given us as provision for life's journey—to us, the very young people who looked to them for principles of true knowledge and just action—and we saw that what we held in our hands was but death and dust. . . . Could we at eighteen or at twenty set up a personal doctrine in opposition to . . . [their] doctrines? Could we refute them systematically, or see clearly for ourselves in what ways they were erroneous?"

52. See esp. Maritain's two major philosophical works, which are composed of essays he wrote on Bergson approximately from 1910 to 1930: *La philosophie bergsonienne* (Paris, 1914), and *Distinguer pour unir ou les degrés du savoir* (Paris, 1932).

53. For the Maritains' writings on Bloy, see Jacques Maritain, *Carnets*, 35, 56, 71, *passim*; Raïssa Maritain, *Memoirs*, 87-141, *passim*; Jacques Maritain, "Le mendiant ingrat," *Léon Bloy* (Neuchâtel, 1946), 31-39; Jacques Maritain, *Quelques pages sur Léon Bloy* (Paris, 1927); Jacques et Raïssa Maritain, eds., *Pilgrim of the Absolute* (New York, 1947).

54. I have relied primarily for my construction of Bloy's view of modern history on Marie-Claire Bancquart, *Les écrivains et l'histoire: Maurice Barrès, Léon Bloy, Anatole France, Charles Péguy* (Paris, 1966). See also the work of Mounier's successor at *Esprit*, Albert Beguin's *Léon Bloy: mystique de la douleur* (Paris, 1948).

55. *Ibid.*, 187. For Bloy's own writings on Salette, on history as redemption through suffering, see eds. Maritains, *Pilgrim of the Absolute*, 229-345.

56. For these characteristics of Bloy, see Raïssa Maritain, *Memoirs*, esp. 87-141, and the writings of Maritain's friend and fellow convert of Bloy, Pierre van der Meer de Walcheren, *Rencontres: Léon Bloy, Raïssa Maritain, Christine et Pietke* (Paris, 1961), 13-78, 79-128.

57. Erik Erikson, *Young Man Luther* (New York, 1962), 14.

58. *Ibid.*, 261-262.

59. This quotation is found in Henri Bars, *Maritain en notre temps* (Paris, 1959), 369.

60. Raïssa Maritain, *Memoirs*, 42.

61. Erik Erikson, *Young Man Luther*, 14-15. For an interesting study of Maritain's contemporary Bernard Shaw, which develops the relation of identity crisis and historical milieu, see Erikson's *Identity, Youth and Crisis* (New York, 1968), 142-150, 185-189.

62. For a classic expression of pre-World War One intellectuals' search for the meaning of themselves and their times, see Romain Rolland's *Jean Christophe*, trans. Gilbert Cannan (New York, 1913). For two good secondary studies on these matters, see Brombert, *The Intellectual Hero* and Micheline Tison-Braun, *La crise de l'humanisme: Le conflit de l'individu et de la société dans la littérature française moderne* (Paris, 1958).

63. For some of Maritain's writings on Psichari, see by way of introduction his "Le témoignage d'Ernst Psichari," *Revue des Jeunes*, XI (December 25, 1921), 670-686, and his introduction to Psichari's classic, *Le voyage du centurion* (Paris, 1948), I-XI.

64. For James' classic study of conversions, which was contemporary with Maritain's conversion, see his Gifford Lectures of 1902 on religious experience, published as *The Varieties of Religious Experience* (New York, 1958), esp. the ninth and tenth chapters on conversion, 157-206 and esp. 161-162.

65. Jacques Maritain, "Le neo-vitalisme en Allemagne et le darwinisme," *Revue de philosophie*, XVII (October, 1910), 417-441.

66. Jacques Maritain, "Confession of Faith," 319.

67. For example, see Jacques Maritain, "La science moderne et la raison," *Revue de philosophie*, XVI (June, 1910), 575-603, "L'esprit de la philosophie moderne. I. Les préparations de la réforme cartésienne. II. Descartes et la théologie," *ibid.*, XXIV (June, 1914), 601-625, and "L'esprit de la philosophie moderne. III. L'indépendance de l'esprit," *ibid.*, XXV (July, 1914), 53-82.

68. For details of Maritain's and Péguy's break, see Raïssa Maritain, *Memoirs*, 151-155, 205-236, and Schmitt, *Charles Péguy*, 22-23, 27-28.

69. Charles Péguy, "Note sur M. Bergson et la philosophie bergsonienne," *Oeuvres en prose, 1909-1914*, 1313-1347. For some of the personal and philosophical factors involved in their struggle, see Griffiths, *The Reactionary Revolution*, 35-40.

CHAPTER III

1. In particular, see Maritain's *Théonas ou les entretiens d'un sage et de deux philosophes, diverses matières inégalement actuelles* (Paris, 1921), and *Antimoderne* (Paris, 1922).

2. During the War Maritain actively engaged himself in writing an affirmative study of the Virgin's supposed appearance at Salette, and thus he was substantiating in his own mind the most reactionary and prophetic elements in Bloy's philosophy of the modern world. Maritain, *Carnets* (Paris, 1965), 113-118.

3. For the weakening of anti-clericalism, see René Rémond, "L'évolution de la notion de laïcité entre 1919-1939," *Cahiers d'Histoire*, IV (No. 1, 1959), 71-87.

4. For these points on the French Catholic right and left, see Jacques Chastenet, *Histoire de la troisième République*, Vol. V: *Les années d'illusions, 1918-1931* (Paris, 1960), 257-258.

5. For some aspects of this Catholic Revival or Renaissance, see *Cinquante ans de pensée catholique française* (Paris, 1955), and Richard Griffiths, *The Reactionary Revolution: The Catholic Revival in French Literature, 1870-1914* (New York, 1965).

6. For some of these men and the Maritains' relations to them, see Maritain's *Carnets*, 183-154.

7. For two short introductions to French intellectual life of the 1920s, see Chastenet, *Les années d'illusion*, 250-281 and Jean de Fabrègues, "Le mouvement des idées," *Trente ans, 1914-1948: De Clemenceau à de Gaulle* (Paris, 1949), 337-352. For Maritain's place in the 1920s, see Helen Iswolsky, *Light Before Dusk: A Russian Catholic in France, 1923-1941* (New York, 1942), 70-87, 184-199; Jean Pierre Maxence, *Histoire de dix ans, 1927-1937* (Paris, 1939), 50-63, 87, 134, 143, 196, and Nicolas Berdyaev, *Dream and Reality*, trans. Katharine Lampert (New York, 1962), 250-254.

8. What is unique about Maritain's Thomism is that it was developed in opposition to Bergson's thought. Anxious to defend reason against Bergson's concept of intuition and the unity of nature against his *élan vital*, Maritain, on one hand, gave special attention to Thomas' thought on epistemological matters pertaining to the intellect and the formation of concepts and, on the other hand, gave particular concern to the questions of change, causality, and potency in Thomas' doctrine. For an introduction to Maritain's Thomism, English readers can consult Jacques Maritain, *Distinguish to Unite or Degrees of Knowledge*, trans. Gerald Phelan (London, 1959), Jacques Maritain, *Preface to Metaphysics* (New York, 1962), and Joseph Evans and Leo Ward, eds., *Challenges and Renewals* (New York, 1968). For an excellent work which views various Thomisms comparatively, see Helen John, *The Thomist Spectrum* (New York, 1966).

9. It must be remembered that Thomas was consciously and progressively revived in the course of the nineteenth century by Catholics and the Vatican, and that Thomism was more than simply a philosophical or theological doctrine. The Church's selection of Thomas, formalized and propagated by Leo XIII's encyclical, *Aeternis Patris* (1879), was not simply his choice, nor was it a decision reached on a singular plane of thought and experience. Instead, it was a total response to the problems the Church found itself facing in nineteenth century Europe. Thomas provided the Church with a tie to the Middle Ages, offered a criticism of numerous philosophical, social, and political errors which threatened Church doctrine and authority without committing it to a definite position in the modern world (conservatism, monarchy, etc.), gave the Church a means to define itself internally with reference to acceptable theology, and offered the Church a means to claim its primacy in both matters of faith and politics without sacrificing itself to feared Protestant and democratic relativism and subjectivism, and without admitting scientific and historical doctrines which would historicize the meaning of the Church as an institution and faith. In effect, Thomism served the

Church's world view; it was a "science," a statement of the unity and transcendence of the Church and its message, a vehicle to define orthodoxy, and a manner to analyze the changes in contemporary thought and society. For an excellent historical introduction to many of the reasons for the Church's adoption of Thomism as an official philosophy, see Louis Foucher, *La philosophie catholique en France au XIXe siècle avant la renaissance thomiste et dans son rapport avec elle, 1800-1880* (Paris, 1955); also of general use is Edgar Hocédèz, *Histoire de la théologie au XIXe siècle*, Vol. III: *Le règne de Léon XIII, 1878-1903* (Paris, 1947), 45-52.

10. The original French edition is Jacques Maritain, *Trois réformateurs: Luther, Descartes, Rousseau* (Paris, 1925). The English translation utilized here is *Three Reformers: Luther, Descartes, Rousseau* (New York, 1955). No translator is mentioned.

11. *Ibid.*, 4.

12. This section title, like the following two, is taken from Maritain's *Three Reformers*.

13. *Ibid.*, 14. Underlining in the original is Maritain's.

14. *Ibid.*

15. Maritain based his interpretation on Catholic Henri Denifle's innovative but polemical psychological study, *Luther et luthérianisme*, trans. and ed. Paquier (4 vols., Paris, 1913). Denifle's work and Maritain's work drew the attention of one of the great twentieth century French historians, Lucien Febvre (see his *Un destin, Martin Luther* [Paris, 1928], and the well known German Protestant scholar, Karl Holl, in "Martin Luther à propos de l'étude de M. Jacques Maritain," *Revue de Théologie et de Philosophie*, new series XV, No. 64-65 [August-December, 1927], 260-270, and Maritain's reply "Réponse à Karl Holl à propos de Luther," *Nova et Vetera*, III [October-December, 1928], 423-427). Consequently, the lengthy notes appended to Maritain's *Three Reformers* (167-209) suggest part of an interesting 1920s debate over Luther between French and German, Catholic and Protestant, religious and secular scholarship. This debate also terrifyingly suggests how, despite the good will of the participants, much of contemporary scholarship is tied to the conflict of nations and ideologies.

16. *Three Reformers*, 18.

17. *Ibid.*, 19.

18. For instance, Maritain rejected what he considered the ultimate historicism of such thinkers as Cassirer and Lévy-Bruhl, and the ultimate existentialism of such thinkers as Heidegger and Husserl. For Maritain both of these errors were implicit in Descartes. That is, on one hand, Maritain found a historicizing notion of human progress and reason, and on the other, a subjectivizing egotism of the self and its own reason.

19. *Three Reformers*, 54-63, *passim*.

20. For a classic warning against the Cartesian error of uprooting man's knowledge from its historical sources, see Giambattista Vico, *The New Science of Giambattista Vico*, trans. by Thomas Bergin and Max Fisch from the 3rd edition of 1744 (New York, 1961), esp. 52-53.

21. For a work that suggests in the broadest philosophical and cultural terms how significant Descartes was in causing the crisis of Western consciousness of the

late seventeenth century, which for one thing marks the great divide between the age of religion and the age of reason; see Paul Hazard's *La crise de la conscicnce européene* (Paris, 1935).

22. *Ibid.,* 79-81.

23. *Ibid.,* 80-81, *passim.* For a later and fuller development of this theme, see Jacques Maritain, *Dream of Descartes*, trans. Mabelle Andison (New York, 1944), 33-57, 61-103.

24. The quotation is from *Three Reformers,* 86.

25. For an excellent history of nineteenth and twentieth century European and French criticisms of Rousseau and, in particular, for a history of the conservative and reactionary traditions Maritain drew upon, see Albert Schinz, *Etat présent des travaux sur Jean-Jacques Rousseau* (New York, 1941). This conservative and reactionary tradition made up at the turn of the century of such men as Lemaître, Maurras, and Seillière was implicitly responded to by such men as Lévy-Bruhl, Jaurès, Boutroux, Bosanquet, and Höffding in a special bicentennial issue of the *Revue Métaphysique et de Morale* (May, 1912). A great portion of this pre-War debate is seen in Maritain's notes to his section in the *Three Reformers* on Rousseau, 219-234. Ernst Cassirer's *The Question of Jean-Jacques Rousseau,* trans. Peter Gay (New York, 1954), written from a decided Kantian point of view, is a valuable contrast to Maritain's treatment.

26. Maritain, *Three Reformers,* 95-96.

27. *Ibid.,* 126-129.

28. Maritain's concern with the destructive confusion in modern thought between natural law and naturalism anticipates the work of several contemporary political theorists; see, for example, Leo Strauss, *Natural Right and History* (Chicago, 1965), Hannah Arendt, *The Human Condition* (Garden City, New York, 1959), and A. P. d'Entrèves, *Natural Law: An Introduction to Legal Philosophy* (London, 1951).

29. *Three Reformers,* 133.

30. On these points Maritain not only reechoes the nineteenth century Vatican criticisms of democracy, liberalism, and socialism but he also anticipates in varying degrees a host of contemporary European political thinkers' analyses of totalitarian politics and society. For an introduction to the Church's political theory, see first Leo XIII's *Immortale Dei,* 1885, which is one of the clearest authoritative Catholic expositions of the problem of Church and state, and liberty (*The Church Speaks to the Modern World: The Social Teachings of Leo XIII*, ed. Etienne Gilson [Garden City, New York, 1954], 157-187), and also Luigi Sturzo's profound study, *Church and State,* trans. Barbara Carter, Vol. II (Notre Dame, Indiana, 1962). For a few contemporary thinkers whose concerns with the tyranny of democracy are on certain points similar to Maritain's, see José Ortega y Gasset, *The Revolt of the Masses* (New York, 1932); Bertrand de Jouvenel, *On Power: Its Nature and the History of Its Growth* (Boston, 1962); Simone Weil, *Selected Essays, 1934-43,* trans. and ed. Richard Rees (London, 1962); Albert Camus, *The Rebel,* trans. Anthony Bower (New York, 1956); and J. L. Talmon, *The Origins of Totalitarian Democracy* (New York, 1960).

31. For a discussion of the Condemnation of *Action Française,* see Eugen Weber's *Action Française: Royalism and Reaction in the Twentieth Century* (Stan-

ford, California, 1962), 106-115; see also Harry W. Paul, *The Second Ralliement: The Rapprochement Between Church and State in Twentieth Century France* (Washington, D.C., 1967), 148-185, 213-220.

32. For a good general discussion of this convergence, see René Rémond, *The Right Wing in France,* trans. James Laux (Philadelphia, 1966), 247-253.

33. It is possible to conceive the *Action Française* as both a reaction against the modern world and as a forerunner of fascism and national socialism. Eugen Weber correctly cautions against unthinking application of the older terms conservative and liberal, right and left, with regard to contemporary French political life in general and such movements as the *Action Française* in particular. For example, see his "Nationalism, Socialism and National-Socialism in France," *French Historical Studies,* Vol. II (No. 3, 1962), 273-307, and "France," in Hans Rogger and Eugen Weber, eds., *The European Right* (Berkeley, 1966), 71-127.

34. For the roots of Maurras' thoughts, see Samuel Osgood, *French Royalism under the Third Republic* (The Hague, 1960), 59, and Ernst Nolte, *Three Faces of Fascism,* trans. Leile Vennewitz (New York, 1966), 30-53.

35. The two major sources for Maritain's tie to the *Action Française* are Raïssa's *Memoirs,* 292-315, and Henri Massis' *Maurras et Notre Temps,* 2 vols., Paris, 1951), I, 156-177. Writing at the outbreak of the Second World War, Raïssa denied that her husband had any profound ties with the *Action Française* and argued that he was primarily concerned with philosophy and religion at this time. Massis, conversely, argued that Maritain was a convinced supporter of the *Action Française,* but did not grasp its fundamental meaning, and both his acceptance and later rejection of it was a matter of religious obedience. While both positions are polemical, they do, however, make it clear that even though the Church was uppermost in Maritain's mind, he shared the *Action Française's* criticism of contemporary society and thought.

36. Maritain, *Carnets,* 179.

37. For Maritain's ties to *Parti de l'Intelligence,* see Henri Bars, *Maritain en notre temps* (Paris, 1959), 373. For its manifesto, see Henri Massis and François Hepp, "La confédération professionale des intellectuels catholiques," *Documentation Catholique* (No. 108, 1921), 325-329. Of special interest is an extensive interview in 1923 of Maritain and Massis together on contemporary French culture and the *Nouvelle Revue Française,* by Frederic Lefèvre, "Jacques Maritain et Henri Massis," *Une heure avec. . . .* Second series (Paris, 1924), 43-63.

38. Henri Bars, *Maritain en notre temps* (Paris, 1959), 116-117.

CHAPTER IV

1. This quotation was taken from Mounier's essay "Comment on conduit une vie: l'exemple de Descartes," 8, as found in the folder of Mounier's pre-*Esprit* writings, held at the Mounier Library Châtenay-Malabry. It was published as Jean Sylvestre [Emmanuel Mounier] "Comment on conduit une vie: l'exemple de Descartes," *Aux Davidées,* I (December, 1929), 83-89.

2. While Candide Moix's *Emmanuel Mounier* (Paris, 1960) is the most complete biography of Mounier, it does not deal adequately with the formation of the young Mounier.

3. Emmanuel Mounier, *Mounier et sa génération, Oeuvres de Mounier* (4 vols., Paris, 1961-1963), IV, 417. Collected within this very important posthumous work are many of Mounier's unpublished letters and reflections during the years 1925 to 1950.

4. For the relations between Mounier and Chevalier, see *ibid.,* IV, 418-425, and Chevalier's *Entretiens avec Bergson* (Paris, 1959), 63, 78, *passim.*

5. Emmanuel Mounier, "Jacques Chevalier: un penseur français," *La Vie Catholique,* No. 79 (April, 1926), 1.

6. *Ibid.*

7. Mounier, *Mounier et sa génération,*IV, 445-446.

8. See Jacques Chevalier, *Les événements d'Espagne* (Paris, 1937), and Mounier's "Lettre autour de la guerre d'Espagne," *Esprit,* No. 68 (May, 1938), 235-251.

9. For Chevalier's place in Vichy, see Robert Aron, *The Vichy Regime, 1940-1944,* trans. Humphrey Hare (Boston, 1969). For his writings just prior to Vichy, in Vichy, and his resignation because of Vichy's treatment of Bergson, see various essays in his *Cadences* (2 vols., Paris, 1951) and his *Entretiens avec Bergson,* 296-301.

10. This quotation is from Mounier's notebook, titled *Entretiens* I, dated November, 1926 to May, 1927; it is specifically located within the notebook under the title, *Une discussion sur Maritain et la nature de la philosophie chrétienne,* dated December 15, 1926, 7-12. It was generously shown to me by Madame Mounier at Mounier's Library, Châtenay-Malabry, and is here translated and published with her permission.

11. See in general Maritain's *Bergsonian Philosophy and Thomism* (Paris, 1914) and in particular his criticism of Chevalier's work on Aristotle, "Aristotle et la critique moderne," XII (November, 1921), 337-386; and for one of Chevalier's criticisms of Maritain's interpretation of Aristotle, see "Réponse de Jacques Chevalier à Jacques Maritain," *Les Lettres* (June, 1920), 179-201.

12. For a contemporary work which reveals many of the fundamental concerns and questions involved in the formulation of a Catholic philosophy, see Henri de Lubac's *Mystery of the Supernatural,* trans. Rosemary Sheed (New York, 1967). Also for a general introduction to twentieth century Catholic philosophy, see Robert Caponigri, ed., *Modern Catholic Thinkers* (2 vols., New York, 1960); I. M. Bochenski, *Contemporary European Philosophy,* trans. Donald Nicholl and Karl Aschenbrenner (Berkeley, 1961); and Helen James John, *The Thomist Spectrum* (New York, 1966).

13. For these schools and their debate over Catholic philosophy, see Maritain, *De la philosophie chrétienne* (Paris, 1933); Etienne Gilson, *Spirit of Mediaeval Philosophy,* trans. A. H. C. Downes (New York, 1940, orig. date, 1932); Maurice Blondel, *Le problème de la philosophie catholique* (Paris, 1932); Jacques Chevalier, *L'idée et le réel* (Paris, 1932). For yet another approach to Christian philosophy, and in particular the relation of faith and reason, see Gabriel Marcel's diary for the years 1928-1933: *Being and Having* (New York, 1965).

14. For Chevalier's ties to Bergson, see Chevalier's *Entretiens avec Bergson, Henri Bergson,* trans. Lilial A. Clare (New York, 1928), and *Bergson et le Père Pouget* (Paris, 1954).

15. Chevalier, "Histoire de mes idées," *Cadences* II, 3-12.

16. See his *L'idée et le réel*. Chevalier believed this insight came to him independently from his early studies of crystallography in England, *Entretiens avec Bergson*, 9-10.

17. *Cadences*, II, II.

18. *Ibid.*, III.

19. In my opinion Chevalier's philosophy of the individual, like Bergson's philosophy, was in great part a restatement of Romanticism. Its concerns for process, the ineffability of the individual and its intuitional epistemology are some of the evidence. Its concern for a sacral and hierarchical cosmos in change as well as its lyrical treatment of history (see esp. his *Pour une science de l'individuel: Introduction à un essai sur la formation de la nationalité et les réveils religieux au pays de galles des origines à la fin du sixième siècle* [Paris, 1923]) and man's tie to nature (see esp. his *La forêt: Troncâis-en-Bourbonnais* [Paris, 1930]) are further evidence of this. In conformity with orthodox Christian theology, Chevalier's science of the individual is predicated on the notion that only the introduction of a personal God and His Creation can account for reality; in contradiction to orthodox theology, Chevalier's science of the individual conceals a Hegelian drive for total knowledge. In the end, the success of Chevalier's philosophical project is doubtful because it is predicated on the contradictory notion of a science of revelation and creation, which, by definition, exist because of the singular and inscrutable acts of God.

20. Chevalier, *L'idée et le réel*, 15.

21. *Ibid.*, 18.

22. Chevalier's nationalism was far more extreme than that found in either Mounier's or Maritain's writings. It had its roots in a romantic conception of the unity between a country, its traditions, and its thought. The most classic expression of Chevalier's nationalism is found in his *Descartes* (Paris, 1921), 7: "We find the highest expression of the Cartesian spirit in our times in General Foch."

23. *Ibid.*, 5.

24. *Ibid.*, 5-6.

25. For a complete listing of Mounier's early writings, see Mounier bibliography, *Oeuvres*, IV, 837-839. Many of these articles were used in manuscript form at Mounier's Library at Châtenay-Malabry. Because of this, and because all the points made are clear throughout most of Mounier's early writings, I have taken the liberty to cite the titles of the most appropriate articles on a given idea in accordance with this bibliography found in Mounier's *Oeuvres*.

26. Emmanuel Mounier, "A propos d'une thèse sur Maine de Biran: la leçon d'une vie," *La Vie Catholique* (September 3, 1927), and Jean Sylvestre [Emmanuel Mounier], "De l'esprit philosophique," *Aux Davidées* (November, 1929), 83-89.

27. Emmanuel Mounier, "Pourquoi parlons-nous? Langage animal et langage humain," *Après ma Classe* (March 20, 1930).

28. Emmanuel Mounier, "L'intuition bergsonienne," *Après ma Classe* (July 20, 1929).

29. Jean Sylvestre [Emmanuel Mounier], L'événement et nous, *Aux Davidées* (December, 1930), 145-150, and Jean Sylvestre [Emmanuel Mounier], "L'étranger," *Aux Davidées* (May, 1930), 466-470.

30. Un Ami [Emmanuel Mounier], "Cause et conditions," *Après ma Classe* (January 20, 1929).

31. Un Ami [Emmanuel Mounier], "Contraires et contradictoires," *Après ma Classe* (February 20, 1929).

32. Emmanuel Mounier, "L'idée d'irrationnel," *Après ma Classe* (March 20, 1929).

33. Emmanuel Mounier, "Subtilité et pureté," *Après ma Classe* (April 20, 1929); Emmanuel Mounier, "Prouver, ou de l'honnêteté intellectuelle," *Après ma Classe* (July 20, 1929).

34. Emmanuel Mounier, "A propos d'une thèse sur Maine de Biran: la leçon d'une vie," *La Vie Catholique* (September 3, 1927); Jean Sylvestre [Emmanuel Mounier], "Comment on conduit une vie: l'exemple de Descartes," *Aux Davidées*, II (January, 1930), 208-211.

35. Emmanuel Mounier, "Le conflit de l'anthropocentrisme et du théocentrisme dans la philosophie de Descartes" (unpublished thesis for D.E.S., University of Grenoble, 1927). Its conclusion was republished under same title in *Etudes Philosophiques*, No. 3 (July-September, 1966), 319-324.

36. Mounier, "Le conflit de l'anthropocentrisme et du théocentrisme" (1927), 5-10.

37. *Ibid.*, 13.

38. Mounier, "Le conflit de l'anthropocentrisme et du théocentrisme," *Etudes Philosophiques*, No. 3, 319.

39. *Ibid.*, 321.

CHAPTER V

1. Mounier, *Mounier et sa génération*, 427.

2. Mounier worked for seven years with this blind Lazarist, who was trained under the modernist Loisy, universally educated, and foremost a student of the Bible. For Mounier and Pouget, see *ibid.*, 428-429; Moix, *La pensée d'Emmanuel Mounier*, 14. For Pouget himself and his relations with Bergson and Chevalier, see Père Pouget, *Logia: Propos et enseignements* ed. Jacques Chevalier (Paris, 1955) and Jacques Chevalier (ed.), *Bergson et le Père Pouget* (Paris, 1954).

3. For *Les Davidées* and Mounier's tie to them, see Mounier, *Mounier et sa génération*, 444, 449. François Chauvières [Emmanuel Mounier], "Une amité spirituelle: Les Davidées," *La vie spirituelle* (Paris, April 1931), 66-91. Jean Guitton, *Les Davidées: Histoire d'un mouvement d'apostolat laïc, 1916-1966* (Paris, 1967).

4. The *agrégation* is an annual national competition held at the *Ecole Normale* for the recruitment of *lycée* and certain college faculty.

5. Mounier, *Mounier et sa génération*, 434.

6. *Ibid.*, 433.

7. *Ibid.*, 434-435.

8. *Ibid.*, 429.

9. *Ibid.*, 431.

10. *Ibid.*, 429.

11. *Ibid.*, 430.

12. *Ibid.*

13. *Ibid.*, 431.

14. *Ibid.*, 434.

15. *Ibid.*, 427.

16. For the reasons for this decision, see his letter of November 7, 1930, to Jacques Chevalier, *ibid.*, 471-472.

17. *Ibid.*, 463-467.

18. *Ibid.*, 464.

19. *Ibid.*

20. *Ibid.*

21. *Ibid.*, 465.

22. *Ibid.*

23. *Ibid.*, 466.

24. While Maritain obviously continued to write philosophy (as is shown by his major work, *Distinguer pour unir*, 1932, as well as by his *De la philosophie chrétienne*, 1932, and *Sept leçons sur l'être*, 1934) his growing concern for political and social matters is revealed by his *Religion and Culture* (Paris, 1930), and *Du régime temporel et de la liberté* (Paris, 1933).

25. Mounier, *Mounier et sa génération*, 425.

26. *Ibid.*, 442, 445, 454-455, 471, *passim*. Also of importance, as is later suggested, is an unpublished Maritain and Mounier correspondence which extends from 1930 to 1950, and in particular, the period 1930 to 1933. Madame Mounier, who was good enough to show me these letters, has recently published what I believe to be the most significant part of them: "Naissance et début de la revue *Esprit*, evoqués à travers les rapports de Maritain et de Mounier: Lettres, notes, articles," *Bulletin des Amis d'E. Mounier*, No. 34-35 (November, 1969). With this publication and what already exists in *Mounier et sa génération*, the essentials of their relations can be adequately grasped.

27. Cited in Moix's *La pensée d'Emmanuel Mounier*, 18.

28. For a fine short study of Mounier's relations with Péguy, see Chapter One, "Alle origini della filosofia della rivoluzione: la lezione di Péguy," of Giorgio Campini's *La rivoluzione cristiana. Il pensiero politico di Emmanuel Mounier.* Brescia, 1968, 41-67.

29. Mounier, *Mounier et sa génération*, 468.

30. *Ibid.*, 452.

31. In preparing his study of Péguy, Mounier and Maritain discussed Péguy four or five times. On one particular occasion, revealing what was later to prove a significant difference of attitude and doctrine between the two, Mounier chose to stress the virtue of Péguy's conception of an incarnate Christianity. While Maritain concurred on this aspect of Péguy's thought, he cautioned Mounier about Péguy's failure to give sufficient attention to the eternal and absolute character of Christianity. See *ibid.*, 459-461.

32. For a short discussion of the revival of Péguy after the First World War, see Bernard Guyon, *Péguy* (Paris, 1960), 272-281.

33. Mounier, "Péguy ressuscité," *Bulletin des Amis d'E. Mounier*, No. 12 (June, 1958), 5-6.

34. Emmanuel Mounier, "Charles Péguy et le problème de l'enseignement," *Revue de Culture Générale*, Vol. I (Aix en Provence, November 20, 1930), 76-84; *ibid.*, Vol. II (December 20, 1930), 144-148; *ibid.*, Vol. III (January 20, 1931),

209-213; *ibid.,* Vol. IV (March 20, 1931), 342-343; *ibid.* (May 20, 1931), 453-461.

35. Quotation from this already cited article was taken from Mounier's draft for it, found in a binder of Mounier's pre-*Esprit* articles, 1929 to 1932, held at Mounier Library, Châtenay-Malabry, 4.

36. Emmanuel Mounier, "L'événement et nous," *Bulletin des Amis d'Emmanuel Mounier,* No. 3 (April, 1953), 11.

37. Emmanuel Mounier, "L'action intellectuelle ou de l'influence," *ibid.,* No. 4 (January, 1954), 2-16. Originally published in *Revue de Culture Générale,* Vol. I (October 20, 1931), 4-9; *ibid.* (November 20, 1931), 67-74; *ibid.,* Vol. III (December 20, 1931), 132-134; *ibid.,* Vol. IV (January 20, 1932), 198-202; *ibid.,* Vol. V (May 20, 1932), 132-134.

38. Emmanuel Mounier, "Défense de la civilization," *Revue de la Culture Générale,* No. 1 (October 20, 1930), 14-21.

39. Mounier, *La pensée de Charles Péguy, Oeuvres* (4 vols., Paris, 1961-1963), I, 19-28.

40. Emmanuel Mounier, "Péguy, médiateur de Bergson," *Bulletin des Amis d'Emmanuel Mounier,* No. 20 (July, 1963), 7. Original publication of this article is in *Henri Bergson,* eds. A. Béguin and P. Thévanez (Neuchâtel, 1941), 319-328.

41. Mounier, *La pensée de Charles Péguy,* 20.

42. *Ibid.,* 102, 111, 112, 119.

CHAPTER VI

1. Quoted in Robert Graves' and Alan Hodge's *The Long Week-End* (New York, 1963), 200.

2. Quoted in *ibid.,* 202.

3. Mounier, *Mounier et sa génération,* 476-477.

4. Aside from *Mounier et sa génération,* also absolutely essential for a study of the founding of *Esprit* and the climate in which it was founded, is Jean Louis Loubet del Bayle's *Les non-conformistes des années 30. Une tentative de renouvellement de la pensée politique française* (Paris, 1969) and Edmond Lipiansky's "L'Ordre Nouveau," in his and Bernard Rettenbach's *Ordre et démocratie. Deux sociétés de pensée: De l'Ordre Nouveau au Club Jean-Moulin* (Paris, 1967), 1-102.

5. For Maritain's important role in the founding of *Esprit,* see Mounier, *Mounier et sa génération,* 473, 486, 487, *passim,* and "Naissance et début de la revue *Esprit* evoqués à travers les rapports de Maritain et de Mounier," *Bulletin des Amis d'Emmanuel Mounier,* No. 34-35 (November, 1964), 3-64.

6. From 1925 when Berdyaev arrived in France until 1933 when Maritain left for Canada, they were in close contact. While they strongly disagreed over modern philosophy, Berdyaev working in the tradition of German idealism and Maritain in Thomism, they both agreed on the importance of mysticism, the destructiveness of contemporary bourgeois civilization, and the challenge of the Russian Revolution to Christianity. For their basic agreement on this last point, see Berdyaev's influential work, *Un nouveau moyen âge* (Paris, 1927). For an introduction to their relations, see Nicolas Berdyaev, *Dream and Reality: An Essay in Autobiography,* trans. Katharine Lampert (New York, 1962), 250-255; Maritain, *Carnets*

(Paris, 1965), 220, 224; Eugène Porret, *Berdiaeff: Prophète des temps nouveaux* (Paris, 1951), 138-139; and Helen Iswolsky, *Light Before the Dusk: A Russian Catholic in France, 1923-1941* (New York, 1942), 70-103.

7. Jacques Maritain, *Religion et culture* (Paris, 1930), 46-47.

8. For studies of the *Nouveau Ordre* and its relation to Mounier and *Esprit*, see Loubet del Bayle, *Les non-conformistes des années 30*, 141-142, 153-154, and Lipiansky, *Ordre et démocratie*, 18-19. For an excellent introduction to its doctrine, see Robert Aron and Arnaud Dandieu, *La révolution nécessaire* (Paris, 1933).

9. For these early contributors to *Esprit* see particularly Mounier, *Mounier et sa génération*; also see Loubet Del Bayle, *Les non-conformistes des années 30*, 140-141, *passim.* For Berdyaev's and Mounier's relations, see esp. Berdyaev, *Dream and Reality*, 255, 263-264; and "Correspondance Mounier-Berdiaeff," *Bulletin des Amis d'Emmanuel Mounier*, No. 33 (February, 1969), 5-20. For Berdyaev's two articles in *Esprit*, see Berdyaev, "Verité et mensonge du communisme," *Esprit*, No. 1 (October, 1932), 104-128; and Berdyaev, "Le christianisme russe et le monde bourgeois," *ibid.*, No. 6 (March, 1934), 933-941.

10. The Mounier and Maritain correspondence shows Maritain counseling Mounier about contributors to *Esprit* in 1934 and advising Mounier regarding the possibility of an impending condemnation of *Esprit* as late as 1936 (see letters, May 23, 1936, November, 1936, and others). Despite this, already in the year 1933 Maritain had (as the letters of May 24, 25, 28 and June 7 make clear) limited his association with *Esprit*. For his few contributions, which corroborate his limited commitment to it, see Jacques Maritain, "Religion et Culture II," *Esprit*, No. 4 (January, 1933), 523-545; and Jacques Maritain, "Lettre sur le monde bourgeois," *ibid.*, No. 6 (March, 1933), 523-545.

11. Cited in Loubet del Bayle, *Les non-conformistes des années 30*, 152.

12. Hajo Holborn, *The Political Collapse of Europe* (New York, 1951), 134-137.

13. Pierre Renouvin, *Histoire des rélations internationales*, Vol. VIII, Part II: *Les crises du XXᵉ siècle, de 1929 à 1945* (Paris, 1958), 11, 15-16.

14. Jacques Chastenet, *Histoire de la troisième république*, Vol. VI: *Déclin de la troisième, 1931-1938* (Paris, 1962), 45-46.

15. For a discussion of these three challenges, see Gordon Wright, *France in the Twentieth Century* (Washington, 1965), 3-4.

16. H. Stuart Hughes, *Contemporary Europe: A History* (Englewood Cliffs, New Jersey, 1961), 264. Hughes cites the men noted parenthetically above in *ibid.*, 264-266.

17. This new mood was not restricted to Europe alone. For instance, in the United States during this period of the early 1930s, Lewis Mumford called for a new relation between culture and technology in his *Civilization and Technics* (New York, 1934) and Protestant theologian Reinhold Niebuhr declared that a tragic gap lay between personal values and the necessities of collective life in his *Moral Man and Immoral Society* (New York, 1932).

18. Karl Jaspers, *Man in the Modern Age*, trans. Eden and Cedar Paul (Garden City, New York, 1951), 15. This is a slightly revised edition of the original 1933 English translation of *Die Geiste Situation der Zeit* (Berlin, 1931).

19. For this theme, see some of his important writings of the 1920s, partially collected in his *The Modern Theme*, trans. James Cleugh (New York, 1961), esp. 19-51.

20. José Ortega y Gasset, *The Revolt of the Masses* (New York, 1957), 11.

21. Paul Valéry, "The Crisis of the Mind," *History and Politics* (New York, 1962), 23. The ellipses in this quotation are Valéry's.

22. See my earlier discussion of Christian philosophy and this debate in reference to Mounier's education as a philosopher, Chapter IV, pp. 82-84.

23. Loubet de Bayle, *Les non-conformistes des années 30*, 29.

24. See Roy Pierce's *Contemporary French Political Thought* (New York, 1966), which makes a study of the political thought of Mounier, as well as five of his important contemporaries, Weil, Camus, Sartre, De Jouvenel, and Aron.

25. See specifically Lipiansky, *Ordre et démocratie*, 4, as well as Pierre Maxence's own *Histoire de dix ans* (Paris, 1939), which is one of the best overall introductions to Mounier's generation.

26. Cited in Lipiansky, *Ordre et démocratie*, 13.

27. This quotation was taken from Jean Lacroix's response to Marxist Roger Garaudy's comments on Personalism; it is found in the latter's *Perspectives de l'homme: Existentialisme, pensée catholique, marxisme* (Paris, 1961), 167.

28. All subsequent references to "Refaire la Renaissance" will be to it as it is found in Mounier, *Oeuvres*, I, 137-174. It was originally published in *Esprit*, No. 1 (October, 1932), 5-51. A longer version of it, which was the substance of the text he delivered at the founding conference at Font-Romeu in April, 1932, is found in Emmanuel Mounier's "Les directions spirituelles du mouvement *Esprit*," *Bulletin des Amis d'E. Mounier*, No. 13-14 (March, 1959), 1-48.

29. Mounier, "Refaire la Renaissance," *Oeuvres*, I, 138.

30. *Ibid.*, 146.

31. *Ibid.*

32. *Ibid.*, 148.

33. *Ibid.*, 151.

34. *Ibid.*, 150.

35. This is a section heading, *ibid.*, 153-158.

36. *Ibid.*, 157.

37. This is also a section heading, *ibid.*, 158-166.

38. *Ibid.*, 158-159.

39. For two criticisms of Mounier's thought on these grounds, see Garaudy, *Perspectives de l'homme*, esp. 158-165, and Noureddine Zaza, *Etude critique de la notion d'engagement chez Emmanuel Mounier* (Geneva, 1955), 85-99.

40. For a developed interpretation of this type, see Hoffman, "Paradoxes of the French Political Community," *In Search of France* (New York, 1965), esp. 26-32.

41. For these points regarding the Church in the modern world, see Luigi Sturzo, *Church and State*, trans. Barbara Barclay Carter (2 vols., Notre Dame, Indiana, 1962 [orig. date, 1938]), II, 552-553.

42. *Ibid.*, 553.

CHAPTER VII

1. Geoffrey Warner, "The Stavisky Affair," *The Shaping of Modern France: Writings on French History since 1715*, ed. James Friguglietti and Emmet Kennedy (London, 1969), 465.

2. See François Goguel's "Positions politiques," *Esprit*, No. 174 (December, 1950), 804-805; and David Lewis' "Emmanuel Mounier and the Politics of Moral Revolution: Aspects of Political Crisis in French Liberal Catholicism, 1935-1938," *Catholic Historical Review*, vol. LV, No. 4 (January, 1970), 272-273. Also see Emmanuel Mounier, "Leçons de l'émeute ou la révolution contre les mythes," *Oeuvres de Mounier* (4 vols., Paris, 1961-1963), I, 361-369, which appeared as "La révolution contre les mythes," *Esprit*, No. 18 (March, 1934), 314-325.

3. Mounier, "Leçons de l'émeute," 367.

4. For Mounier's comments on Izard's *Troisième Force*, its joining with Bergery's *Front Commune* to form the *"Front Social,"* and then the birth of the *Rassemblement Populaire*, see Goguel, "Positions politiques," 807-809; Lewis, "Emmanuel Mounier and the Politics of Moral Revolution," 282-287; and Mounier, "Rassemblement populaire," *Esprit*, No. 45 (June, 1936), 441-449.

5. Goguel, "Positions politiques," 809. For Mounier's analyses of its failure, see "Le front populaire: Bilan, avenir, et maintenant," *Esprit*, No. 66 (March, 1938), 801-806, and one of Mounier's most penetrating analyses of the "myths" of French political life, "Bilan spirituel: court traité de la mythique gauche," *ibid.*, 873-890.

6. Mounier's most extended treatment of peace is "Les chrétiens devant le problème de la paix," *Oeuvres*, I, 783-837; this work originally appeared in the wake of Munich as *Pacifistes ou Bellicistes* (Paris, 1939).

7. The Manifesto is summarized in Goguel, "Positions politiques," 812-813.

8. For Mounier's writings, see "Espagne, signe de contradiction," *Esprit*, No. 49 (October, 1936), 1-3; "Terre libre," *ibid.*, No. 50 (November, 1936), 286-290; "Guernica ou la technique du mensonge," *ibid.*, No. 57 (June, 1937), 449-473; "Espoir au peuple basque," *ibid.*, No. 58 (July, 1937), 643-649; and esp. "Lettre autour de la guerre d'Espagne," *ibid.*, No. 68 (May, 1938), 235-251. For Maritain, see his "War and the Bombardment of Cities," *Commonweal*, XXVIII (September 2, 1938), 460-461; and esp. "De la guerre sainte," *La Nouvelle Revue Française*, XLIX (July 1, 1937), 21-37. For a general discussion of French Catholics' reaction to the War, see Rémond's *Les catholiques, le communisme et les crises, 1920-1939* (Paris, 1960), 175-212.

9. This phrase is found in Robert Graves' and Alan Hodges' *Long Weekend* (New York, 1953), 337. For one well done study of the influence of the War on European intellectuals, see Frederick Benson's *Writers in Arms: The Literary Impact of the Spanish Civil War* (New York, 1967).

10. All subsequent references to and translations of the *Manifeste au service du personnalisme, Oeuvres de Mounier*, I, 481-649, will be to the English translation, *A Personalist Manifesto*, trans. by the monks of Saint John's Abbey at Collegeville, Minnesota (New York, 1938).

11. Such aesthetic attacks on the bourgeois were widespread throughout European intellectual life in the 1920s and 1930s. For examples of this in Germany,

see Peter Gay's *Weimar Culture* (New York, 1968), especially Chapter Four, "The Hunger for Wholeness: Trials of Modernity," 70-96.

12. Mounier was one of numerous French intellectuals who from the early 1930s on took an interest in the rediscovery of writings of the young Marx. Of particular interest, aside from constant references to the young Marx across all of Mounier's writings, is Marcel Moré's *Accords et dissonances* (Paris, 1967). Therein Moré describes how he came to see a profound unity between Bloy's and Marx's concerns for the poor (11-12), suggests which steps led him to *Esprit* in 1934 (12), and reproduces his review article in *Esprit* on Auguste Cornu's *Karl Marx* (Paris, 1935), which more than any other book, called the intellectuals' attention to the young man Marx (86-99).

13. Mounier, *Manifesto*, 17-18.

14. *Ibid.*, 15-18.

15. *Ibid.*, 19-23.

16. *Ibid.*, 24-27.

17. *Ibid.*, 24.

18. For example, see *ibid.*, 87-91. At this point Mounier had no real understanding of or sympathy for liberalism. Both he and Maritain treated liberalism under the rubric of the failure of all modern history. Some of the reasons for this were: religious and conservative sources inspired in great part their criticisms of the modern world; French intellectuals from the late nineteenth century onward did not appreciate English political experience and confused liberalism with Manchester liberalism, anarchic individualism, capitalism, and their own malfunctioning Republic; they lived in an epoch when nearly everyone turned against the notions of progress, science and reason which were essential assumptions of eighteenth and nineteenth century liberalism. For an essay that has historiographically inspired this analysis, see A. William Salomone, "The Risorgimento between Ideology and History: The Political Myth of *rivoluzione mancata,*" *American Historical Review*, LXVIII (October, 1962), 38-56.

19. Mounier, *Manifesto*, 25.

20. *Ibid.*, 29-30.

21. For Mounier the denial of transcendence was the essence of the modern world. For three works which, in conjunction with Mounier's, make a strong contribution to a discussion of modern society's antithetical disposition towards transcendence, see Herbert Marcuse, *Reason and Revolution* (New York, 1960), esp. 3-29, 409-419, Ernst Nolte, *Three Faces of Fascism: Action Française, Italian Fascism, National Socialism*, trans. Leila Vennewitz (New York, 1966), esp. 429-454, and Ernst Cassirer, *The Myth of the State* (New Haven, 1961), esp. 277-298.

22. *Ibid.*, 65-66.

23. For Mounier's treatment of Marxism in the *Manifesto*, see Chapter Four, "The New Marxist Man," 44-66.

24. *Ibid.*, 46.

25. *Ibid.*, 7-8.

26. *Ibid.*, 107-108. Mounier borrowed this notion from Maritain.

27. *Ibid.*, 10. Underlining in the original is Mounier's.

28. *Ibid.*, 69.

29. *Ibid.*, 68.

30. See esp. Chapter Six, "A Personalist Communitarian Civilization," *ibid.*, 89-101.

31. For Mounier's treatment of the family, see Chapter Nine, "The Private Life," *ibid.*, 124-129.

32. Mounier treats education in Chapter Eight, "The Education of the Person," *Manifesto*, 111-123. For the issues involved in the educational policy of the Third Republic, see William Bosworth, *Catholicism and Crisis in Modern France: French Catholic Groups at the Threshold of the Third Republic* (Princeton, New Jersey, 1962), 13-43, 279-308; and René Rémond, "L'évolution de la notion de laïcité entre 1919 et 1939," *Cahiers d'Histoire*, Vol. IV (No. 1, 1959), 71-87.

33. The question of culture was central to Mounier, for indeed his first criticism of the modern world was cultural and religious. He wrote: "By civilization in the strict sense we mean the progress of man's biological and social adaptation to his body and environment. By culture we mean the enlargement of his consciousness, the ease he acquires in the exercising of his spirit, his participation in a certain way of reacting and of thinking. . . . By spirituality we mean the unfolding of the deeper life of his person. We have therewith defined the three ascending levels of an *integral humanism*," *Manifesto*, 6-7. For Mounier's treatment of culture see esp. Chapter Ten, "The Culture of the Person," *ibid.*, 150-164.

34. For these points and this quotation, see *ibid.*, 162-163.

35. For Mounier's description of capitalism under the rubric of "the primacy of economics," see *Manifesto*, 165-169; for his general treatment of capitalism, see Chapter Eleven, "Capitalism as the Enemy of the Person," *ibid.*, 165-188.

36. *Ibid.*, 165-166.

37. Mounier leveled these attacks against capitalism under the following subtitles: "Capitalist Subversion," "Capitalist Profit: The Fecundity of Money," "Capital, Enemy of Labor and of Responsibility," "Capital as Enemy of the Consumer," "Capitalism, the Enemy of Liberty," and "Capitalism, the Enemy of Private Property," *ibid.*, 165-187.

38. For these points, see *ibid.*, 169-182.

39. For Mounier's conception of work and labor see *ibid.*, esp. 196-199. For more general aspects of a Personalist economics, see *ibid.*, 189-224.

40. A Personalist politics are treated primarily in Chapter Thirteen, "The Political Society," *ibid.*, 225-252.

41. *Ibid.*, 231.

42. *Ibid.*, 232.

43. *Ibid.*

44. For Mounier's concept of a "pluralist state," see *ibid.*, 215-218, 232-239; also see Mounier's "Anarchie et personnalisme," *Oeuvres de Mounier*, I, 653-725, and his "De la propriété capitaliste à la propriété humaine," *ibid.*, 419-477.

45. The concept "Personalist Democracy" is discussed in *ibid.*, 239-250.

46. *Ibid.*, 246.

47. See Chapter Fourteen, "International and Interracial Society," *ibid.*, 253-265.

48. *Ibid.*, 254.

49. For Mounier's treatment of pacifism in the *Manifesto*, see 257-260. See also his "Les chrétiens devant le problème de la paix," *Oeuvres de Mounier*, I, 783-837.

50. Mounier, *Manifesto,* 261.

51. All these points are found in *ibid.,* 260-261; underlinings in the original are Mounier's.

52. Throughout the 1920s and 1930s, Berdyaev voiced the need for a Christianity which would accept the positive social program of Marxism, transcend the West's materialism and positivism, and prepare the way for a new human order. For his views and their influence see esp. his important *Nouvel moyen âge* (Paris, 1927) and his "Young France and Social Justice," *Dublin Review,* CXCVI (January, 1935), 37-46 in which he speaks of the reception of his book *The New Middle Ages* by *Esprit* and the *Nouveau Ordre.*

53. The original French edition, composed in great part of lectures given by Maritain in Spain in 1934, was published as *Humanisme integral* (Paris, 1936). The work used here, and to which all subsequent references are made, is the slightly revised and recently translated *Integral Humanism,* trans. Joseph Evans (New York, 1968).

54. It is possible to trace Maritain's political evolution from the reactionary *Action Française* to a democratic pluralism in the mid-1930s in terms of the books he wrote. See his *Primauté du spirituel* (Paris, 1927); "Le sens de la condemnation," *Pourquoi Rome a parlé* (Paris, 1927), 329-385; "Le joug du Christ," *Clairvoyance de Rome* (Paris, 1929), 269-290; *Religion et culture* (Paris, 1930); and *Du régime temporel et de la liberté* (Paris, 1933). For a study of this evolution, see Henri Bars, *Maritain en notre temps* (Paris, 1959), 113-140.

55. Maritain, *Integral Humanism,* p. 28.

56. *Ibid.,* 15, 18, 24-26. Of course, both Maritain's conception and use of history are open to serious questions. For instance, while Maritain alluded frequently to the Renaissance in his writings, nowhere to my knowledge did he explore its origin or meaning in any systematic historical sense, but rather he consistently treated it as part of a polemical history of ideas. Indicative of this is what he wrote in *Integral Humanism* (15): "The catastrophe of the Middle Ages thus opens the epoch of modern humanism. The radiating dissolution of the Middle Ages and its *sacral* forms is the engendering of a *secular* civilization—of a civilization not only secular, but which *separates itself* progressively from the Incarnation." (Underlining is Maritain's.) The same is true in the case of the Reformation. While Maritain became more open to the possibility and even desirability of cultural and religious freedom, his theological and "historical" attacks on the Reformation and Protestant thought were in no way softened. As late as 1964, in his *Moral Philosophy* (London, 1964) his passing references to Luther and Calvin remained untempered by historical understanding, *ibid.,* 29, 92. For an example of his continued attacks against Kant, Hegel, Marx, and Comte, see *ibid.,* 92-118, 149-208, 209-260, 261-349.

57. Maritain, *Integral Humanism,* 28-29.

58. *Ibid.,* 30.

59. *Ibid.,* 35-40. Throughout *Integral Humanism* there are frequent references to Marxism; see esp. Chapter II, "A New Humanism" (35-94), the first half of which is dedicated primarily to Marxism.

60. See Chapter Four, "The Historical Ideal of a New Christendom I," and Chapter Five, "The Historical Ideal of a New Christendom II," *ibid.,* 127-161, 162-210.

61. For these points see *ibid.*, 178-180, 203- 204. In terms of the concept of personalist democracy, as will be seen later, Maritain found the essential bridge from his early conservative views to what broadly can be called American liberalism as expressed in his *Man and State* (Chicago, 1951).

62. Maritain, *Integral Humanism*, 128.

63. *Ibid.*

64. Mounier's and Maritain's search for an organic, pluralist and decentralized society can on numerous points be said to have varying parallels with such diverse thinkers as Lammenais, Proudhon, the young Marx, Mazzini, and De Tocqueville. It might be further suggested that the crises of Europe from 1929 on opened before them, as the French Revolution once did for all of Europe, the need for and possibility of a new relation between state and society and a new European order. If, in fact, the period 1848 to 1871 did open the door irreversibly to nationalism, realism, and centralization (as is suggested by Robert C. Binkley's *Realism and Nationalism, 1852-1871* [New York, 1935]), then not only are Maritain's and Mounier's political thought utopian, but so, in varying degrees, are liberalism, conservatism, and socialism.

65. The best treatment of these dilemmas of the Church in the modern world is found in Luigi Sturzo's *Church and State* (2 vols., Notre Dame, Indiana, 1962), II, 375-466.

CONCLUSION

1. Each of these authors in his own way calls attention to the massive and uncontrollable forces which man has unleashed upon himself. For example, see Bertrand de Jouvenel, *On Power: Its Nature and the History of its Growth*, trans. J. F. Hunington (Boston, 1962 [originally published in Geneva, 1945]); Simone Weil, *Selected Essays, 1934-1943*, trans. and ed. Richard Rees (London, 1963), esp. 44-54, 89-144; Albert Camus, *The Rebel: An Essay on Man in Revolt*, trans. Anthony Bower (New York, 1956 [originally published in Paris, 1951]); and Raymond Aron, *The Century of Total War* (Boston, 1955).

2. For Mounier's and Maritain's central works on existentialism, see respectively Jacques Maritain, *Existence and the Existent*, trans. Lewis Galantière and Gerald Phelan (Garden City, New York, 1957 [originally published in Paris, 1948]); and Emmanuel Mounier, *Introduction aux existentialismes, Oeuvres de Mounier*, III, 69-175.

3. For the use of the doctrine of the Incarnation for justifying more radical and liberal social and political thought with specific references to *Esprit*, see Roger Aubert, *La théologie au milieu du XXe siècle* (Paris, 1954), 65-70. For an even broader discussion of the interrelation between theological concepts and political and social doctrines, see Réné Rémond, "Droite et gauche dans le catholicisme français contemporaine," *Revue Française de Science Politique*, Nos. III and IV (September and December, 1958), 529-544, 803-820.

4. *Cf.* Marc Bloch's *Strange Defeat of France: A Statement of Evidence Written in 1940*, trans. Gerard Hopkins (New York, 1968) with Maritain's *France, My Country, Through the Disaster* (New York, 1941), esp. 1-61 and Mounier's "The Structures of Liberation," *The Commonweal*, XLII (May 18, 1945), 112-114.

5. For Maritain on Vichy, see his *France, My Country, Through the Disaster*, 67-107, *passim* and his *Messages, 1941-1944* (Paris, 1945), 123-126; the later works are part of the radio messages that Maritain broadcast from the United States to France during the War. For Mounier, see his "France in the Catacombs," *The Commonweal*, XLII (May 11, 1945), 85-87.

6. For Mounier on the Resistance, see "The Resistance," *ibid.*, 136-138. For Maritain on the same subject, see his *Messages*, 186, 189, *passim*.

7. For Maritain's and Mounier's indirect roles in helping form the milieu out of which the *Mouvement Républicain Populaire* was born, see Mario Enaudi and François Goguel, *Christian Democracy in Italy and France* (Notre Dame, Indiana, 1952), 107-131, and Charles Micaud, "The Politics of French Catholics in the Fourth Republic," in Joseph Moody, *Church and Society: Catholic Social and Political Thought and Movements, 1789-1950* (New York, 1953), 187-202. For a discussion of Maritain's and Mounier's basic assumptions regarding a Christian political party, see Donald Wolf, "Emmanuel Mounier: A Catholic of the Left," *Review of Politics*, XXII, No. 3 (July, 1960), 324-344, and Henri Bars, *La politique selon Jacques Maritain* (Paris, 1961), 218-235.

8. For Mounier's relations to Marxism in the post-War period, see Candide Moix, *La pensée d'Emmanuel Mounier* (Paris, 1960), 211-302; Roy Pierce, *Contemporary French Political Thought* (New York, 1966), 77-84; and Giorgio Campanini, *La rivoluzione cristiana. Il pensiero politico di Emmanuel Mounier* (Brescia, 1968), 139-164. For Maritain's position on Marxism, see Bars, *La politique selon Maritain*, 89-105.

9. Wolf, "Emmanuel Mounier," 329-333 and Pierce, *Contemporary French Political Thought*, 73-77.

10. For one of Mounier's views of the post-War world at large, see his *La petite peur du XXe siècle, Oeuvres de Mounier* (4 vols., Paris, 1961-1963), III, 341-425. For Maritain, see his *Messages*, his *Pour la justice, articles et discours, 1940-1945* (New York, 1945) and his *Man and State* (Chicago, 1951).

11. This is the title of one of Maritain's writings on the eve of the Second World War: *Le crépuscule de la civilisation* (Paris, 1939). All subsequent references to it will be to the English translation, *Twilight of Civilization*, trans. Lionel Landry (New York, 1943).

12. *Ibid.*, 64.

13. Maritain, *France, My Country*, 2-5.

14. Maritain, *Pour la justice*, 14.

15. Maritain, *France, My Country*, 93.

16. *Ibid.*, 21. Maritain, in annexing Péguy to his point of view, has mistakenly seen Péguy considering the *monde moderne* as the last four centuries of European history. Péguy, in fact, saw *le monde moderne* beginning in 1880 with what he considered the full emergence of the doctrines of positivism and secularism.

17. Maritain, *Messages*, 170-171.

18. For Maritain's analogy of the French to the Jews and Poles, see *France, My Country*, 107; for his vision of France's potential in post-World War Europe, see his *Messages*, 135, 137, *passim*.

19. For these points, see esp. Mounier's "Frontières du parti," *Esprit*, No. 80 (May, 1939), 258-263; and also "Conditions de paix pour l'été," *Esprit*, No. 83

(August, 1939), 657-692; "La France est-elle finie?" *Le Voltigeur* (September 29, 1938); and "1789-1939," *Esprit*, No. 84 (September, 1939), 697-700.

20. Pierce, *Contemporary French Political Thought*, 20.

21. Mounier, "1940," *Esprit*, No. 88 (January, 1940), 114. Italics are mine.

22. Mounier, "Gardons-nous de notre ennemi, l'Ennemi," *ibid.*, 118.

23. Mounier's actual role in the Resistance and his relation to *Combat* are an open question. For what I consider the best discussions of these matters, see Pierce, *Contemporary French Political Thought*, 140-141. *Cf.* Moix, *La pensée d'Emmanuel Mounier*, 31-44.

24. For Mounier's plan to make *Esprit* a full community and create a Personalist college, see Emmanuel Mounier, "Une nouvelle réalisation," *Esprit*, No. 81 (June, 1939), 414-418. To see Mounier's full plan after the War for creation of a Personalist college, which would have its own distinct anthropology, philosophy of society, politics and revolution, see an unpublished piece titled "Formation d'un collège personnaliste," dated December, 1945, found in *Dossier Three* of Mounier's writings and radio addresses from the years 1944 and 1945, at the Mounier Library, Châtenay-Malabry.

25. This quotation is taken from Adrien Dansette, "Contemporary French Catholicism," *The Catholic Church in World Affairs*, ed. Waldemar Gurian and M. A. Fitzsimons (Notre Dame, Indiana, 1954), 257.

26. Maritain, *France, My Country*, 29.

27. Maritain, *Messages*, 20.

28. Jacques Maritain, *Reflections on America* (Garden City, New York, 1964 [original date, 1958]), 101-102. This work gathers together Maritain's views on America which otherwise would have to be culled from Maritain's writings, in particular, his *Scholasticism and Politics*, ed. and trans. Mortimer Adler (New York, 1940), *Christianisme et démocratie* (New York, 1943), and *Education at the Crossroads* (New Haven, 1943), as well as his *Messages* and *Pour la justice* and *Man and State*.

29. For these quotations, see Maritain, *Reflections on America*, 104 and 106; for these points, *ibid.*, 101-116. Italics and parentheses are mine.

30. *Ibid.*, 105.

31. *Ibid.*, 110, 111.

32. *Ibid.*, 12.

33. For two points in Maritain's evolution from what can be considered a nineteenth century European conservatism to twentieth century American liberalism, see Jacques Maritain, " 'Right' and 'Left,' " *Blackfriars*, XVIII (November, 1937), 807-812, and *Man and State* (Chicago, 1951), esp. 76-187. In order to grasp in part how Maritain's evolution to democracy was in conjunction with that of the whole Church, see *Devant la crise mondiale. Manifeste de Catholiques européens séjournant en Amerique* (New York, n.d. [1941], and William Fitzgerald, "The Idea of Democracy in Contemporary Catholicism," *Review of Religion*, XII (January, 1948), 148-165.

34. For this last point, see esp. Maritain, *La voie de la paix, discours prononcé à la séance inaugurale de la seconde conférence internationale de l'UNESCO*, Mexico, November 6, 1947 (Mexico City, 1947).

35. See Jacques Maritain, *Education at the Crossroads* (New Haven, 1967 [orig. in English, 1943]), esp. 88-118.

36. For Mounier's admission that *Esprit* had been too divorced from political considerations, see Mounier's first post-War editorial, *Esprit*, nouvelle serie, No. 105 (December, 1944), 1-2.

37. For Mounier's comments on Christian Democrats, Socialists, Radicals, and De Gaulle, as well as his efforts to form an independent party, see Donald Wolf, "Emmanuel Mounier: A Catholic of the Left."

38. For Mounier's views on the Cold War, Russia and the United States, Marshall Plan and Atlantic Pact and nuclear war, see esp. an essay he wrote with Paul Fraisse and Jean-Marie Domenach, the future editor of *Esprit*, "La pacte atlantique," No. 155 (May, 1949), 215-226,; also see Mounier, "Les équivoques du pacifisme," *Esprit*, No. 153 (February, 1949), 181-198.

39. For the use of the concept real socialism and Mounier's conscious awareness of the development of this thought in this direction, see Emmanuel Mounier, "Les cinq étapes d'*Esprit*," *Dieu Vivant* (No. 16, 1950), 37-53.

40. It should be noted, however, that Mounier never stopped making criticisms of specific acts of all European Communist parties as is shown by his reaction to the Mindszenty trial and the Petkov case (Mounier, *Les certitudes difficiles, Oeuvres*, IV, 107-189); nor did Mounier abandon his basic philosophical and theological objections to Marxism or attempt to fuse the Church and Christianity to Marxism as he believed the *chrétiens progressistes* were in the destructive course of doing, as is shown for example in his article "Les chrétiens progressistes," *Esprit*, No. 154 (March-April, 1949), 572.

41. Jacques Maritain, *The Peasant of the Garonne: An Old Layman Questions Himself about the Present Time*, trans. Michael Cuddihy and Elizabeth Hughes (New York, 1968 [orig. date of French publication was 1966]).

BIBLIOGRAPHY

THIS BIBLIOGRAPHY is intended primarily to list the materials that have been used and cited in this study and to offer a bibliographical introduction to the works of Maritain and Mounier. Given the numerous themes this study has touched in seeking to trace the development of Maritain's and Mounier's understanding of the modern world, the following arrangement of materials has been adopted.

I. Mounier
II. Maritain
III. French and European Society and Politics
IV. French and European Thought and Culture
V. Catholicism and French Catholicism
VI. Catholic and French Catholic Thought

While obviously certain works could fall into two or more of the last four general categories, I have placed them in the category which best describes their use in this study. For instance, while Croce's *History of Europe in the Nineteenth Century* could be placed in either the category of French and European Society and Politics or in French and European Thought and Culture, I have placed it in the latter because it was used here as a vision of the modern world which contrasts with the visions of Maritain and Mounier. To take one more example, the works of Nicolas Berdyaev were placed with Catholic and French Catholic Thought, even though Berdyaev himself was not Catholic. The reason for this choice was Berdyaev's influence on French Catholic thought from the late 1920s onward. I hope the occasional inconvenience that might result from this arrangement will be compensated for by its greater suggestiveness.

Because of the important place of Bergson, Péguy and Chevalier in this study, a bibliographical word should be mentioned about each of them. The entries in this bibliography have been restricted to citing what I directly used in preparing this study. For a bibliography of Bergson, the reader can see Rose Marie Mosse-Bastide, *Bergson éducateur* (Paris: Presses Universitaires, 1955), 359-448. For Péguy's writings and works on Péguy, in addition to what is given here in section IV, the reader can see Hans Schmitt, *Péguy: Decline of an Idealist* (Baton Rouge: Louisiana State University Press, 1967), 193-205. For a bibliography of Chevalier,

the reader can use Chevalier's own five page bibliography, *Bibliographie,*
1903-1931 (Paris, 1931), and *Bibliothèque Nationale, catalogue général des livres
imprimés: Auteurs* (Paris: Impr. Nationale, 1900-1963).
There is need also for a few bibliographical statements on Mounier and Maritain.
Emmanuel Mounier's major writings are found in his four volume *Oeuvres* (Paris:
Seuil, 1961-1963). Volume One contains the books Mounier wrote in the 1930s.
Volume Two contains the *Traité,* in addition to notes Mounier had taken for later
editions of it. Volume Three contains the books Mounier wrote from 1944 to
1950. Volume Four contains three works published posthumously: *Les certitudes
difficiles* (Paris: Seuil, 1950), *L'espoir des désespérés* (Paris: Seuil, 1953), and an
enlarged version of *Mounier et sa génération* (Paris: Seuil, 1956), which contains
parts of Mounier's large and important correspondence and notebooks from the
mid-1920s until his death in 1950. Also in Volume Four is a complete bibliography of Mounier's writings, 835-876; slight corrections of the bibliography were
made in the 1967 edition of Volume Four.
The great majority of Mounier's published and unpublished writings are located
at a small library at the *Esprit* community, Châtenay-Malabry, France. In the
Mounier library there, in addition to Mounier's published writings, there are a
complete set of *Esprit* and numerous books, articles, addresses and theses on Mounier, as well as copies of all his articles (1929-1950) and radio addresses (1945-
1948). These articles and addresses are arranged chronologically in *Dossiers One
to Six.* Madame Mounier, who resides at Châtenay-Malabry and directs the Mounier Library, has Mounier's complete notebooks, correspondence, and personal
library. It should be mentioned here that Madame Mounier generously allowed me
to see Mounier's first *Carnet* which contains his reflections on his days with Chevalier, and the entirety of the Maritain-Mounier correspondence. During my two
week stay at Châtenay-Malabry, October 1 to October 14, 1968, I spoke with
Madame Mounier several times and with other members of the *Esprit* community,
especially historian Henri Marrou (October 13), Paul Fraisse (October 14), and
the present editor of *Esprit,* Jean-Marie Domenach (October 7).
It should be pointed out that the *Association des Amis d'Emmanuel Mounier*
(19 rue d'Antony, Châtenay-Malabry and 19 rue Jacob, Paris) has published since
1952 an annual or biannual bulletin titled *Bulletin des Amis d'Emmanuel Mounier.* These *Bulletins* have important materials for the Mounier scholar: (1) Bibliographical data on recent works, articles, conferences, as well as completed and
projected theses on Mounier (No. 6 [April, 1955] ,No. 21 [December, 1963], No.
22 [June, 1964], and No. 27 [January, 1966]); (2) Republications of many of
Mounier's pre-*Esprit* articles (No. 3 [April, 1953], and No. 4 [January, 1954]);
(3) First publication of some of Mounier's radio addresses on diverse subjects (No.
9-10 [December, 1956] and No. 12 [June, 1958]); (4) Unpublished correspondence, such as "Naissance et début de la revue *Esprit* evoqués à travers les rapports
de Maritain et Mounier, 1931-1933," No. 34-35 (November, 1969), "Correspondance Mounier-Berdiaeff," No. 33 (February, 1969), and "Lettres de Teilhard de
Chardin à Mounier," No. 27 (January, 1966), and (5) important writings of Mounier which are not easily obtained, such as "Péguy, médiateur de Bergson," No.
20 (July, 1963), and "Péguy ressuscité," No. 12 (June, 1958).
The beginning point of a biographical study of Mounier is still the commemorative issue of *Esprit* No. 174 (December, 1950), dedicated to Mounier at the time

of his death. Particularly valuable therein are Pierre-Aimé Touchard's "Dernier dialogue," 777-787, François Goguel's "Positions politiques," 797-819, Jean-Marie Domenach's "Les principes de choix politiques," 820-838, Paul Ricoeur's "Une philosophie personnaliste," 860-887, Henri Marrou's "Un homme dans l'église," 888-904, and Jean Lacroix's "Mounier éducateur," 839-851. For two other sympathetic and important collections of essays on Mounier, see *Emmanuel Mounier ou le combat du juste* (Bordeaux: Guy Ducros, 1968), which is a series of articles taken from the journal *Frères du Monde*, 1964-1967; and a recent special issue of *Esprit*, "Mounier de nouveau" (April, 1970). The standard biography of Mounier remains Candide Moix, *La pensée d'Emmanuel Mounier* (Paris: Seuil, 1968); a useful and short introduction to Mounier's thought has been done by Madame Mounier under the title of *L'engagement de la foi* (Paris: Seuil, 1968).

In contrast to Mounier's *Oeuvres*, there is no single collection of Maritain's works. The English reader, however, does have available to him three works that synthesize much of what is best in Maritain's writings: *The Social and Political Philosophy of Jacques Maritain*, ed. Joseph Evans and Leo Ward (Garden City, New York: Doubleday and Company, 1965), *A Maritain Reader*, ed. Donald and Idella Gallagher (Garden City, New York: Doubleday and Company, 1966), and *Jacques Maritain: Challenges and Renewals*, ed. Joseph Evans and Leo Ward (Cleveland: The World Publishing Company, 1968). For the student of Maritain, there are two indispensable books: Henri Bar's *Maritain en notre temps* (Paris: Grasset, 1959) is not only the standard biography of the mature Maritain but offers in its appendix a very useful chronology of Maritain's life and works. Donald and Idella Gallagher's *The Achievement of Jacques and Raïssa Maritain: A Bibliography* (Garden City, New York: Doubleday and Company, 1962) offers what can be considered a complete bibliography of the Maritains, which gives cross references to his books and articles and cites most major translations of his works in most foreign languages. For the American scholar of Maritain, the Jacques Maritain Library at the University of Notre Dame, Indiana, under the supervision of Joseph Evans, has made an impressive attempt to gather all of Maritain's writings, the works that influenced him and formed his milieu, and the works of some of his disciples such as Yves Simon.

In conclusion, it should be pointed out that the sections on Maritain and Mounier have each been divided into three subsections. First their major books are listed chronologically with some of their important English translations. (In Maritain's case there are necessary omissions because of the number of books, and included is Paul VI's [G. B. Montini's] Italian translation of Maritain's *Three Reformers*.) Second, their articles used in this study are also listed chronologically. (Mounier's pre-*Esprit* articles cited in the text and found in *Dossier One* have been omitted.) Third, selected articles and books that were helpful in preparing this study are listed in alphabetical order.

I. Mounier

A. The major works of Emmanuel Mounier.
Original editions in chronological order of their appearance, with mention of some English translations.

La pensée de Charles Péguy. Written in collaboration with Marcel Péguy and Georges Izard. Paris: Plon, 1931.

Révolution personnaliste et communautaire. Paris: Montaigne, 1935.

De la propriété capitaliste à la propriété humaine. Paris: Desclée de Brouwer, 1936.

Manifeste au service du personnalisme. Paris: Montaigne, 1936. *A Personalist Manifesto.* Trans. by the monks of Saint John's Abbey at Collegeville, Minn. New York: Longmans Green and Company, 1938.

Pacifistes ou bellicistes? Paris: Cerf, 1939.

L'affrontement chrétien. Neuchâtel: Baconnière, 1945.

Liberté sous conditions. Paris: Seuil, 1946.

Traité du caractère. Paris: Seuil, 1946. *The Character of Man.* Trans. Cynthia Rowland. Abridged. London: Rockliff, 1956.

Introduction aux existentialismes. Paris: Denoël, 1946. *Existentialist Philosophies.* Trans. Eric Blow. London: Rockliff, 1948.

Qu'est-ce que le personnalisme? Paris: Seuil, 1947.

L'éveil de l'Afrique noire. Paris: Seuil, 1948.

La petite peur du XXe siècle. Paris: Seuil, 1948. *Be Not Afraid: A Denunciation of Despair.* Also includes *What is Personalism?* Trans. Cynthia Rowland. London: Rockliff, 1951.

Le personnalisme. Paris: Presses Universitaires de France, 1949. *Personalism.* Trans. Philip Mairet. London: Routledge and Kegan Paul, 1952; republished by the University of Notre Dame Press, 1970.

Feu la Chrétienté. Paris: Seuil, 1950.

Les certitudes difficiles. Paris: Seuil, 1951.

L'espoir des désespérés. Paris: Seuil, 1953.

Mounier et sa génération. Paris: Seuil, 1956.

Oeuvres de Mounier. 4 vols. Paris: Seuil, 1961-1963.

B. A chronological list of articles and other writings of Mounier which were used within the text.

"Un penseur français: Jacques Chevalier," *La vie catholique*, April 3, 1926.

"A propos d'une thèse sur Maine de Biran: la leçon d'une vie," *La vie catholique*, Sept. 3, 1927.

"Refaire la renaissance," *Esprit*, No. 1 (October, 1932), 5-51.

"Espagne, signe de contradiction," *Esprit*, No. 49 (October, 1936), 1-3.

"Terre libre," *Esprit*, No. 50 (November, 1936), 286-290.

"Guernica ou la technique du mensonge," *Esprit*, No. 57 (June, 1937), 449-473.

"Espoir au peuple basque," *Esprit*, No. 58 (July, 1937), 643-649.

"Action temporelle des Catholiques," *Regards catholiques sur le monde,* eds. Dominique Auvergne [pseud.] and Geneviève d'Harcourt. Paris: Desclée de Brouwer, 1938, 77-91.

"Le Front Populaire: Bilan, avenir, et maintenant," *Esprit,* No. 66 (March, 1938), 801-806.

"Lettre autour de la guerre d'Espagne," *Esprit,* No. 68 (May, 1938), 235-251.

"La France est-elle finie?" *Le Voltigeur,* September 29, 1938.

"Vers un volonté française," *Esprit,* No. 80 (May, 1939), 297-300.

"Frontières du parti," *Esprit,* No. 80 (May, 1939), 258-263.

"Une nouvelle réalisation," *Esprit,* No. 81 (June, 1939), 414-418.

"Observations on the Traditions of French Personalism," *Personalist,* XX (Summer, 1939), 280-287.

"Conditions de paix pour l'été," *Esprit,* No. 83 (August, 1939), 657-692.

"1789-1939," *Esprit,* No. 84 (September, 1939), 697-700.

"1940," *Esprit,* No. 88 (January, 1940), 113-114.

"Gardons-nous de notre ennemi, l'Ennemi," *Esprit,* No. 88 (January, 1940), 115-119.

"Letter from France," *Commonweal,* XXXIII, No. 1 (October, 1940), 8-11.

"Péguy, médiateur de Bergson," *Henri Bergson,* eds. A. Béguin and P. Thévanez. Neuchâtel: La Baconnière, 1941, 319-328.

"*Esprit, nouvelle série,*" *Esprit,* No. 105 (December, 1944), 1-2.

"France in the Catacombs," *Commonweal,* XLII (May 11, 1945), 85-87.

"The Structures of Liberation," *Commonweal,* XLII (May 18, 1945), 112-114.

"The Resistance," *Commonweal,* XLII (May 25, 1945), 136-138.

"Les équivoques du pacifisme," *Esprit,* No. 153 (February, 1949), 181-198.

"Les chrétiens progressistes," *Esprit* No. 154 (March-April, 1949), 567-576.

"Le pacte atlantique," *Esprit,* No. 155 (May, 1949), 215-266.

"Les cinq étapes d'*Esprit,*" *Dieu Vivant* (No. 16, 1950), 37-53.

C. Selected articles and books on Mounier

Campanini, Giorgio. *La rivoluzione cristiana. Il pensiero politico di Emmanuel Mounier.* Brescia: Morcelliana, 1968.

Coll-Vinent, Roberto. *Mounier y el desorden establecido.* Barcelona: Ediciones Península, 1968.

Conilh, Jean. *Emmanuel Mounier, sa vie, son oeuvre avec un exposé de sa philosophie.* Paris: Presses Universitaires de France, 1966.

Dunphy, Jocelyn. "Emmanuel Mounier et la crise de l'humanisme, 1932-1950." Unpublished Master's thesis, Department of French, University of Melbourne, 1964.

"Emmanuel Mounier," *Esprit,* a commemorative issue, No. 174 (December, 1950).

Guissard, Lucien. *Emmanuel Mounier.* Paris: Editions Universitaires, 1962.

Hellman, John. "Emmanuel Mounier and *Esprit*: Personalist Dialogue with Existentialism, Marxism and Christianity." Unpublished doctoral thesis, Department of History, Harvard University, 1969.

———. "The Opening to the Left in French Catholicism: The Role of the Personalists," *The Journal of the History of Ideas*, XXXIV, No. 3 (July-Sept., 1973), 381-390.

Hill, Patrick J. "Emmanuel Mounier: Total Christianity and Practical Marxism," *Cross Currents*, XVIII, No. 1 (Winter, 1968), 77-104.

Kelly, M. H. "The Fate of Mounier: A Bibliographic Essay," *Journal of European Studies*, II, No. 2 (Sept., 1972), 256-267.

Lewis, David. "Emmanuel Mounier and the Politics of Moral Revolution: Aspects of Political Crises in French Liberal Catholicism, 1935-1938," *Catholic Historical Review*, LX, No. 4 (January, 1970), 266-290.

Loubet de Bayle, J. *Les non-conformistes des années 30. Une tentative de renouvellement de la pensée française.* Paris: Seuil, 1969.

Moix, Candide. *La pensée d'Emmanuel Mounier.* Paris: Seuil, 1960.

Pierce, Roy. *Contemporary French Political Thought.* New York: Oxford University Press, 1966.

Rauch, William. *Politics and Belief in Modern France: Emmanuel Mounier and the Christian Democratic Movement, 1932-1950.* New York: Humanities Press, 1972.

Simon, Pierre-Henri. "Mounier et l'*Esprit*," *Le Monde*, April 20, 1956.

Wolf, Donald. "Emmanuel Mounier: A Catholic of the Left," *Review of Politics*, XXII, No. 3 (July, 1960), 324-344.

Zaza, Noureddine. *Etude critique de la notion d'engagement chez E. Mounier.* Geneva: Librairie Droz, 1955.

II. Maritain

A. The major works of Jacques Maritain.

Selected original editions in chronological order of their appearance, with mention of some English translations.

La philosophie bergsonienne: Etudes critiques. Paris: Marcel Rivière et Cie., 1914. *Bergsonian Philosophy and Thomism.* Trans. by Mabelle L. Andison. New York: Philosophical Library, 1955.

Art et scholastique. Paris: Librairie de l'Art Catholique, 1920. *Art and Scholasticism.* Trans. by J. F. Scanlan. London: Sheed and Ward, 1930.

Théonas, ou les entretiens d'un sage et de deux philosophes sur diverses matières inégalement actuelles. Paris: Nouvelle Librairie Nationale, 1921. *Théonas: Conversations of a Sage.* Trans. by F. J. Sheed with a preface by the author. New York: Sheed and Ward, 1933.

Antimoderne. Paris: Editions de la Revue des Jeunes, 1922.

Réflexions sur l'intelligence et sur sa vie propre. Paris: Nouvelle Nationale, 1924.

Trois réformateurs: Luther, Descartes, Rousseau. Paris: Librairie Plon, 1925. *Three Reformers: Luther, Descartes, Rousseau.* New York: Charles Scribner's Sons, 1929. *Tre riformatori.* Trans. G. B. Montini. Brescia: Morcelliana, 1928.

Réponse à Jean Cocteau. Paris: Librairie Stock, 1926.

Une opinion sur Charles Maurras et le devoir des catholiques. Paris: Librairie Plon, 1926.

Primauté du spirituel. Paris: Librairie Plon, 1927. *The Things That Are Not Caesar's.* Trans. J. F. Scanlan. London: Sheed and Ward, 1930.

Quelques pages sur Léon Bloy. Paris: L'Artisan du Livre, 1927.

Le docteur angélique. Paris: Desclée de Brouwer, 1930. *The Angelic Doctor: The Life and Thought of Saint Thomas Aquinas.* Trans. by J. F. Scanlan. Toronto: Longmans, Green and Co., 1931.

Religion et culture. Paris: Desclée de Brouwer, 1930. *Religion and Culture.* Intro. by Christopher Dawson. Trans. by J. F. Scanlan. London: Sheed and Ward, 1931.

Distinguer pour unir: Ou, les degrés du savoir. Paris: Desclée de Brouwer, 1932. *Distinguish To Unite: Or The Degrees of Knowledge.* Trans. under the supervision of Gerald B. Phelan from 4th French Edition. London: Geoffrey Bles, 1959.

Le songe de Descartes, suivi de quelques essais. Paris: Corrêa, 1932. *The Dream of Descartes, Together With Some Other Essays.* Trans. by Mabelle L. Andison. New York: Philosophical Library, 1944.

De la philosophie chrétienne. Paris: Desclée de Brouwer, 1933.

Du régime temporel et de la liberté. Paris: Desclée de Brouwer, 1933. *Freedom in the Modern World.* Trans. by Richard O'Sullivan. London: Sheed and Ward, 1936.

Sept leçons sur l'être et les premiers principes de la raison spéculative. Paris: Pierre Téqui, 1934. *A Preface to Metaphysics: Seven Lectures on Being.* New York: New American Library, 1962.

Lettre sur l'indépendance. Paris: Desclée de Brouwer, 1935.

Science et sagesse, suivi d'éclaircissements sur la philosophie morale. Paris: Labergerie, 1935. *Science and Wisdom.* Trans. by Bernard Wall. New York: Charles Scribner's Sons, 1940.

Humanisme intégral: Problèmes temporels et spirituels d'une nouvelle chrétienté. Paris: Fernand Aubier, 1936. *Integral Humanism.* Trans. by Joseph Evans from revised French edition. New York: Charles Scribner's Sons, 1968.

Les juifs parmi les nations. Paris: Cerf, 1938. *A Christian Looks at the Jewish Question.* New York and Toronto: Longmans, Green and Co., 1939.

Le crépuscule de la civilisation. Paris: Editions Les Nouvelles Lettres, 1939. *The Twilight of Civilization.* Trans. by Lionel Landry. New York: Sheed and Ward, 1943.

Scholasticism and Politics. Trans. and ed. by Mortimer J. Adler. New York: The Macmillan Company, 1940.

A travers le désastre. New York: Editions de la Maison Française, 1941. *France, My Country, Through the Disaster.* New York and Toronto: Longmans, Green and Co., 1941.

Les droits de l'homme et la loi naturelle. New York: Editions de la Maison Française, 1942. *The Rights of Man and Natural Law.* Trans. by Doris C. Anson. New York: Charles Scribner's Sons, 1943.

Christianisme et démocratie. New York: Editions de la Maison Française, 1943. *Christianity and Democracy.* Trans. by Doris C. Anson. New York: Charles Scribner's Sons, 1944.

Education at the Crossroads. New Haven: Yale University Press, 1943.

A travers la victoire. Paris: Paul Hartmann, 1945.

Messages, 1941-1945. New York: Editions de la Maison Française, 1945.

Pour la justice, articles et discours (1940-1945). New York: Editions de la Maison Française, 1945.

Court traité de l'existence et de l'existant. Paris: Paul Hartmann, 1947. *Existence and the Existent.* Trans. by Lewis Galantière and Gerald B. Phelan. Garden City, New York: Doubleday and Company, 1957.

La personne et le bien commun. Paris: Desclée de Bouwer, 1947. *The Person and the Common Good.* trans. by John J. Fitzgerald. New York: Charles Scribner's Sons, 1947.

Raison et raisons: essais détachés. Paris: Egloff, 1947. *The Range of Reason.* New York: Charles Scribner's Sons, 1952.

Man and the State. Chicago: University of Chicago Press, 1951.

Neuf leçons sur les notions premières de la philosophie morale. Paris: Pierre Téqui, 1951.

Approches de Dieu. Paris: Alsatia, 1953. *Approaches to God.* Trans. by Peter O'Reilly. New York: Harper and Brothers, 1954.

Creative Intuition in Art and Poetry. New York: Pantheon Books, 1953.

On the Philosophy of History. Ed. by Joseph Evans. New York: Charles Scribner's Sons, 1957.

Reflections on America. New York: Charles Scribner's Sons, 1958.

Le philosophe dans la cité. Paris: Alsatia, 1960.

La philosophie morale; examen historique et critique des grands systèmes. Paris: Librairie Gallimard, 1960. *Moral Philosophy. An Historical and Critical Survey of the Great Systems.* London: Geoffrey Bles, 1964.

Carnet de notes. Paris: Desclée de Brouwer, 1965.

Le paysan de la Garonne: Un vieux laïc s'interroge à propos du temps présent. Paris: Desclée de Brouwer, 1966. *The Peasant of the Garonne.* Trans. by Michael Cuddihy and Elizabeth Hughes. New York: Holt, Rinehart and Winston, 1968.

De l'Eglise du Christ. Paris: Desclée de Brouwer, 1970.

B. Articles and other writings of Maritain used within the text.

"La science moderne et la raison," *Revue de la philosophie,* XVI (June, 1910), 575-603.

"Le néo-vitalisme en Allemagne et le darwinisme," *Revue de philosophie.* XVII (October, 1910), 417-444.

"L'esprit de la philosophie moderne. I. Les préparations de la réforme cartésienne. II. Descartes et la théologie," *Revue de la philosophie,* XXIV (June, 1914), 601-625.

"L'esprit de la philosophie moderne. III. L'indépendance de l'esprit," *Revue de la philosophie,* XXV (July, 1914), 53-82.

"L'Allemagne et la philosophie moderne," *La Foi Catholique,* XVI (1915), 5-30.

"L'état actuel de la philosophie allemande," *La Revue Universelle,* IV (March 15, 1921), 705-720.

"Le témoignage d'Ernst Psichari," *Revue de Jeunes,* XI (December 25, 1921), 670-686.

"Ernst Psichari," *La Revue Universelle,* VII (March 1, 1922), 609-633.

"Le sens de la condemnation," Jacques Maritain *et al., Pourquoi Rome a parlé.* Paris: Spes, 1927, 329-385.

"Réponse à Karl Hall à propos de Luther," *Nova et Vetera,* III (October-December, 1928), 423-427.

"Le joug du Christ," *Clairvoyance de Rome.* Maritain *et al.* Paris: Spes, 1929, 269-290.

"Religion et culture II," *Esprit,* No. 4 (January, 1933), 523-545.

"Lettre sur le monde bourgeois," *Esprit,* No. 6 (March, 1933), 523-545.

"De la guerre sainte," *La Nouvelle Revue Française,* XLIX (July 1, 1937), 21-37.

"'Right' and 'Left,'" *Blackfriars,* XVIII (November, 1937), 807-812.

"War and the Bombardment of Cities," *Commonweal,* XXVIII (September 2, 1938), 460-461.

"I Believe," *I Believe.* Ed. by Clifton Fadiman. New York: Simon and Schuster, 1939, 197-210.

"Le mendiant ingrat," *Léon Bloy.* Neuchâtel: Baconnière, 1946, 31-37.

C. Selected articles and books on Maritain.

Bars, Henry. *Maritain en notre temps.* Paris: Bernard Grasset, 1959.

——. *La politique selon Jacques Maritain.* Paris: Editions Ouvrières, 1961.

Coulton, G. G., "The Historical Background of Maritain's Humanism," *Journal of the History of Ideas,* V (October, 1944), 415-433.

Croteau, Jacques. *Les fondements thomistes du personnalisme de Maritain.* Ottawa: Editions de l'Université d'Ottawa, 1955.

Evans, Joseph W. "Jacques Maritain and the Problem of Pluralism in Political Life," *The Review of Politics,* XXII (July, 1960), 307-323.

——. "Jacques Maritain's Personalism," *The Review of Politics,* XIV (April, 1952), 166-177.

Holl, Karl. "Martin Luther à propos de l'étude de M. Jacques Maritain," *Revue de Théologie et de Philosophie,* N. S. XV, No. 64-65 (August-December 1927), 260-270.

"Hommage à Jacques Maritain," *La Nouvelle Relevé* (Montreal), II (December, 1942).

Hook, Sidney, "The Integral Humanism of Jacques Maritain," *Partisan Review,* VII (May-June, 1940), 204-229.

Iswolsky, Helen. "The House in Meudon" and "The Philosophies in the World," *Light Before Dusk: A Russian Catholic in France, 1923-1941.* New York: Longmans, Green and Co., 1942, 70-87, 184-199.

"Jacques Maritain, son oeuvre philosophique," *Revue Thomiste,* XLVIII, Nos. 1-2 (1948).

Journet, Charles. "La philosophie de l'histoire," *Recherches et Débats,* No. 19 (Maritain Issue of July, 1957), 166-176.

Jung, Hwa Yol. *The Foundation of Jacques Maritain's Political Philosophy.* Gainesville, Florida: University of Florida Press, 1960.

Kelsen, Hans. "Foundations of Democracy," *Ethics,* LXVI (October, 1955), 62-67.

Lefevre, Frédéric, ed. "Jacques Maritain et Henri Massis," *Une Heure Avec.* Paris: Editions de Nouvelle Revue Française, 1924.

Maritain, Raïssa. *The Memoirs of Raïssa Maritain: We Have Been Friends Together and Adventures in Grace.* Trans. by Julie Kernan. Garden City, New York: Doubleday and Company, 1961.

The Maritain Volume of the Thomist. Dedicated to Jacques Maritain on the occasion of his Sixtieth Anniversary. Published January 1943 as Volume V of the Thomist. New York: Sheed and Ward, 1943.

Massis, Henri. *Maurras et notre temps.* 2 vols., Paris-Geneva: La Palatine, 1951.

Meer de Walcheren, Pierre van de. *Rencontres: Léon Bloy, Raïssa Maritain, Christine et Pietke.* Paris: Desclée de Brouwer, 1961.

Meinvielle, Julio. *De Lammenais à Maritain.* Buenos Aires: Nuestro Tiempo, 1945.

O'Donnell, Charles. "The Idea of a New Christendom: The Cultural and Political Philosophy of Jacques Maritain." 2 vols. Unpublished doctoral dissertation, Harvard University, 1940.

Rommen, Heinrich A. "Church and State," *The Review of Politics,* XII (July, 1950), 321-340.

Rouquette, Robert. "Filleuls de Léon Bloy. Le cheminement spirituelle de Raïssa et Jacques Maritain," *Etudes,* CCIX (February, 1949), 200-216.

III. *French and European Society and Politics*

Aron, Robert. *The Vichy Regime, 1940-1944.* Trans. by Humphrey Hare. Boston: Beacon Press, 1969.

Bloch, Marc. *Strange Defeat.* Trans. by Gerard Hopkins. New York: W. W. Norton, 1968.

Chastenet, Jacques. *Histoire de la troisième république.* 7 vols. Paris: Hachette, 1952-1963.

Cobban, Alfred. *A History of Modern France.* Vol. II: *1799-1945.* Baltimore: Penguin, 1961.

Earle, Edward M., ed. *Modern France: Problems of the Third and Fourth Republics.* Princeton: Princeton University Press, 1951.

Elbow, Matthew. *French Corporate Theory, 1789-1848.* New York: Columbia University Press, 1953.

Goguel, François. *La politique des partis sous la IIIe république.* Paris: Seuil, 1946.

——. "Six Authors in Search of a National Character," *In Search of France.* Stanley Hoffmann et al. New York: Harper and Row, 1965, 359-405.

Hale, Oron. *The Great Illusion, 1900-1914.* New York: Harper and Row, 1971.

Hoffmann, Stanley. "Paradoxes of the French Political Community," *In Search of France.* Stanley Hoffmann et al. New York: Harper and Row, 1965, 33-117.

Holborn, Hajo. *The Political Collapse of Europe.* New York: Alfred Knopf, 1951.

Hughes, H. Stuart. *Contemporary Europe: A History.* Englewood Cliffs, New Jersey: Prentice Hall, 1961.

Julliard, Jacques, "La politique religieuse de Charles Maurras," *Esprit,* Vol. XXVI, No. 259 (January-March, 1958), 359-384.

Larmour, Peter J. *The French Radical Party in the 1930s.* Stanford: Stanford University Press, 1964.

Lichtheim, George. *Marxism in Modern France.* New York: Columbia University Press, 1966.

Luethy, Herbert. *France Against Herself.* New York: Praeger, 1955.

Mayer, Arno. *Wilson vs. Lenin: The Political Origins of the New Diplomacy.* New York: World Publishing Company, 1964.

Osgood, Samuel M. *French Royalism Under the Third and Fourth Republics.* The Hague: Nijhoff, 1960.

Panichar, George A., ed. *Promise of Greatness. The War of 1914-1918.* New York: John Hay, 1968.

Plumyène, Jean and Lasierra, R. *Les fascismes français, 1923-1963.* Paris: Seuil, 1963.

Rémond, René. *The Right Wing in France from 1815 to de Gaulle.* Trans. by James Laux. Philadelphia: University of Pennsylvania Press, 1966.

Renouvin, Pierre. *Histoire des rélations internationales,* Vol. VIII, Part II, *Les crises du XXᵉ siècle, de 1929 à 1945.* Paris: Librairie Hachette, 1958.

Sontag, Raymond. *A Broken World, 1919-1939.* New York: Harper and Row, 1971.

Stillman, Edmund and Pfaff, William. *The Politics of Hysteria.* New York: Harper and Row, 1964.

Thomson, David. *Democracy in France Since 1870.* 4th ed. New York: Oxford University Press, 1964.

Warner, Geoffrey. "The Stavisky Affair and the Riots of February Sixth, 1934." *The Shaping of Modern France: Writings on French History since 1715,* ed. by James Friguglietti and Emmet Kennedy. London: MacMillan, 1969.

Weber, Eugen. *Action Française: Royalism and Reaction in the Twentieth Century.* Palo Alto: Stanford University Press, 1962.

——— . "France," in Hans Rogger and Eugen Weber, *et al. The European Right.* Berkeley: University of California Press, 1966.

——— . "Nationalism, Socialism and National Socialism in France," *French Historical Studies,* II (No. 3, 1962), 273-307.

——— . *Varieties of Fascism: Doctrines of Revolution in the Twentieth Century.* New York: D. Van Nostrand Company, 1964.

Werth, Alexander. *France 1940-1955.* New York: Holt, 1956.

——— . *The Twilight of France 1933-1940.* New York: Harper and Row, 1942.

Williams, Philip M. *Crisis and Compromise: Politics in the Fourth Republic.* London: Longmans, 1964.

Wright, Gordon. *France in Modern Times: 1760 to the Present.* Chicago: Rand McNally, 1960.

——— . *The Ordeal of Total War, 1939-1945.* New York: Harper and Row, 1968.

——— . *The Reshaping of French Democracy.* London: Methuen and Company, 1950.

IV. French and European Thought and Culture

Agathon, pseud. [Henry Massis]. *Enquête des jeunes gens d'aujourd'hui.* Paris: Librairie Plon, 1913.

Alberés, R. M., pseud. [René Marrill]. *L'aventure intellectuelle du XXᵉ siècle.* Paris: La nouvelle édition, 1950.

Arbour, Romeo. *Henri Bergson et les lettres françaises.* Paris: Librairie José Corti, 1955.

Arendt, Hannah. *The Human Condition.* Garden City, New York: Doubleday and Company, 1959.

——. *Men in Dark Times.* New York: Harcourt, Brace and World, 1968.

——. *The Origins of Totalitarianism.* Cleveland: World Publishing Company, 1958.

Aron, Raymond. *The Century of Total War.* Boston: Beacon Press, 1955.

——. *The Opium of the Intellectual.* Trans. by Terence Kilmartin. New York: Norton and Company, 1962.

Aron, Robert and Dandieu, Arnaud. *La révolution nécessaire.* Paris: Grasset, 1933.

Bancquart, Marie-Claire, *Les écrivains et l'histoire: Maurice Barrès, Léon Bloy, Anatole France, Charles Péguy.* Paris: A. G. Nizet, 1966.

Barthélemy-Madaule, Madeleine. *Bergson, adversaire de Kant, étude critique de la conception bergsonienne du kantisme.* Paris: Presse Universitaires de France, 1966.

Béguin, Albert and Thévanez, P., ed. *Henri Bergson.* Neuchâtel: Baconnièr, 1941.

Benda, Julien. *The Betrayal of the Intellectuals.* Trans. by Richard Aldington. Boston: Beacon Press, 1959.

Benson, Frederick. *Writers in Arms. Literary Impact of the Spanish Civil War.* New York: New York University Press, 1967.

Bergson, Henri. *Creative Evolution.* Trans. by Arthur Mitchell. New York: Modern Library, 1944.

——. *The Creative Mind.* Trans. by Mabelle Andison. New York: Greenwood Press, 1968.

——. *Duration and Simultaneity.* Trans. by Leon Jacobson. New York: Bobbs-Merrill Company, 1965.

——. *An Introduction to Metaphysics.* Trans. by T. E. Hulme. Revised edition. New York: G. P. Putman's Sons, 1912.

——. *Matter and Memory.* Trans. by Nancy Paul and W. Scott Palmer. Garden City, New York: Doubleday and Company, 1959.

——. *Time and Free Will: An Essay on the Immediate Data of Consciousness.* Trans. by F. L. Pogson. New York: Harper and Row, 1960.

Binkley, Robert C. *Realism and Nationalism, 1852-1871.* New York: Harper and Row, 1935.

Bochenski, I. M. *Contemporary European Philosophy.* Trans. by Donald Nicholl and Karl Aschenbrenner. Berkeley: University of California Press, 1961.

Bourdieu, Pierre and Passeron, Jean-Claude, "Sociology and Philosophy Since 1945—Death and Resurrection of a Philosophy without Subject," *Social Research,* XXXIV (Nov. 7, 1967), 162-212.

Brombert, Victor. *The Intellectual Hero: Studies in the French Novel, 1880-1955.* Philadelphia: Lippincott, 1961.

Brunschvicg, Léon. *Descartes et Pascal, lectures de Montaigne.* New York: Brentano, 1944.

Burnier, Michel-Antoine, *Choice of Action. The French Existentialists on the Political Front Line.* Trans. Bernard Murchland. New York: Random House, 1968.

Camus, Albert. *The Rebel: An Essay on Man in Revolt.* trans. by Anthony Bower. New York: Alfred A. Knopf, 1956.

Cassirer, Ernst. *The Philosophy of the Enlightenment.* Trans. by Fritz C. A. Koellen and James Pettegrove. Boston: Beacon Press, 1955.

———. *The Question of Jean-Jacques Rousseau.* Trans. by Peter Gay. New York: Columbia University Press, 1954.

Catemario, Armando, *La società malata. Saggio sulla filosofia di Fromm.* Naples: Gianni, 1962.

Caute, David. *Communism and the French Intellectuals, 1914-1960.* New York: Macmillan, 1964.

Colton, Joel. *Léon Blum: Humanist in Politics.* New York: Alfred A. Knopf, 1966.

Cornu, Auguste. *Karl Marx. L'homme et l'oeuvre.* Paris: Félix Alcan, 1935.

Croce, Benedetto. *History of Europe in the Nineteenth Century.* Trans. by Henry Furst. New York: Harcourt, Brace and World, 1963.

Curtis, Michael. *Three Against the Republic: Sorel, Barrès and Maurras.* Princeton, New Jersey: Princeton University Press, 1959.

Curtius, Robert. *The Civilization of France.* Trans. by Olive Wyon. New York: Random House, 1962.

Digeon, Claude. *La crise allemande de la pensée française.* Paris: Presses Universitaires de France, 1959.

Domenach, Jean-Marie. *Barrès par lui-même.* Paris: Seuil, 1954.

Entrèves, A. P. d'. *Natural Law: An Introduction to Legal Philosophy.* London: Hutchinson University Library, 1951.

Erikson, Erik. *Identity, Youth and Crisis.* New York: W. W. Norton, 1968.

———. *Young Man Luther.* New York: W. W. Norton, 1962.

Fabrègues, Jean de. "Le mouvement des idées," *Trente ans, 1914-1948: de Clemenceau à de Gaulle.* Paris: Nouvelle Librairie de France, 1949, 337-352.

Febvre, Lucien. *Un Destin: Martin Luther.* Paris: Rieder, 1928.

Fonsegrive, Georges. *L'évolution des idées dans la France contemporaine.* Paris: Bloud et Gay, 1920.

Fowlie, Wallace. *A Guide to Contemporary French Literature.* New York: Meridian, 1957.

Garaudy, Roger. *Perspectives de l'homme: existentialisme, pensée catholique, marxisme.* Paris: Presses Universitaires de France, 1961.

Gay, Peter. *Weimar Culture.* New York: Harper and Row, 1968.

Goldberg, Harvey. *The Life of Jean Jaurès.* Madison: The University of Wisconsin Press, 1968.

Graves, Robert and Hodges, Alan. *The Long Week-end. A Social History of Great Britain, 1918-1939.* New York: Norton, 1963.

Hazard, Paul. *La crise de la conscience européenne.* Paris: Boivin, 1935.

Hegel, George Wilhelm Friedrich. *The Philosophy of Hegel.* Ed. and Trans. by Carl J. Friedrick. New York: Random House, 1954.

Heidegger, Martin. *Being and Time.* Trans. by John Macquarrie and Edward Robinson. Oxford: Blackwells, 1967.

Henry, André. *Bergson: Maître de Péguy.* Paris: Elzéver, 1948.

Hughes, H. Stuart. *Consciousness and Society. The Reconstruction of European Social Thought, 1890-1930.* New York: Knopf, 1961.

———. *The Obstructed Path. French Social Thought in the Years of Desperation.* New York: Harper and Row, 1968.

Husserl, Edmund. *Cartesian Meditations.* Trans. by Dorion Cairns. The Hague: Nijhoff, 1967.

James, William. *Varieties of Religious Experience.* New York: The New American Library, 1958.

Jankélévitch, Vladimir. *Bergson.* Paris: F. Alcan, 1931.

Jaspers, Karl. *Man in the Modern Age.* Trans. by Eden and Cedar Paul. Garden City, New York: Doubleday and Company, 1951.

Jones, W. T., *A History of Western Philosophy.* Vol. II. New York: Harcourt Brace and World, 1952.

Jouvenel, Betrand de. *On Power: Its Nature and the History of Its Growth.* Trans. by J. F. Hunington. Boston: Beacon Press, 1962.

Kahler, Erich. *The Tower and the Abyss.* New York: The Viking Press, 1967.

Lavelle, Louis. *La philosophie entre les deux guerres.* Paris: Aubier, 1949.

Lipiansky, Edmond. *"L'Ordre Nouveau,"* Lipiansky and Bernard Rettenbach, *Ordre et démocratie: Deux sociétés de pensées: De l'Ordre Nouveau au Club Moulin.* Paris: Presses Universitaires de France, 1967, 1-102.

Loubet del Bayle, Jean Louis. *Les non-conformistes des années 30. Une tentative de renouvellement de la pensée politique française.* Paris: Seuil, 1969.

Marcuse, Herbert, *Reason and Revolution.* Boston: Beacon Press, 1960.

Masur, Gerhard. *Prophets of Yesterday: Studies in European Culture.* New York: Harper and Row, 1966.

Maxence, Jean-Pierre. *Histoire de dix ans, 1927-1937.* Paris: Gallimard, 1939.

Molnar, Thomas. *The Decline of the Intellectual.* New York: World Publishing Company, 1965.

Moré, Marcel. *Accords et dissonances, 1932-1944.* Paris: Gallimard, 1967.

Muchielli, Roger. *Le mythe de la cité idéale.* Paris: Presses Universitaires, 1960.

Mumford, Lewis. *Technics and Civilization.* New York: Harcourt Brace and World, 1934.

Niebuhr, Reinhold. *Moral Man and Immoral Society.* New York: Charles Scribner's Sons, 1932.

Nisbet, Robert. *Community and Power.* New York: Oxford University Press, 1962.

———. *Social Change and History: Aspects of the Western Theory of Development.* New York: Oxford University Press, 1969.

Nolte, Ernst. *Three Faces of Fascism: Action Française, Italian Fascism, National Socialism.* Trans. by Leile Vennewitz. New York: Holt, Rinehart and Winston, 1966.

Ortega y Gasset, José. *The Modern Theme.* Trans. by James Cleugh. New York: Harper and Row, 1961.

———. *The Revolt of the Masses.* 25th ed. New York: W. W. Norton, 1957.

Park. Julien, ed. *The Culture of France in Our Time.* Ithaca: Cornell University Press, 1954.

Perry, Ralph Barton. *The Thought and Character of William James.* 2 vols. Boston: Little, Brown and Company, 1935.

Pierce, Roy. *Contemporary French Political Thought.* New York: Oxford University Press, 1966.

Ricoeur, Paul. *History and Truth.* Trans. by Charles A. Kelbey. Evanston: North-western University Press, 1965.

Rolland, Romain. *Jean Christophe.* Trans. by Gilbert Cannan. New York: Modern Library, 1913.

Rougemont, Denis de. *The Idea of Europe.* Trans. by Norman Guterman. New York: World Publishing Company, 1968.

——. *Penser avec les mains.* Paris: Albin Michel, 1936.

Ruggiero, Guido de. *A History of European Liberalism.* Trans. by R. G. Colling-wood. Boston: Beacon Press, 1959.

Salomone, A. William. "The Risorgimento between Ideology and History: The Political Myth of 'Rivoluzione Mancata,'" *American Historical Review,* LXVIII (October, 1962), 38-56.

Schinz, Albert. *Etat présent des travaux sur Jean-Jacques Rousseau.* New York: Modern Language Association, 1941.

Sciacca, M. F., ed. *Les grands courants de la pensée mondiale contemporaine.* 6 vols. Milan: Marzorati, 1964.

Sebba, Gregor. *Bibliographia Cartesiana: A Critical Introduction to Descartes Literature, 1880-1960.* The Hague: Nijhoff, 1964.

Shattuck, Roger. *The Banquet Years: The Origins of the Avant-Garde, 1885 to World War One.* Garden City, New York: Doubleday and Company, 1961.

Shestov, Léon. *Athens and Jerusalem.* Trans. by Bernard Martin. Athens, Ohio: Ohio University Press, 1966.

Simon, Pierre-Henri. *Histoire de la littérature française au XXe siècle.* 2 vols. 8th ed. Paris: Librarie Armand Colin, 1965.

—— *L'homme en procès: Malraux, Sartre, Camus, Saint-Exupéry.* 6th ed. Paris: Petite Bibliothèque Payot, 1950.

Sorel, Georges. *Reflections on Violence.* Introduction by Edward Shils. Trans. by J. Roth and T. E. Hulme. New York: Collier Books, 1961.

Stern, Fritz. *Politics of Cultural Despair: A Study in the Rise of Germanic Ideology.* New York: Doubleday and Company, 1965.

Strauss, Leo. *Natural Right and History.* Chicago: University of Chicago Press, 1965.

Stock, Phyllis, "Students versus the University in Pre-World War I Paris," *French Historical Studies,* VIII, No. 1 (Spring, 1971), 93-110.

Swart, Konrad. *The Sense of Decadence in Nineteenth Century France.* The Hague: Nijhoff, 1964.

Talmon, J. L. *The Origins of Totalitarian Democracy.* New York: Frederick A. Praeger, 1960.

Tison-Braun, Micheline. *La crise de l'humanisme: Le conflit de l'individu et de la société dans la littérature française moderne.* Paris: Librairie Nizet, 1958.

Touchard, Jean. "L'esprit des années 30: Une tentative de renouvellement de la pensée politique française," *Tendances politiques dans la vie française depuis 1789.* Paris: Hachette, 1960.

——. *Histoire des idées politiques.* Vol. II: *Du XVIIIe siècle à nos jours.* Paris: Presses Universitaires, 1959.

Valéry, Paul. *History and Politics.* Introduction by Salvador de Madariaga. Trans. by Denise Folliot and Jackson Mathews. New York: Bollingen Foundation, 1962.

Vico, Giambattista. *The New Science of Giambattista Vico.* Trans. and ed. by Thomas Bergin and Max Fisch from the 3rd edition of 1744. New York: Doubleday and Company, 1966.

Weber, Eugen. "The Secret World of Jean Barois: Notes on the Portrait of an Age," *The Origins of Modern Consciousness.* Ed. by John Weiss. Detroit: Wayne State University Press, 1965.

Wilson, Edmund. *Axel's Castle: A Study of the Imaginative Literature of 1870-1930.* New York: Charles Scribner's Sons, 1959.

Windelband, Wilhelm. *A History of Philosophy.* Vol. II. New York: Harper and Row, 1958.

V. *Catholicism and French Catholicism*

Bosworth, William. *Catholicism and Crisis in Modern France: French Catholic Groups at the Threshold of the Third Republic.* Princeton: Princeton University Press, 1962.

Daniel-Rops, Henri. *A Fight for God, 1870-1939.* Trans. by John Warrington. 2 vols. Garden City, New York: Doubleday and Company, 1967.

Dansette, Adrien, "Contemporary French Catholicism," *The Catholic Church in the Modern World.* Ed. by Waldemar Gurian and M. A. Fitzsimmons. Notre Dame, Indiana: Notre Dame University Press, 1954.

———. *Religious History of Modern France.* Vol. II. New York: Herder, 1961.

Einaudi, Mario and Goguel, François. *Christian Democracy in Italy and France.* Notre Dame, Indiana: Notre Dame University Press, 1952.

Falconi, Carlo. *The Popes in the Twentieth Century.* Trans. by Muriel Grindrod. Boston: Little, Brown and Company, 1967.

Fremantle, Anne, ed. *The Papal Encyclicals in Their Historical Context.* New York: New American Library, 1956.

Gilson, Etienne, ed. *The Church Speaks to the Modern World. The Social Teachings of Leo XIII.* Garden City, New York: Doubleday and Company, 1954.

Guitton, Jean. *Les Davidées: Histoire d'un mouvement d'apostolat laïc, 1916-1966.* Paris: Casterman, 1967.

Hales, E. E. Y. *The Catholic Church in the Modern World.* Garden City, New York: Doubleday and Company, 1960.

———. *Pope John and His Revolution.* Garden City, New York: Doubleday and Company, 1966.

McLaughlin, Terence, ed. *The Church and the Reconstruction of the Modern World: The Social Encyclicals of Pius XI.* Garden City, New York: Doubleday and Company, 1957.

Moody, Joseph. *Church and Society: Catholic Social and Political Thought and Movements, 1789-1950.* New York: Arts Inc., 1950.

Paul, Harry W. *The Second Ralliement: The Rapprochement Between Church and State in France in the Twentieth Century.* Washington, D.C.: Catholic University of America Press, 1967.

Rauch, R. William, Jr. "From the Sillon to the Mouvement Républicain Populaire," *The Catholic Historical Review,* LVIII, No. 1 (April, 1972), 25-66.

Rémond, René. *Les catholiques, le communisme et les crises, 1929-1939.* Paris: Armand Colin, 1960.

——. "Droite et gauche dans le catholicisme français contemporain," *Revue Française de Science Politique.* Nos. III and IV (September and December, 1958), 529-544 and 803-820.

——. "L'évolution de la notion de laïcité entre 1919 et 1939," *Cahiers d'Histoire,* IV (No. 1, 1959), 71-87.

Sturzo, Luigi. *Church and State.* Trans. by Barbara Barclay Carter. Vol. II. Notre Dame, Indiana: University of Notre Dame Press, 1962.

VI. *Catholic and French Catholic Thought.*

Aubert, Roger. *La théologie catholique au milieu du XXe siècle.* Paris: Casterman, 1954.

Barthélemy-Madaule, M. *La personne et le drame humain chez Teilhard de Chardin.* Paris: Seuil, 1967.

Béguin, Albert. *Léon Bloy, mystique de la douleur.* Paris: Labergerie, 1948.

Berdyaev, Nicolas. "Bourgeois Spirit," *Dublin Review,* CXCIII (October, 1933), 169-180.

——. "The Crisis of Christianity," *Christendom,* II, No. 2 (Spring, 1937), 228-240.

——. *Dream and Reality: An Essay in Autobiography.* Trans. by Katharine Lampert. New York: Collier, 1962.

——. *Un nouveau moyen âge.* Paris: Rouseau d'Or, 1927.

——. *The Origin of Russian Communism.* Trans. by R. M. French. Ann Arbor: University of Michigan Press, 1960.

——. "Young France and Social Justice," *Dublin Review,* CXCVI (January, 1935), 37-46.

Bernanos, George. *Last Essays.* Chicago: Henry Regnery Company, 1955.

——. *Tradition of Freedom.* New York: Roy Publishers, 1950.

Blondel, Maurice. *L'action.* 4th ed. 2 vols. Paris: Presses Universitaires de France, 1949.

——. "Le christianisme de Descartes," *Revue Métaphysique et Morale,* IV (1896), 551-567.

——. *Le problème de la philosophie catholique.* Paris: Bloud and Gay, 1932.

Bloy, Léon. *Au seuil de l'apocalypse.* Paris: Mercure de France, 1916.

——. *La femme pauvre.* Paris: Mercure de France, 1937.

——. *Pilgrim of the Absolute.* Intro. and ed. by Jacques and Raïssa Maritain, trans. by John Coleman and Harry Binsse. New York: Pantheon, 1947.

Bollery, Joseph. *Léon Bloy: Essai de biographie avec de nombreux documents inédits.* 2 vols. Paris: A. Michel, 1947.

Bouillard, Henri. *Blondel et le christianisme.* Paris: Seuil, 1961.

Brunetière, Ferdinand. *La science et la religion.* 2nd ed. Paris: Perrin, 1906.

Caponigri, Robert, ed. *Modern Catholic Thinkers.* 2 vols. New York: Harper and Row, 1960.

Challaye, Félicien. *Péguy socialiste.* Paris: Amiot Dumont, 1954.

Chevalier, Jacques. "A propos de la philosophie bergsonienne," *Les Lettres* (April 1, 1920), 88-91.

—— "Bergson et Aristote: Réponse à Jacques Maritain," *Les Lettres* (June 1, 1920), 179-201.

——. *Bergson et le Père Pouget*. Paris: Plon, 1954.

——. *Cadences*. 2 vols. Paris: Librairie Plon, 1951.

——. *Descartes*. Paris: Plon, 1921.

——. *Entretiens avec Bergson*. Paris: Librairie Plon, 1959.

——. *Les evénements d'Espagne*. Paris, 1937.

——. *La Forêt Tronçâis-en-Bourbonnais*. Paris: Aux Horizons de France, 1930.

——. *Henri Bergson*. Trans. by Lilian A. Clare. New York: Macmillan and Company, 1928.

——. "Henri Bergson," *Les grands courants de la pensée mondiale contemporaine*. Vol. I: *Portraits*. Ed. by M. F. Sciacca. Milan: Marzorati, 1964, 123-152.

——. *L'idée et le réel*. Paris: B. Arthaud, n.d.

——. *La notion du nécessaire chez Aristotle et chez ses prédécesseurs*. Lyon: A. Rey, 1914.

——. *Pascal*. Paris: Plon, 1922.

——. *Pour une science de l'individuel: Introduction à un essai sur la formation de la nationalité et les réveils relieux au pays de galles des origines à la fin du sixième siècle*. Paris: Alcan, 1923.

Cinquante ans de pensée catholique française. Paris: Arthème Fayard, 1955.

Coutrot, Aline. *Un courant de la pensée catholique: L'hebdomadaire Sept*. Paris: Cerf, 1961.

Denifle, Henri. *Luther et le luthéranisme*. 4 vols., 2nd ed. Paris: Paquier, 1913.

Devant la crise mondiale. Manifeste de Catholiques européens séjournant en Amérique. New York: Editions de la Maison Française, [1941].

Domenach, Jean-Marie and Montvalon, Robert de. *The Catholic Avant-Garde: French Catholicism Since World War II*. Trans. by Brigid Elson ,et al., New York: Holt, Rinehart and Winston, 1967.

——. *Gilbert Dru, celui qui croyait au ciel*. Paris: E.L.F., 1947.

Fitzgerald, William. "The Idea of Democracy in Contemporary Catholicism," *Review of Religion*, XII (January, 1948), 148-165.

Foucher, Louis. *La philosophie catholique en France au XIXe siècle avant le renaissance thomiste et dans son rapport avec elle (1800)1880)*. Paris: V. Uren, 1955.

Fowlie, Wallace. *Ernst Psichari: A Study in Religious Conversion*. New York: Longmans, Green, 1939.

——. *Jacob's Night: The Religious Renaissance in France*. New York: Sheed and Ward, 1947.

Gilson, Etienne, "Le Descartes de Lucien Lévy-Bruhl," *Revue philosophique de la France et de l'Etranger*, 147 (No. 4, 1957), 432-452.

——. *La liberté chez Descartes et le théologie*. Paris: Alcan, 1913.

——. *The Philosopher and Theology*. Trans. by Cécile Gilson. New York: Random House, 1962.

——. *The Spirit of Mediaeval Philosophy*. Trans. by A.H.C. Downes. New York: Charles Scribner's Sons, 1940.

Griffiths, Richard. *The Reactionary Revolution: The Catholic Revival in French Literature, 1870-1914*. New York: Frederick Ungar Publishing Company, 1965.

Guardini, Romano. *The End of the Modern World*. Trans. by Joseph Theman and Herbert Burke. Chicago: Henry Regnery Company, 1968.

Guyon, Bernard. *Péguy*. Paris: Hatier, 1960.

Halévy, Daniel. *Péguy et les Cahiers de la Quinzaine*. Paris: Bernard Grasset, 1941.

Hocedez, Edgar. *Histoire de la théologie au XIXᵉ siècle*. Vol. III: *Le règne de Léon XIII, 1878-1903*. Paris: Desclée de Brouwer, 1947.

Isaac, Jules, *Expériences de ma vie*. Paris: Calmann-Levy, 1959.

John, Helen James. *The Thomist Spectrum*. New York: Fordham University Press, 1966.

Jussem-Wilson, Nelly. *Charles Péguy*. London: Bowes and Bowes, 1965.

Lacroix, Jean. *Histoire et mystère*. Paris: Casterman, 1962.

——— *Marxisme, existentialisme, personnalisme. Présence de l'éternité dans le temps*. Paris: Presses Universitaires de France, 1951.

———. *The Meaning of Modern Atheism*. Trans. by M. H. Gill. New York: Macmillan and Company, 1965.

———. *Panorama de la philosophie française contemporaine*. Paris: Presses Universitaires de France, 1966.

Landsberg, Paul-Louis. *The Experience of Death. The Moral Problem of Suicide*. Trans. by Cynthia Rowland. London: Rockliff, 1953.

———. *Problèmes du personnalisme*. Paris: Seuil, 1952.

Lestavel, Jean. *Les prophètes de l'église contemporaine*. Paris: EPI, 1969.

Ligneul, André. *Teilhard and Personalism*. Trans. by Paul Oligny and Michael Meilach. New York: Paulist Press, 1968.

Lubac, Henri de. *The Mystery of the Supernatural*. Trans. by Rosemary Sheed. New York: Herder and Herder, 1967.

Marcel, Gabriel. *Being and Having*. New York: Harper and Row, 1965.

———. *Man Against Mass Society*. Trans. by G. S. Fraser. Chicago: Henry Regnery, 1965.

Marrou, Henri-Irénée, *De la connaissance historique*. Paris: Seuil, 1954.

Massis, Henri and Hepp, François, "La confédération professionale des intellectuels catholiques," *Documentation Catholique*, No. 108 (May 14, 1921), 325-329.

Mayeur, Françoise. *L'Aube. Etude d'un journal d'opinion, 1932-1940*. Paris: Armand Colin, 1966.

Molnar, Thomas. *Bernanos: His Political Thought and Prophecy*. New York: Sheed and Ward, 1960.

Moody, Joseph N. *The Church as Enemy: Anticlericalism in Nineteenth Century French Literature*. Washington: Corpus Books, 1968.

Nédoncelle, Maurice. *La réciprocité des consciences*. Paris: Aubier, 1942.

Onimus, Jean. *La route de Charles Péguy*. Paris: Plon, 1962.

Péguy, Charles. "A propos des affaires d'Orient," *La Revue Socialiste*, XXV (1897), 258-261.

———. "L'Affaire Dreyfus et la crise du parti socialiste," *La Revue Blanche*, XX (1899), 127-139.

———. *Basic Verities*. Trans. by Anne and Julien Green. New York: Pantheon Books, 1943.

———. "De la cité socialiste," *La Revue Socialiste*, XXVI (1898), 186-190.

———. "La crise et le parti socialiste," *La Revue Blanche*, XIX (1899), 462-468.

——. "La crise du parti socialiste et l'Affaire Dreyfus," *La Revue Blanche,* XIX (1899), 626-632.

——. "Durkheim's 'Le suicide,' étude de sociologie," *La Revue Socialiste,* XXVI (1898), 635-636.

——. "Un économiste socialiste, M. Léon Walras," *La Revue Socialiste,* XXV (1897), 174-186.

——. *Oeuvres en prose, 1898-1908.* Paris: Pléiade, 1959.

——. *Oeuvres en prose, 1909-1914.* Paris: Pléiade, 1961.

——. *Oeuvres poétiques complètes.* Paris: Pléiade, 1957.

——. "Le ravage et la réparation," *La Revue Blanche,* XX (1899), 417-432.

Pouget, Guillaume. *Logia: Propos et enseignements du Père Pouget.* Ed. Jacques Chevalier. Paris: Grasset, 1955.

Porret, Eugène. *Berdiaeff: Prophète des temps nouveau.* Paris: Delachaux et Niestlé, 1951.

Psichari, Ernest. *Lettres du centurion; l'adolescent, le voyageur, le croyant.* Paris: L. Conard, 1947.

Reclus, Maurice. *Le Péguy que j'ai connu.* Paris: Hachette, 1951.

Rivière, Jacques. *La trace de Dieu.* Paris: Gallimard, 1925.

Rolland, Romain. *Péguy.* 2 vols. Paris: Albin Michel, 1944.

Schmitt, Hans. *Charles Péguy: Decline of an Idealist.* Baton Rouge: Louisiana State University Press, 1966.

Sertillanges, A.–D. *La vie intellectuelle.* Paris: Cerf, 1966.

Teilhard de Chardin, Pierre. *Phenomenon of Man.* Trans. by Bernard Wall. London: Harper and Row, 1959.

Tharaud, Jérome and Jean. *Notre cher Péguy.* 2 vols. Paris: Librairie Plon, 1926.

Weil, Simone. *Selected Essays, 1934-1943.* Trans. and ed. by Richard Rees. London: Oxford University Press, 1962.

INDEX